DEVA BHUMI

The Abode of the Gods in India

DEVA BHUMI

The Abode of the Gods in India

by Krishna Kumar (K.K.) Sah

Ram Dass
love serve remember foundation

Ane Books Pvt. Ltd.
New Delhi ♦ Chennai

FIRST EDITION

This edition published by
Ane Books Pvt. Ltd.
4821, Parwana Bhawan, 1st Floor, 24 Ansari Road, Darya Ganj,
New Delhi - 110002, India

Under licence from
Love Serve Remember Foundation, USA.

ISBN: 978-93-8546-254-2

Designed by Anthony Bellemare

Library of Congress Cataloging-in-Publication Data is available upon request.

Printed at : Sagar Color Scan.

DEDICATION

To the Supreme Unseen Power that propelled me along the path of devotion and became the inspiration for this book.

K.K. at old Shiva temple in Kakrighat below banyan tree and Sombari Baba's seat

Binu Hari Kripa Milahi Nahin Santa

Without God's grace, you cannot meet any saint.

—RAMAYANA

Contents

Foreword
By Ram Dass

K.K. and Ram Dass

When I had my first *darshan* of Maharajji, K.K. Sah was my translator—the first person I met from Maharajji's family of devotees. My first impression of him was how familiar he was with Maharajji, so free with him, not holding anything back.

When Maharajji sent me to stay with K.K. at his house, I began to see his spiritual side. I saw all the pictures of holy people on his wall and in his altar room, as well as the books he had and the way he turned our discussions to spiritual topics. K.K. was so at ease talking about spirit.

Ram Dass and K.K. with Neem Karoli Baba

He lived in an old house with many floors and narrow staircases. I was used to considerably more comfort back in America. Maharajji told K.K. to feed me "double *roti*" (toast). I thought I was being punished. On the physical plane it was all very unfamiliar, but after some time we got to laughing about the cultural differences around food. They took great joy in feeding me, and distracting me while they piled more food on my plate. With that feeding and loving care, I started to feel like part of the family, a familiar family.

That family feeling made my discomfort vanish and my perceptions shifted. I began to understand the Hindu aphorism, "A guest in the home is God." I was going from middle class professor to family member. I had missed the feeling of this type of family love when I grew up.

I was reminded of what Maharajji said, "I feed the Westerners love through food."

K.K. behaved no differently with me than with Maharajji. He treated him like a regular human, yet he knew at the same time that Maharajji was not a regular person. K.K.'s humor, warmth, fearlessness, and honesty were infectious. When Maharajji had K.K. take me into his home, he also had him take me into his heart. K.K. became my brother. I truly felt the bond beyond this lifetime with K.K., something I had never before felt. He was never impressed with my western credentials. Instead, we had unconditional love.

He was drawn to my father and step-mother as they were familiar to him. He was so happy that my Dad treated him like family. Actually he brought out that quality in my father. In fact K.K.'s *siddhi* (spiritual power) is that he is able to make everyone feel like family.

His child-like quality is so infectious. I was not surprised when I heard that Maharajji gave him the blessing that he would always remain child-like.

Whenever I have been at K.K.'s house in his family temple room, I can feel the legacy of the *siddhas* (perfected ones) that permeates the room. This book represents K.K.'s persona—his love of the siddhas, from Hairakhan Baba to Neem Karoli Baba.

I can hear K.K. speaking to me when I read this book, which is an introduction to the *bhav* (spiritual feeling) we all got when we spent time living with his family in India.

Many people say to me that I was so lucky to be with Maharajji. The revelation of this book is that it transmits his love and spirit and, in fact, the soul of the entire Kumaon area, or Deva Bhumi, the abode of the gods, as it's called.

When you read this book, you will understand why K.K. Sah is my deepest friend and brother.

Ram Dass, George Alpert (Ram Dass's father),
K.K., Phyllis (George's wife)

Preface
By Raghu Markus

In 1970, I traveled to India after meeting Ram Dass. I had asked him to connect me with his guru, Neem Karoli Baba. Little did I know that not only would I meet Maharajji, as we called him, but I'd also meet a family of his devotees who were to become as dear to me as my own blood family. Before that fateful trip to the East, I could only think of family as a broken part of my life. Not that my parents did not care for me, but they were too wounded from their own history and cultural boundaries to provide that space of unconditional acceptance and love.

Soon after I arrived in India, I met up with Ram Dass at Swami Muktananda's ashram. Ram Dass told me that he had found Maharajji's whereabouts; he tucked a note into my pocket with the address of a hotel in the foothills of the Himalayas.

Two days later, I arrived in Nainital and was ushered into the hands of M.L. Sah, one of the two brothers who owned the hotel. I had no idea what to expect from this perfect stranger, and I certainly was not familiar with Indian customs. I was promptly served a cup of chai and M.L. welcomed me as if I were a long lost relative. He regaled me with stories of Maharajji and the other saints who had walked this sacred land for so many centuries. It was as if I had entered a dream world, at least until the next day when I met Maharajji for the first time and realized I had, in fact, come *home*. The dream was real.

Next I was introduced to M.L.'s cousin, K.K. Sah, and their large extended family, through whom all of us Westerners were brought into a new reality: unconditional family love. At K.K.'s house, we were fed in a temple room where Hairakhan Baba, Bal Brahmachari Maharaj, Neem Karoli Baba, and other saints had all been fed. Their family tradition included living with the saints! And guests were treated as if they were God. We learned to be like children, demanding food and comfort from our parents.

I remember at one point thinking that this felt more like home than the home I had left on the other side of the world. That feeling has persisted for all these decades. Maharajji left his body in 1973, but the unconditional love that we received from him, and which was extended to us from his Indian family, has spread like a benevolent virus through our Western community. As Meher Baba said, "Love is like a disease. Those who have it give it to those who don't."

Deva Bhumi, this book from K.K. Sah, is a gift from the immense heart of the region in northern India known as the Kumaon. It's K.K.'s story of growing up in the lap of the siddhas. K.K.'s father traveled yearly the narrow trails on horseback to the sacred temple of Badrinath and encountered many of these realized beings along the way. Stories about them graced the lives of his family. This book is primarily the story of one of these siddhas, Sombari Baba, whose tale has never before been told.

Above all, this book is permeated with the highest spiritual emotion, or *bhav* as it's called in India, that leaves us with the feeling of unconditional love and the possibility for our own realization of true kindness and compassion.

Maharajji with the Westerners

Introduction

Deva Bhumi is a region in the Northwest foothills of the Himalayas (Uttarakhand), where gods and saints have lived for thousands of years, where they performed their *leelas* (divine play) and inspired their devotees along the path of *bhakti*, *dharma*, and *karma*. (*Bhakti* is the path of devotion, *dharma* is the principle of cosmic order and righteousness, and *karma* is the spiritual principle of cause and effect that influences the future of a person.) I have always lived in Nainital, in the Kumaon hills, and grew up inclined towards the spiritual path, mainly through listening to the stories of the saints of this region since childhood. It is my hope that through this book Westerners can feel and understand the glory of the saints and siddhas. And that future generations in India will maintain the tradition of love and bhakti and the glory of the saints.

The Kurmanchal mountains have been blessed with the presence of many amazing siddhas over the centuries. However, their stories are not always known, and often get forgotten. Especially with the fast pace of modern life, the younger generation is not fully aware of the wonderful heritage, life, and teachings of these siddha masters. The intention behind this book is to make them aware of the lives of the great masters who have lived in this very area.

The stories in this book have been collected from eyewitnesses and first-hand accounts. Most of those people are now very old (and many have passed away since the articles were collected), so there may be some discrepancies in dates. However, I have tried to be as faithful as possible to exact facts. It is my hope that readers may get to know a little (a drop in the ocean) about the qualities of the siddhas who shower unconditional grace on us.

The root message of the saints is to love and serve and remember the Divine, but in the presence of unconditional grace, a devotee does not need to do even that! Simply by being in the presence of these saints, all the work is done. It is my hope that reading about these saints in this book will bring exactly that blessing to readers: that of being in the blessed presence of these great masters.

In the past, people in this area of the Himalayas were not very educated. They were simple, god-fearing people, sharing the stories of saints and siddhas among themselves. Going to see these beings (having darshan) was to pray for prosperity, to solve family problems, to get their children married—all worldly desires. No one wrote down anything about the saints of Deva Bhumi. For their part, the saints never encouraged crowds; they had no desire for name and fame. Their teachings were indirect. Sometimes there were miracles. In other parts of India, where the devotees were well-educated and could understand the glory of the saints, books were written about them, such as those about Ramakrishna, Ramana Maharshi, and Shirdi Sai Baba. But nothing was ever written about the saints of the Himalayas.

Even the early Westerners who lived in the region did not write about their experiences. For example, Jim Corbett (who was born in Nainital), the legendary British hunter of man-eating tigers, went to Tanakpur, where the Purnagiri Temple sits on the banks of the Sarda River in the Kumaon district. There he saw the lights of the Goddess. The temple priest fell at his feet and said, "We have been here for the last fifty years and do worship every day, but we could never see that light. You, who are a hunter, you could see that light." After that, Corbett never fired on tigers again and became a noted conservationist and naturalist, who spoke out about protecting

India's wildlife. He created a reserve for the endangered Bengal tiger, which was renamed Jim Corbett National Park in his honor. But he never wrote about his spiritual experiences.

Even in today's materialistic world, a trip through the Himalayas brings great peace and inspires the heart. Those who are in search of truth and inner peace are always attracted to these mountains.

The Himalayas extend over thousands of miles, from Kashmir in the Northwest to Arunachal Pradesh in the Northeast. The area of Uttarakhand (formerly Uttarakhand) is a state in northern India that has special significance in the heart of Indians, especially in the Kumaon division. Many holy shrines such as Gangotri, Yamnotri, Badrinath, Kedarnath and Bageshwar—varying from the very famousto the almost unknown—lie in this area, which attracts saints, spiritual teachers, and seekers from all over India.

SADHUS, SAINTS, AND SIDDHAS

From the times of Adi Shankaracharya in the early 8th century to Swami Vivekananda and Swami Ram Tirtha in the 19th century and Neem Karoli Baba in the 20th century, many great beings have come to Uttarakhand. (The great follower of truth and the "father of the Nation," Mahatma Gandhi, wrote his book Anasakti Yoga while staying in Kausani in Uttarakhand.)

What is the difference between a saint, a sadhu, and a siddha? A *sadhu* or *sadhaka* is a renunciate, one who has been initiated in a particular sect and does his *sadhana* (spiritual practices). Anyone can be called a sadhu. Even I have been known as a sadhu because of my devotion and spiritual practices. If someone is living in a family, if he is leading a very simple life based on spiritual values, he will be known as a sadhu type of person.

In India, when you go to the *Kumbha mela*—a great gathering of more than 80-90 million people—there are millions upon millions of sadhus. Not all of them have holy aspirations, but they are practicing a lifestyle that is encouraged and protected by their sect at the mela. The heads of these sects, or *mahants*, may be wearing garlands of flowers, holding big malas, and be carried in palanquins in procession, but their self-realization may be limited.

An advanced sadhu may be called a saint—someone who has a certain level of attainment—while a sadhu can be either just beginning on the path or far along it. Someone who is living a simple life of devotion and spiritual practice, doing their morning and evening prayers, may be called a saint—treading the path towards God. You may receive wonderful teachings from these saints. They may even do so-called miracles. But siddhas, perfected beings, are above and beyond sadhus and saints. (Often, the terms saint and siddha are used interchangeably, which does create some confusion.) Siddhas use their power not for name or fame, as some saints do, but as a form of teaching for their devotees. The ways of a real siddha cannot be known, but their devotees will experience their grace and love. If we have love, we can conquer everything.

The stage of siddha is attained after a long, long process. I have heard a siddha comes along once in thousands of saints. A sad hu or saint has to do many *pujas* (rituals/ceremonies) to attain God. He will have to maintain all the standards of a saintly person, taking his bath, doing *japa* (reciting a mantra on a mala), doing sadhana, doing rituals. But when the saint is fully cooked, he reaches the stage of *purna siddha*. He may take a bath, or not. He doesn't do any puja or go to temples. His life is now lived for others, not for himself. Neem Karoli Baba only needed one *dhoti* (cloth wrapped around the waist), one blanket. He passed the stage of doing sadhana; he had attained perfection. Maharajji (Neem Karoli Baba) used to say: "What's the use of doing rituals when people are dying of hunger? Feed people, then do puja."

A siddha can do anything, but a sadhu or beginner on the path has to maintain the *niyam*, the laws of nature. That is the difference between a siddha and an ordinary saint. An ordinary saint will put on the sacred thread and *vibhuti* (sacred ash) and do japa, but Maharajji was never seen wearing the thread or doing puja in his adult life. During his earlier *tapasya* time, he would pass through temples and often *pranaam* to the *murtis* (statues of deities) because he was always one with all the gods.

Those who understand the stage of a real siddha know so only when the siddha allows the devotee to understand these things. That is the problem in the West: everyone that comes there from India is treated as if they were on the same level—a sadhu, a saint, or a siddha. A saint may lecture and preach, but a siddha can be silent. It is the vibration of his presence, a look that can change your whole being without anything seeming to be done. A devotee came to Bal Brahmachari Maharaj who had many problems in his mind. As he sat in front of Brahmachari, he received answers to each of his questions without asking a single one out loud. That is the power of a siddha.

A siddha might do a miracle for the sake of instilling faith in his devotees, while a saint might do a miracle to attract a crowd. The siddha will generally avoid a crowd. The siddha knows who is deserving and who is not, so he will act according to his devotee's karma (*sanskaras*, the history and traits that influence that person). Whenever Neem Karoli Maharaj did a miracle, he always said, "I am nobody. God did it."

If you visit the places where the siddhas have lived, you can feel the intense vibrations that are still there. Places like Padampuri, Kainchi, Khairna, Kakrighat—where saints stayed and performed their leelas—if you go there with a pure heart, you can feel the siddha's *ananda* (bliss).

Sitting in front of a siddha, even if he doesn't talk, you will realize a kind of joy. Your mind and heart are the best judge. In the Ramayana it talks about the four *yugas*, the vast ages of the past. We are in the Kali Yuga, the lowest vibratory age. The Ramayana says that in the Kali Yuga, only those persons with good sanskaras will be able to have darshan of a siddha, for they are hidden nowadays.

IN THIS BOOK

I am taking you on an exploration of the saints and siddhas of the Kumaon region, going back over a hundred years. From family stories, I learned that my father had a special connection, love, and devotion for Sombari Baba. My Uncle Hubba told me many stories, and I read others from a monthly magazine that was published in Almora in the 1930s. I started by soliciting accounts from his original devotees and translated many of them from the Pahari hill dialect.

No one can claim that he or she can write about the saints. Writing about them is just like a drop of the ocean—an indescribable experience of grace. As Tulsi Das has said in the *Ramayana*: "*Vidhi Hari Har Kavi Kovid Bani, Kahat Sadhu Mahima Sakuchani.*" "Even the speech of deities like Brahma, Vishnu, and Mahesh, poets and men of wisdom, falters in depicting the glory of pious souls (saints)."

True devotees like nothing better than to sit together and hear stories of those who have inspired them along the path to God. May these recollections, many from people who have since passed on, inspire your path.

Part I
K.K.'s Story

I was born from the *prasad* (blessed substance) of the siddhas into a very spiritual family in the Kumaon Hills of India. My father, Bhawani Das Sah, had four daughters from his first marriage, but he had the desire that his last rites be performed by a son, as is our religious tradition. When he married my mother, it was through the grace and blessings of Bal Brahmachari Baba that I was born.

In 1944, Devi Datt Kabdwal brought a message from Bal Brahmachari Baba, who was staying at our *kutir* (hut). He said, "Tell Bhawani Das to get his son's thread ceremony performed immediately." I was only ten years old. Usually, the sacred thread ceremony is done when a boy is at least fifteen or sixteen years old, sometimes later. And there are certain hours and days that are fixed for that ceremony. Everything was prepared and my thread ceremony was performed. Hundreds of people were invited, and they all were fed sitting on the road in back of the Himalaya Hotel in Nainital.

On the 30th day after the thread ceremony, there is another part when the gold earrings, which had been put into the ear piercings that are done during the thread ceremony, are then taken out. This completes the ceremony and the boy is now qualified to perform religious rites.

Exactly on the 30th day after my thread ceremony, my father died. My head was shaved. I was so nervous. My father's body was taken out of the house and with S.L.'s help, I performed his last rites according to the ways of our Hindu religion.

My father had been in the Police Service in Nainital district. I was born after he had retired from his service. After his retirement, he would mostly stay in town, looking after the family and the farm.

When he was a police officer during British Rule, he held the post of Circle Inspector of Police. He was assigned the duty of "opening the doors" of the Badrinath Temple, which used to be closed for the winter in the month of October or November and then, after the heavy snow melted, he would reopen it in May. In those days there were no buses or roads. Pilgrims traveled on foot, walking uphill and making stops every three to four miles. The pilgrimage would take a month or more. Nowadays there are motor roads and hotels, restaurants, and conveyances, and one can do the pilgrimage in a day or two. But people who took that journey in those early days experienced the true joy of pilgrimage.

My father was given four or five attendants and horses for the journey. On the way, he would meet many saints and siddhas, which was a great boon for him. Hundreds of saints and sadhus would be going on foot and the pilgrims could get darshan while walking to the shrine. In Badrinath, there was a saint known as Sundarnath Baba, whom my father met. After his return from the pilgrimage, my father would tell all about it in the family (before I was born).

When I grew up, my stepsisters would tell me about the experiences of my father as they had been related by him in the family gatherings.

The family was my father, mother, three sisters, and one younger brother. I had four stepsisters who all lived in town. One of these (the fourth) was living in my house with her two sons, and the other sister (the third) was living in the back half of our house with her husband and children. Thus we had a big family in that house and the adjoining portion. The other two stepsisters (the eldest and the second) lived with their husbands and families about a mile or so from our house. The eldest was married to I.L. Sah; the third was married to P.L. Sah, who was in charge of a private bus company (K.M.O.U.) in Nainital. The buses ran from Nainital to Haldwani.

Every evening, a dozen or so people would come to sit in the big room on the first floor of our house. They would talk with my father about the news, as we had the only radio in our home. Then they would talk about the saints and siddhas, so our house was permeated with that atmosphere.

I was not mature enough to understand the talks that were going on. I used to see my father doing puja in the temple without knowing what it was. There were pictures of gods, goddesses, and saints in the temple room, but I didn't know anything about all that. Sometimes my stepsister (the one living in our house) used to tell me about the saints. Gradually, gradually, watching and hearing, I came to know about the magical power of a saint. I heard that these saints can help you pass your exams and they could bring prosperity (money, food, etc.) to your family. I had the faith that even if I didn't study, I would get through my exams. All such thoughts used to come in my mind, but I never paid them any heed. I myself didn't know how I had the desire to meet siddhas. Even today it is a puzzle for me!

Time passed and my eagerness increased. My father told us to respect these gods and saints, although I had never seen any saints. What little I had heard of Sombari Baba, Hairakhan Baba, and Bal Brahmachari Baba gave me further appetite to meet saints and siddhas.

In 1939-40, when I was five to six years old, my father, my brother-in-law I.L. Sah, my father's friend Devi Babu (as Devi Datt Kabdwal was known), and I all went to Haldwani. I have very little memory of that trip. From the bus stand in Haldwani, we went in a horse cart (*tonga*) to a place known as Katgharia. There was a saint sitting under a tree. Everyone pranaamed (bowed); my father asked me to pranaam and I did. We were there for a few hours. I was a bit confused. This was my first darshan of a saint. Later I came to know that he was known as Shri Bal Brahmachari Maharajji. All I knew at the time was that I was given fruit and sweets to eat!

In 1943 or so, a saint came to my house. Some people, including my brother-in-law I.L. Sah and other friends of my father, were accompanying him. I remember my father washed his feet and then there was a prayer and fruits and sweets were distributed. It was Papa Ram Dass from Kasargod, South India, as I later came to know.

My father died soon afterwards, when I was ten years old, and my new life started. After my father's death, his old friend Devi Datt Kabdwal (Devi Babu) was appointed as our guardian. We were all minors. My stepsister's family was living in a different apartment of the house. Devi Babu and my father were close devotees of Sombari Baba, and close friends. Devi Babu looked after our family very well. He used to tell stories about the saints and their grace. Slowly, I began to know the "glory" of the saints, and by their grace my respect towards them increased. Devi Babu also had written some articles in *Pahari* (the hill dialect), which were published in the magazine ACHAL (from Almora).

On 20th February 1950, Shri Kabdwal left his body. He is

remembered by people of Nainital for his amazing memory, firm decisions, and perseverance. Whenever he decided to undertake a task, he would not rest until he had completed it successfully. He always carried out his work with great diligence, and was known to almost all the people of Nainital.

My stepsisters also told us stories from our father when he would return from Padampuri after having darshan of Sombari Baba. This was before I was born. All these stories made me so excited that I used to take much interest in the saints. This was the foundation of my life: receiving the grace of the saints.

From left to right: Bina, Bhabhi, S.L.Sah with Gudhu in the frontat Padampuri

The teenage years are a time when you are supposed to enjoy

worldly pleasures—movies, tours, fun with friends—but in my case it was nothing like that. I always preferred to be with persons who would tell stories about the saints and siddhas. Thus my interest went on increasing. From time to time, such moments happened automatically when I found myself in that atmosphere.

By the grace of these saints, I was able to meet some of their original devotees. There was an old person named Hardattji who spent all his life with Shri Sombari Baba and had met many saints like Hairakhan Baba, Bal Brahmachari Baba, and others. Whenever he was in town, he would stay in our house. He was about a hundred years old! He would relate stories of Sombari Maharajji in such a beautiful way, as if that incident was taking place right there before our eyes. That kept me attracted toward the company of saints, toward love and regards for saints. And in return I received their grace and blessings.

My mother died in 1951. After the teenage years, I used to go to have darshan of Shri Bal Brahmachari Maharajji, whom the devotees regarded as the incarnation of Shri Sombari Baba (as predicted by Sombari Baba before leaving his body at Padampuri in 1919).

Neem Karoli Baba Maharaj

In 1940-41, when I was six or seven years old, my father asked my stepsister's elder son (who was about ten or twelve years older than me) to take me to see a siddha who had come to my stepsister's house, the one right in back of ours. So I went, and like the others I pranaamed.

I thought sadhus did not come to family houses. They are supposed to live away from people in the forests. I was curious why that saint was there. I whispered in the ear of my nephew who had accompanied me, "What type of saint visits the houses in town?" Lying on a cot in the room, he suddenly asked my nephew what I was saying. My nephew was embarrassed to tell him what I had said, but he insisted, "Tell me, tell me." My nephew told him.

The saint got up from the cot and, then and there, he came to our home. What grace! Here he was, Shri Neem Karoli Baba! It was my father's first darshan. All the family members were excited. He spoke with everyone there. I was standing to one side, as many devotees and relatives flocked to my house. It was like a big celebration. Then he left.

My other nephew (who was nine years older) had been present, and he told me later, "As soon as your father pranaamed to him, Maharajji asked, 'Where is that cot where Hairakhan slept?'" My father was stunned. How did he know that? Then he asked, "Hairakhan Baba gave you a mantra. Do you repeat it?" Oh! My father was shocked. No one knew about that. After that, Maharajji came often to our house and my father was his devotee.

From 1940 to about 1952, there was no ashram in the Nainital area where Maharajji would stay. He used to come for four or five days, walking all over, visiting devotees' houses, and eating a full meal in every home. He would visit our house and, especially on the eve of his departure, he would stay the night. My stepsister's husband, P.L. Sah, was the manager of the bus company and he would arrange for Maharajji's departure the next day. So that night many devotees would gather, knowing that Maharajji was going to leave town the next day. As P.L. Sah was the manager, the bus would wait! People would go to the bus station and pranaam and Maharajji would leave on the bus.

There was always an old man accompanying him from the

plains (maybe from Neem Karoli or Agra village), who also stayed in our house. We brothers and sisters would sit around him and ask about Maharajji. "How old is he? How did he stop the train?" (Maharajji became known as Neem Karoli Baba after boarding a train in first class. When a conductor kicked him off the train for not having a ticket, the train wouldn't move. Finally Maharajji was invited back on. He extracted a promise that sadhus would be treated well and a train station would be built at Neem Karoli. Then the train was able to move again.) We would enjoy the way he would speak, in the village dialect, telling us the stories. It was big fun.

When I was in school, a student could only take his examinations if his attendance rate was 75 or 80 percent. Because of my following Maharajji about, my presence was less than the required percentage. To my surprise, I never got notice that I was ineligible for exams. In college, my class teacher was a devotee of Maharajji. He would mark me "present" in the class even when I was absent, so I could skip the class to spend time with Maharajji.

After college I worked in the local city council office. I would usually finish my work sincerely, smartly, and up to date by noon time, so I could make the 12:30 bus to Kainchi. If someone was trying to find me, he would go to my office. There he would get the reply, "Oh! Go to Kainchi. You'll find him there." I still wonder how I served in that office for 34 years, since I was mostly not there!

I often went on trips with Maharajji. Once I told my sister Bina that I would be home by noon, but when I got to Maharajji, he told me to get in the jeep. He didn't tell me where we were going. We went to Vrindavan and I didn't return for twelve days.

There is a quote from Kabir's poetry: *Duniya me hu duniya ka talabgaar nahin hu bazaar se guzara hu kharidaar nahin.*" (I am passing through the market but I am not purchasing.) Maharajji used to quote this often. For a real siddha, everything is like dust because he has already crossed that level of desire. He can sleep on pebbles and mud or in a five-star hotel.

The only thing you can offer to God or a siddha is the bhav of devotion and love; singing to his glory (as the saint poets of India have done). Mirabai used to sing and see her beloved Krishna through that singing. She would become unconscious because she became one with Krishna. I heard that you could reach God through singing, without doing any sadhana. But to actually sing to God you have to combine the words of the song with the beauty and bliss you feel from what those words are describing. You have to create that vision in your mind.

I remember one devotee singing for Maharajji, and Maharajji was listening seriously. The singer went into *samadhi* (state of absorption in God) because he could see in Maharajji the beauty of that God about whom he was singing. *Bhajan* (songs) should come from the inner core of your heart, and then it will have a real effect on you. It is the bhav that counts. It should go totally towards God, without caring what you sound like. Your whole being can be changed while you are singing bhajan to God. Once Maharajji was in his office in Kainchi and I was singing near the Lakshmi Narayan temple. It was *Janmashtami*, Krishna's birthday. Maharajji went on talking with some devotee at the same time he was listening to that bhajan. A siddha has that power to do many things at a time. He is in this world, but above all these things.

I would spend all my time with Maharajji. I was like a spoiled child on his lap and I would take liberties—getting angry, sulky, or stubborn when he would refuse a certain request—but he would pardon me. When someone wanted to come visit him and, if he refused to see him, then again I would become angry/pouting. Why is he refusing to give darshan?

Sometimes acting like a child and pouting was very useful, like when Jim, Jeff, and Dan wanted to come from America. When those three (Rameshwar Das, Krishna Das, and Jagganath Das) wrote letters in 1970 asking if they could come to see Maharajji, I received those letters and took them to Maharajji. I explained that these were Ram Dass's students, but Maharajji said no, they couldn't come. I had been feeding Maharajji apple slices, but I put them down, looked away, and pouted. He kept asking, "What's wrong? What's wrong?" I would not look up. Finally he said, "Okay, tell them what you want." Soon afterwards, the three arrived in Nainital and the influx of Westerners began.

My love for Maharajji was not always unconditional. He would ask me to get married, sometimes with anger, sometimes politely. Then he would forget. Unpredictable are the ways of these siddhas! Sometimes he would say, "Don't get married." Okay, Maharajji. Such kinds of things went on taking place. So many leelas (plays).

One day, in the evening time, Maharajji was just lying on the *takhat* in the office room and I was sitting there silently. In the meantime, Siddhi Ma entered. (She might have been thinking that Maharajji was insisting on me getting married, although we were not talking about that.) Without any reference, she started speaking to Maharajji, "Why are you forcing K.K. to get married if he does not want?" Oh! Before she could complete the sentence, Maharajji sat straight on the takhat and in harsh tone yelled, "You! Why did you get married and now you are asking him not to?" That was such a wonderful scene, Maharajji murmuring and Siddhi Ma and I smiling—enjoying the mood of Maharajji—full of hidden love!

Another leela happened when Maharajji was going from house to house eating meals. In every house he would take a full meal—*puris*, vegetables, milk, heavy food. But he did not come to

Maharajji with Hira Ballabh Pant, K.K., and other devotees (Mohini, Gudhu, and Pyare Lal Sah)

my house for several weeks. I was upset. I would go daily to Hanumangarh for chai that Baba Hari Das would prepare for me. But even when Maharajji was there, I would ignore him.

Maharajji was staying in a small kutir there at Hanumangarh, Nainital. One day he came out of his kutir and said to Hari Das, "Tonight I will go into town. If anybody wants to take me to his house, he can do so." Hari Das was smiling; he knew that it was meant for me because I was so angry at Maharajji for not coming to my house for such a long time. I ignored him. I was too mad to invite him, and

I went home. Later that night, around midnight, there was a pounding at my front door. I was upstairs, and did not go to open the door. Finally I heard Maharajji's plaintive voice, "Kailash (which is what Maharajji called me), Kailash, I have come, now open the door." I could no longer stay mad. My heart melted and I began to cry. I opened the door and let Maharajji in. He stayed the whole night.

Once I did something that delayed his departure by one hour. It could have been avoided, but I didn't pay any heed. He was a bit upset or annoyed (outwardly) and he said, "You shall ever remain a child." I still don't know if that was a curse or a boon!

Sometimes Maharajji used to behave in a worldly way, as if he was attached to money. There is a farm close to Kainchi temple where vegetables used to be grown. Maharajji instructed me to take those vegetables from that farm to Bhowali, sell them in the market, and get a good price for them. The cost of gas from Kainchi to Bhowali, back and forth, was more than the amount received from selling the vegetables! He said, "Keep an account every day." I was really strict about doing that, writing down how many vegetables were sold and for how much. I thought, "How worldly Maharajji is!"

On the last day, when the fields were empty and everything was sold, I said, "Maharajji, there are no more vegetables," and I brought that account of how much was sold.

Suddenly he said, "I have nothing to do with that list. How much money do you have? Go to Bhowali and bring back woolen sweaters and dhotis for the working men."

I had thought he would praise me for keeping the account in such a sincere way, but he didn't even ask for it. In that moment I could feel what a wrong idea I had had in my mind. I thought he was thinking about the money, but it had nothing at all to do with money. Instead, he showed that a worldly man should be sincere in his job.

There are so many teachings in that. Secondly, he showed me that one should be sincere in keeping accounts. And third he showed that you should not be attached to money. So in one incident, there were four or five teachings, most of which I didn't realize until years later.

Once when I was in Vrindavan with Maharajji, he took off his sweater and said, "Kailash, take out the little balls." The sweater was full of little balls where the wool had pilled. I thought it was a useless task and I neglected it, putting that sweater aside. Maharajji banged at my door at 5 a.m. "Where is my sweater? Have you done it?"

"No, Maharajji. I am working on it. Don't worry." I got up and finished the task in a couple of hours. Now, whenever I wear a sweater and there are pills on it, I think of him. I remember the whole scene in Vrindavan—that night when he took the sweater off, the banging at my door in the morning. It is hard in this Kali Yuga to remember God's name. So for one moment, I remember something that happened with him. I remember him. I enjoy him, not in any spiritual way. He said, "When I take hold of anybody's hand, I will never leave him." He is doing that at every step.

I never asked Maharajji any spiritual questions. I never asked to have darshan of this or that god. What do I have to do with *atma* (the true self)? *Paramatma* (the supreme soul)? I am not a *jnani* (one who follows the path of knowledge). I want to see the form of an ordinary being so I may talk to him. That is my way of bhakti. I have been declared a child, so I can do anything. That is my crazy way of devotion.

There was a devotee, Kishori Raman Acharya from Vrindavan. He was signed up to recite the *Bhagavad Gita* for ten days at the temple in Kainchi. Many people came to listen to the recitation every day. Although I am not interested in these things, as a formality I went and sat in the veranda of the temple to listen to the *Bhagavad*

Gita. Maharajji said to me, "You need not go over there. Stay here." So only we two were sitting near the takhat. Kishori Raman Acharya was reciting the Gita and, in between, he was relating stories from here and there, going away from the main bhav of the Gita. Maharajji, who notices everything, said, "He is doing a good job in reciting the Gita, but sometimes he's talking about this and that. It is not good."

I didn't know anything, but just to appease him I said, "Yes, Maharajji." I didn't know what the Acharya was reciting. When that recitation ended, everybody came to the takhat and pranaamed to Maharajji. Kishori Raman Acharya came over last. Maharajji said, "You do good recitation. But sometimes you go this way, that way, useless talks, and praising me, just read."

"No, Maharajji, I do not do that," Kishori Raman said. Maharajji pointed towards me and said, "He said it." Kishori Raman looked at me with anger. I thought, "Maharajji doesn't want to hurt the feelings of Kishori Raman Acharya so he made me the scapegoat."

A few days later, I went there again and sat there listening to his Gita recitation. There were about a hundred people there. Kishori Raman Acharya said, "Look at this, Kailash." He complained to Maharajji that sometime I go away from the recitation. I blushed as everybody was looking at me. This was the way of Maharajji.

He enjoyed embarrassing me sometimes, but always out of love.

Maharajji took K.C. Tewari, Jivan Baba, and me to Vrindavan and we were staying at the temple. For a few days Maharajji said, "Don't go outside the boundary of the ashram." After four or five days, he changed his statement to, "What are you people doing inside? You have this jeep. Jivan, put in gas and go to the temples of Nandgaon, Barsana, and Daoji." Then he said to me, "You have no money," and he gave me ten rupees. "You purchase butter and *misri* (rock sugar) and offer it to Daoji, and bring some for me also."

We three started off in the jeep. Nandgaon, on the outskirts of Vrindavan, is where Krishna lived from the age of seven to ten with his mother Yashoda. Barsana is a village not far from Mathura where Krishna's favorite *gopi*, Radha, spent her childhood. We went first to Nandgaon. There were some gopis dancing in their white frocks, with peacocks all around. These milkmaids would sell milk in Vrindavan in the morning and would return back in the afternoon. Before leaving for their respective homes, they would meet together and dance.

I was so attracted. I said, "Nandgaon will always remain, but I will not often get the chance to see these ladies dancing." We went on to Barsana, where we found the same thing: very beautiful girls dancing, their wrists covered in big silver bangles. I said, "Barsana will always be there, but these gopis I can't always see." When Jivan and K.C. walked up to the temple, I stayed where I was to watch the dancing of the milkmaids (Gwalan gopis).

We returned to Vrindavan in the night. The next morning about twenty people were sitting with Maharajji. He first asked Jivan Baba, "How did you like Barsana and Nandgaon?"

Jivan said, "Oh Maharajji, they were so beautiful."

Then Maharajji asked K.C. Tewari, who said, "Yes, they had very good vibrations."

After a pause, Maharajji pointed to me and said, "How did he like the temple?"

K.C. always loved it when Maharajji scolded me, so he said, "Maharajji, he didn't come."

"What?! He didn't come?"

K.C. exaggerated, "Maharajji, these ladies were dancing and he was there..."

Maharajji was the perfect master of exaggeration. He said, "Oh, he didn't go. *Badmash* (rascal). He is like that." He started saying so many insulting things about me.

The next day, Siddhi Ma and all these mothers were sitting with Maharajji when he called me in. He said, "How did you like those places? You didn't go to the temple? You know, Ma, had I not been there he could have been kidnapped by these Gwalan gopis. They had big wrists. He could not have gotten rid of them. He is such a bad person and I was there to protect him, otherwise by this time he would be gone." My face was blushing and I was shaking. I couldn't speak a single word. This is what he repeated to everyone who came.

This happened in the month of October. That year Maharajji stayed in Kainchi through the month of December. He was in his room with a charcoal brazier for warmth. He had about fifteen or twenty mothers in his room and he sent Mohini Ma to call me. I had already forgotten about that incident. He said, "Oh Kailash, you are so devoted. Come, come." He asked me to sit on a side of the room, which meant I had to pass through all the ladies. He must have thought that way I wouldn't be able to run away. First he started praising me, then he said, "You know how badmash he is? You know what happened in Vrindavan? I sent him to these temples and he got involved with the gopis. I saved him. They could have taken him away." Finally, after fifteen or twenty minutes, I was able to run away. Siddhi Ma still laughs about it.

One month before Maharajji left his body, my sister was quite sick and she died in my house. I was so upset with Maharajji that I became mad and said, "I will never go to see Maharajji." I never expected the death of my sister while Maharajji was alive. Generally, these siddhas give a hint to close devotees if there is anything bad going to happen in that family, as had happened with my mother.

When my mother was sick, I was very sad. Maharajji was so kind; it is said that a saint's heart melts just like butter. He never wanted to hurt my feelings. He said, "Don't worry, K.K., she will be all right." Every time he used to say that.

There was a doctor, Dr. Nawal Kishore, staying in the Empire Hotel in Nainital, and he tried to find Maharajji. One day Maharajji was in our house in the morning, and I was worried about my mother. Maharajji said, "There is a doctor, my devotee. He's calling. But he charges a lot. Will you pay him?"

I said, "Yes, Maharajji, I will pay him."

"Okay, call him and tell him to bring the apparatus that is put in the ears," and he showed how it was to be used. He meant the stethoscope. He couldn't speak that word, stethoscope. The doctor was so happy. He took his stethoscope and came running to my house. He fell at the feet of Maharajji and said, "I have been pining to see you."

Maharajji said, "Check out his mother." My mother was lying in that room. There were about six or seven family members there. Without my mother being able to hear, he said to Maharajji, "She is quite ill. She cannot survive more than twenty-six days." I heard that. My face turned red. Then he left.

Now Maharajji called me, "You should not have trusted this doctor. Doctors are not God. She will be all right."

There is depth in this incident. Of course he knew that my mother was going to die, but he didn't want to put me into that kind of sadness. He knew about this death but he never said it in his own voice. He made the doctor the channel to forecast her death. Generally, a doctor would tell the family that the person will survive maybe two or three weeks, but he said twenty-six days. Exactly on the twenty-sixth day, she died.

How dutifully these saints manage to play a double role. On one side, they know that some bad thing is going to happen. On the other side, they see that the family members should not feel sad about that. So this is a very good lesson for me.

A few days before Maharajji left his body, I went to see him. In those days Maharajji sent so many messages that I should come see him. Finally I said I must go. He was on his takhat and everybody was sitting around. I pranaamed. Suddenly he sat up in the lotus position. There were five or six people sitting around him, and pointing to everybody one by one, he said, "You know, you will die, you will die, you will die. I will die. K.K. will not die." My eyes immediately opened. Indirectly he was saying that everybody has to leave his body. And K.K. thinks that he will live long. I can remember that scene as if it were taking place right now. You will die, you will die, you will, and finally I will die. But this Kailash will not die. It was very funny, but at the same time it was eye opening. When at last he pointed to himself and said, "I'm going to die," I pretended not to understand it.

After my sister died, her body was taken to Almora. After the cremation, we were returning from Almora to Nainital at about midnight. We hired a bus that passed through Kainchi. There were about thirty people, including M.L. and my younger sister Bina, in that bus. We pranaamed as we passed the temple. We didn't stop at Kainchi because it was late in the night but, believe me, I saw Maharajji standing with a dhoti and a blanket just in front of his takhat. I said, "M.L., Maharajji is there." It was a little hint for me, "Don't worry, I'm always with you." Nobody else on the bus saw Maharajji.

All of these incidents opened my eyes. He was instructing me to follow the rules of nature. He would teach me indirectly. But I used to take liberties. Oh Maharajji, I am totally different from all other devotees. You have spoiled me and I want to be in a special category in the list of your devotees. I had his curse (or boon): "Kailash, you shall ever remain a child." Brahmachari Maharaj said, "*Pagall* (crazy one), how will you pass the days of your life? You are so simple." It is crazy talk that in my mind I felt I should be treated specially among the devotees. I will do follies, I will make mistakes, but it is the duty of the baba that you'll have to pardon me. I will repeat my mistakes and again you need not scold me, but to pardon me, overlooking my mistakes.

The last visit of Maharajji in my house was about midnight and my sister Janki was alive then. Janki, Bhabi, M.L., and a few devotees were there. Usually, Maharajji was in a very jolly mood, but that night he was talking to us about Hari Das Baba and he said, "I have the keys in my hands. I can turn the minds of anybody in any direction."

I didn't dare ask a question when there were other devotees present. When Maharajji was getting ready to leave, I was in tears. I don't know how I got the courage, but I said, "Maharajji, you said that you can throw anybody out. You can change their minds. You've thrown out a saintly person like Hari Das Baba. So I stand nowhere. The day may come when you throw me out."

He patted me on the back and said, "K.K., I will never never leave you."

Those last words still echo in my mind: "K.K., I will never leave you." So that gives me courage. Sometimes I feel like I didn't do any *seva* (service), but I got so much from Baba without doing anything. Some were jealous of me. Maharajji had given me so much. He pardoned me every time.

I knew that whenever a person wanted to talk with him privately, he would send the others to do something, like bring water, or do this and that. Sometimes he would ask me to bring water and

I would never return back. I still remember one day Maharajji said, "Kailash, I've asked you to bring me water. You didn't bring it." I said, "Maharajji, I know your tricks. You wanted to be alone with that

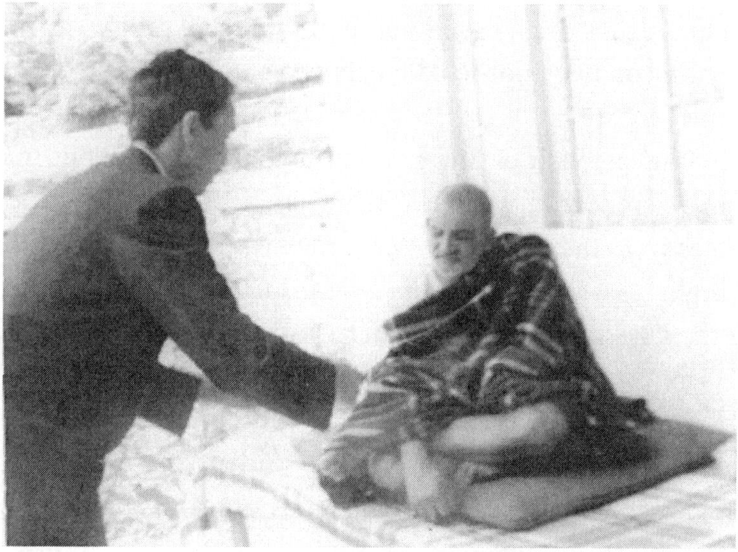

K.K. doing arti to Maharajji

person, so you made excuses to send me away, so it was just your trick to get rid of me." He laughed.

There were so many cases when he used to take me to this or that nearby place. One day in Kainchi he was holding my hand near the gate. I was going to put on my shoes, so I wanted to let go of his hand. "Where are you going?" he asked.

I said, "I am going to put on my shoes."

"What do you mean by that? I am walking barefoot and you need shoes?"

These were minor things, but they were great teachings. I

said, "All right, Baba, I will not put them on."

"No, you have to."

I said, "No, not at all." I walked barefoot up to the jeep and we went to Bhowali. My cousin Shailesh was with us in that jeep.

It was quite late in the night when we returned, so Maharajji said to us both, "You can sleep here."

Maharajji walked into his office room and I said to Shailesh, "Maharajji does not have to come through our room when he gets up early in the morning for his daily bath, although that is the quickest way for him. There is another way for Maharajji to go. You should bolt the door to our room so that he will go the other way." Of course, this was so I would not be woken up so early in the morning. Shailesh bolted our room and we went to sleep, thinking that we would be getting up late. In the morning when I got up, I said, "Now, Shailu, open the bolt because Maharajji might be coming through our room to go take his bath. "

"What are you talking about?" he said. "At about five in the morning, I was awake and Maharajji passed through our room and went to the toilet. "

I said, "Did you open the bolt? "

He said, "Uncle, I swear, I never opened the door."

Often people would come to Kainchi and ask Maharajji if they could stay, and he would say, "No, go home. Your children will be all alone. What are they going to do alone? Go." Yet, every time, he'd say to me, "K.K., stay here." See what foolishness, what an idiot and how proud I was. I would say, "No, Maharajji. I don't want to stay here." But sometimes I would stay there.

One day, after the last evening puja, the mothers were in their rooms and Maharajji and I were sitting together. Most of the time he was lost in his inner self, but in between he'd say, "Kailash, anything to tell?"

I said no. I knew his tricks. I knew that there was nobody to talk with him and he wanted to make me to go on talking. I said, "No, Maharajji. I have nothing to say."

Then he looked serious and sat in the lotus position. He said, "Kailash, you were watching how many people come from morning to evening to me. Everybody talks about his son, his family, the wedding of his children, all worries about his family, worldly things, and nobody ever asks about God." He became quiet.

These were precious moments. It is very hard to express how "lost" he was and how he made me get lost myself. Beautiful moments that I spent with Baba, just he and I near the takhat. Quiet. Everybody was in their rooms and we were talking quietly. Just think about that. Such rare moments!

How rude I was. Instead of expressing my gratitude and saying "Maharajji, there is so much grace and blessing that I'm realizing." I said, "Maharajji, it is your duty to do that," and he would laugh. Had there been someone else in my place, I feel he would have been kicked out right at that moment. In spite of my rude behavior and these kind of things, I would say, "Maharajji, it is your duty to pardon me. I will do wrong things, I will do everything bad. You need not scold me. You should treat me as if I had done nothing wrong." Every time I would say that, he would laugh; he never said a single word. These moments when I received his blessings, his grace, I can tell you that nobody on this Earth, to this day, can claim that he enjoyed so much love from Baba. All His grace, His love!

What I enjoyed most was just Maharajji and me together. So many things happened—very small things to big teachings. Nobody, nobody, can enjoy that much. They may boast that they were with Maharajji for so many years, but what I enjoyed, I can tell you, nobody can enjoy that much in this life. That time with Maharajji was so precious. At that time I couldn't understand much, but now, at every moment, I can interpret what that meant.

All his grace! His love!

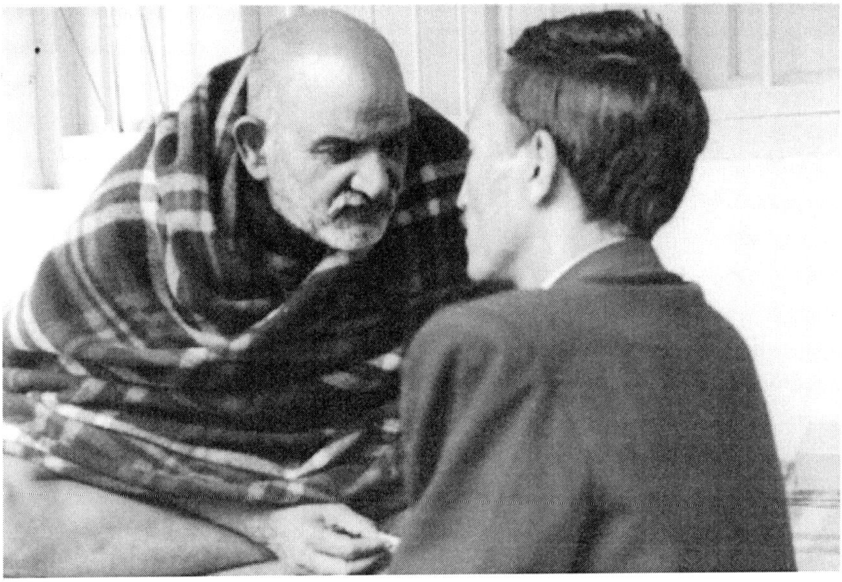

K.K. and Maharajji having a serious talk

How this book came to be

After my father's death, Devi Babu used to tell the stories of saints and siddhas like Sombari Baba, Hairakhan Baba, Bal Brahmachari Baba, and Raukharia Baba, and my interest went on growing and growing. I went to Padampuri with my mother and about ten other devotees to see Brahmachari Maharajji; it was Diwali (the Hindu festival of lights). At that time I did not know much about that place. Next time I went, around 1958, on the occasion of *bhandara* (large feeding) for the samadhi day of Shri Bal Brahmachari, I met Bageshwariji, who spent all his life with Sombari Baba and never left that place. He told me so many stories about my father's meeting with Sombari Maharajji. He was so happy to see me.

K.K. with Bageshwari Baba at Padampuri

There was another close devotee of Sombari Baba named Haridatt Baba, who after Sombari Baba's death would come to our house and give eyewitness accounts of Baba's leela performed in Padampuri and Kakrighat. His way of describing was unique, so simple, with actions. I was impressed. This also increased my respect for Sombari Baba. My brother-in-law I.L Sah had personally met Sombari Baba. He would relate stories. He would also talk about other siddhas, like Anandamayi Ma, Papa RamDas, and a few others.

The stories of siddhas from the old devotees had so much impact upon me that I had the intense desire to write about Sombari Baba. I went to Padampuri with my elder cousin S.L. Sah, his wife Bhabi, and my sister Bina. There we could see all that we had heard and read about Sombari Baba. The place appeared to be neglected. The thought came into our minds about how joyful it used to be when Sombari Baba was in his body—hundreds of people receiving his blessings and witnessing his leelas; alas, today the strong vibrations seem to have disappeared. S.L. Sah said, "Try to collect stories about Sombari Baba and put them into a book."

A few days later, I started working on this book about Sombari Baba. I printed appeals to the devotees to share their stories. I sent more than a hundred letters. I collected many stories and descriptions through these letters, and through the Hill magazine ACHAL, which contained articles about Sombari Baba by Devi Babu and other devotees. I contacted other devotees like Kaka Saheb Kalelkar (a close friend of Mahatma Gandhi), who wrote an encouraging letter to me, together with the article he had written about his short meeting with Sombari Baba in his book, *Himalaya Ki Yatra.*

One day I went to Kainchi and I spoke with Maharajji about writing a book on Sombari Baba (I still have the bus ticket from that day). Maharajji said, "This is a very good thing. First, you should know the name of Kakrighat was mentioned in the village records as Gudarmarhi." Then he related the story of the saint Gudariya Baba, whose cave is still preserved in Kakrighat. *Gudaria* means a torn, dirty quilt filled with cotton. He told me how people would bring their children or themselves with fever or sickness so Gudaria Baba could heal them. He would start shivering in his quilt and the person would become all right.

Maharajji blessed me to write the book. It was a great boon.

PART II
THE SAINTS OF DEVA BHUMI

For many centuries, the Himalayas have been considered the origin and support of some of India's greatest spiritual traditions. Countless great *rishis* (sages), *mahatmas* (great souls) and seekers have carried out their spiritual practices here. Great rivers like the Ganges, Yamuna, Sindhu, Vyas, Shatadru, Chandrabhaga, Sarayu, and Brahmaputra take their birth in the Himalayas. A large number of our great spiritual *dhams* (abodes) are located there.

The Uttarakhand-Kumaon area is the gateway to powerful Himalayan spiritual spots, such as Kedarnath, Badrinath, Gangotri, Yamnotri, and Kailash-Mansarovar. For many centuries, saints and seekers have been visiting these shrines. Passing through Kumaon en route, they would often stay because the peaceful atmosphere was very conducive to their spiritual practices.

Kakrighat, by the bank of the Kosi River, has been frequented by great sages for many centuries, and many of them performed their spiritual practices here. Until the end of the 19th century and even during the beginning of the 20th century, many great sages passed through this area.

This holy land of Uttarakhand has been blessed with the presence of great sages and siddhas throughout the ages. In the 20th century, siddhas like Hairakhan Baba, Sombari Baba, and Bal Brahmachari Maharaj made their home here. There have also been many other great beings, such as Sundarnath Baba, Swami Purnanand in Badrinath, Raukhdiya Baba in Almora, and Gudadi Baba in Kaladhungi. In more recent times, it has been sages like Neem Karoli Baba and Nantin Baba.

THE SAGES DURING THE CHAND DYNASTY[1]

(Contributed by Shri Nityananda Mishra)

In the ninth century, a prince by the name of Somchandra set up his kingdom in a place called Champawat in east Kurmanchal.

It is from Kurmanchal that the term Kumaon is derived. *Kurmanchal* means the land of the Kurmavatar, the incarnation of Lord Vishnu as a tortoise. In that incarnation, Lord Vishnu became a tortoise in order to keep Mt. Mandara afloat during the churning of the ocean until the nectar of immortality came out. Prince Somchandra belonged to the Chandrawanshi lineage, who were also known as the Chandas. This lineage ruled for a thousand years, and many saints stayed in the area during this time.

When the kings of the Chand dynasty came to the plains for the winter months, they would pass through Kakrighat. It was their practice to meet with the sages who stayed there and seek their advice and blessings. Several sages have taken *jeevit* (living) *samadhi* at Kakrighat. When a saint feels that his work in a particular body is done, he sometimes chooses consciously to be "buried alive." The saint enters a room and goes into a state of deep samadhi. The door

1 from an article in *Ramlila Smarika* 1996, issue 17

to the room is then sealed. This practice is only undertaken by saints of the highest order, and their presence continues to bless anyone who comes to the area. The sage's energy remains in and around the body upon death, and the body does not decay over time.

Around the year 1620, a sage called Nagnath, who belonged to the Nath sect of sage Gorakhnath, came to the area. The reigning king at the time was Maharaja Udhanchand, and he asked the sage to become his guru. The sage accepted, and with his guidance, the king was able to make the kingdom peaceful and prosperous. At around the same time, another great sage called Satyanath, also from the same tradition, stayed in the area for some time and then proceeded towards Garhwal, where he became the guru of the rulers of Garhwal, the Parmars.

The Chandas set up a *math* (hermitage) for sages from the Nath tradition. Some of the scriptures from that time refer to this as the *Math of Kumaon*. From the years 1678 to 1698, the reigning king was a person called Maharaja Udhyotchandra. A sage from the Nath tradition called Riddhgiri was his guru. With the blessings of his guru, the king was able to conquer the kingdoms of Garhwal and Nepal. There are many stories about the miracles performed by this sage.

A little distance from the capital, Champawat, was the small city of Almora. In the southern part of the city was a fort called Lal Mandi, and close to the fort was a well, really a *naula* (a depression with a little spring that communities use to collect drinking water). The sage Riddhgiri used to live close to this well. Since those times, the well is known in the area as "the well of the siddhas." To this day, even in years of drought, this well is always full and provides water to a large part of the city. Close to this well is a dark tunnel, above which is a small temple. Maharaja Udhyotchandra had a routine of coming to this spot in the evenings when he could to spend some time with his guru.

Once, during the peak of winter, the king went to visit the sage. It was very cold and the ground was covered with snow. The king went into the sage's hut, and saw that the sage was sitting next to a fire. The king bowed to the sage, and sat in a corner of the hut. When he realized that the sage was sitting naked in such cold weather, he took off his beautiful and expensive warm shawl and put it over the sage's shoulders. The sage took it off and threw it into the fire. The woolen shawl caught fire immediately and within moments was reduced to ashes. On seeing this, the king felt sad, but he did not say anything. After a while, he returned to the palace, but he could not forget the shawl and did not sleep all night.

The next evening, he went to see the sage again. On seeing him, the sage laughed: "Son, were you not able to sleep all night? Oh I see, it was an expensive shawl, that is why! Here, take it back." He put his tongs into the fire and pulled the shawl back out in pristine condition. He gave it to the king and said, "Fakirs like us have no need of something like this."

SAGE RIDDHGIRI RISES AGAIN FROM HIS SAMADHI

(Contributed by Shri Nityananda Mishra)

Some time during the reign of Maharaja Udhyotchandra, the sage took jeevit samadhi in a place called Jageshwar about 26 miles away. A few years after this event, some people from Kurmanchal went to Haridwar for a pilgrimage. While taking a dip in the holy pond called Brahmakund, they saw someone come out from beneath the water. One of the pilgrims recognized the person and said, "That is Sage Riddhgiri. How can this be? He had taken jeevit samadhi at Jageshwar some time ago!" Other pilgrims also saw the sage and confirmed that it was him.

The sage indicated to the pilgrims to come near him. When they came close to him, he took a gold ring off his finger and said, "When you get back to Almora, please give this ring to your king, Maharaja Udhyotchandra. It is like bondage for me." The king recognized the ring and remembered that he has gifted it to the sage some time earlier. He was very curious and had people dig up the samadhi of the sage at Jageshwar. They found no body and no skeleton at the spot.

Shri Raukhdiya Baba

Around the year 1600, a great saint lived by the banks of a seasonal rain-fed river near the village of Kaladhungi. He did not feel the effects of rain, cold, or heat. There was no roof over his hut, and he lived on rocky places near the riverbank, so he was known as "Raukhadiya Baba" (*raukhad* is a rocky place where nothing grows). After living there for about 30 to 40 years, he gave up his body there.

A DESCRIPTION OF THE LIFE OF SHRI RAUKHDIYA BABA

(Contributed by Shri Darshan)

Raukhadiya Baba looked like he was about 45 years old. People who had been seeing him from many years ago said he looked exactly the same as he did back then. He had a slightly dark complexion and looked healthy. Apart from a small *kaupin* (loincloth), he did not wear any clothes. Occasionally, he would have a dark blanket over his shoulder.

He was believed to be an *Avadhoota* (someone who is beyond

ego consciousness and acts with no consideration of usual social etiquette). He was always lost in himself and did not socialize with people. He did not carry anything to hold food, and did not even have anything to carry water. Every two or three days, he would walk from the rocky area by the river to Kaladhungi and ask for alms. He would not go to anyone's house for a meal. He would just walk around the market and say: "Will anyone feed a beggar?" Whatever simple food was offered, he would accept. In this way, he only had one meal every two or three days, and spent the rest of his time on the rocks by the riverside.

He did not smoke, drink, or partake of drugs. It seemed, even during his occasional trips to the market to asks for alms, that he was not interested in the world. Though he knew everything about everyone, he never spoke of it. He would not even bless anyone by saying "May good things happen to you." It is only because of certain incidents it came to light that he was aware of everything that went on in people's minds and in their lives. As no one knew of his powers, there were very few people around him.

Once a learned old lawyer decided to make a roof for Baba's hut. When the roof was built, Baba moved to a different rocky area by the river and started living there. Baba did not like living under a roof or inside walls. He preferred to live in the open under the sky. People from Kaladhungi also saw with their own eyes that even when the river would flood when it rained hard, Baba would not move from his spot. The water of the river would pick him up from one rocky bank and deposit him on another. His entire existence was dependent on Divine Grace.

As Baba did not speak much with anyone, he never gave any sermons or teachings. Simply by looking at him, a person who was ready would start thinking about the purpose of life, and begin to wonder why they were here. It got them moving along the path of inquiring into the nature of life.

Once, Baba was sitting on the bank of the river there with a dark blanket over his shoulder. Some people had come to visit him, among them a doctor. The doctor happened to notice some flies on the blanket and he moved the blanket to shoo them away. On moving the blanket, he noticed that Baba's foot was infected from the knee down, and the wound was infested with flies and worms. The doctor decided to take Baba to the hospital and treat him. When it was time to dress the wounds and remove the worms, Baba said, "This is their food. Let them eat." But the doctor did not listen, and insisted on cleaning the wounds and bandaging them.

A DESCRIPTION OF THE LIFE OF SHRI RAUKHADIYA BABA, CONTINUED ...

(Contributed by Pandit Jagannath Joshi)

Once a gang of thieves stole some shawls from the village of Kaladhungi. One of the thieves gifted one of the shawls to Baba. A few days later, the police were making inquiries in the village bazaar, and as it happened, Baba went to the bazaar that day asking for alms with the shawl over his shoulder. One of the police constables, a strapping young man, saw Baba and asked him where he had gotten the shawl. Baba said, "A man came by one night and gave it to me. If you want it, you keep it; I do not need it." The constable thought that Baba was mixed up with the thieves, and he slapped Baba in the face. Baba started laughing. The constable became angry and slapped Baba again, harder this time. Baba laughed some more. People in the bazaar noticed and stopped the constable. The constable started feeling unwell soon after this, and three days later the young, healthy constable was dead.

This story shows that saints are not really concerned about their bodies, and nothing can be predicted about their ways and of the Divine play that works through them. Shri Hairakhan Baba had met this saint Raukhadiya Baba many years back and described him, saying, "He is always lost in union with the Divine. After achieving complete union, he will leave his body to dissolve in the Divine."

Swami Vivekananda

SWAMI VIVEKANANDA IN DEVA BHUMI

(Contributed by Dhanilal Sah and Shri Nityananda Mishra)

On the road from Almora to Kathgodam, by the banks of the river Kosi, is Kakrighat. The great Swami Vivekananda was traveling from Nainital to Almora in 1890, before his trip to America, accompanied by Bhikshu Gangadhar. He carried just a *kamandalu* (water pot) and a walking staff. One day, while walking in the afternoon heat, they decided to rest under a *peepul* (sacred fig tree) at Kakrighat. While sitting in this peaceful spot by the river, Swami Vivekananda had an experience of samadhi, and he experienced how the entire universe is inside a single atom, how everything from the microcosm to the macrocosm is connected and is one.

He spoke to his traveling companion: "This is a very special place, filled with the vibrations of great beings who lived in the area and did their practices here. I have just had a very special experience, unlike any other before." A small whitewashed temple still stands at the spot and can be seen from the road.

Shri Harshdev Puri Maharaj

SHRI HARSHDEV PURI MAHARAJ TRIES TO SAVE THE KING

(Contributed by Shri Nityananda Mishra)

A little bit further along the river at Kakrighat, hardly visible through the foliage of large trees, is a temple complex established by Neem Karoli Baba. At this very spot were the ashrams of two very famous saints from Kurmanchal.

Shri Harshdev Puri Maharaj had his ashram there around the year 1720. He was very well known in the area during the reign of Maharaj Devichandra. People would visit Kakrighat from faraway places for darshan of this great sage. The king was also a devotee of the sage. As winter began to set in, the king would travel from Almora to a place called Kota Bhabar and then on to Devipur where he would spend the winter.

In the year 1726, the king was heading to Kota Bhabar as usual, on his way to spend the winter in Devipur. On the way, he stopped at Kakrighat to meet Harshdev Puri Maharaj. The sage advised the king not to go to Kota Bhabar that year, saying that something bad was likely to happen if he did. The king replied that a rival king's army had gathered near the plains, and that he had to go. The sage replied: "As you wish, but be careful."

The king went on to Devipur, but in less than a month, he fell prey to a plot and was murdered.

When the king's men were returning to Almora carrying his belongings, the sage looked across the road and said to the people in the ashram: "What was to happen, happened. I had warned him not to go this year, but he would not listen. Go and ask them what transpired." The people from the ashram made inquiries with the king's soldiers and found out that the king has been murdered in his sleep.

For the next many years after that, the situation in Kurmanchal was tense, with plots and murders a regular feature of the political scene.

Khaki Baba

ABOUT KHAKI BABA

(contributed by Shri Kaka Kalelkar)

When someone returns from a visit to the Himalayas, a typical question that they are asked is: "Did you get to meet any saints?" The fact is that just as I had traveled to the Himalayas, many sadhus also travel there. However, people are not interested in hearing about those sadhus; people are interested in hearing about the saints who have great spiritual powers, know all about the past, present and future, and often live without having to take any food. If nothing else, people hope for miraculous healing from such saints. Those interested in politics want to know what such saints have to say about the country's future. I usually reply to the question about meeting saints in one line: "I did not go to the Himalayas seeking to meet saints." I feel that one has to do one's own spiritual practices, but meeting saints can definitely give rise to faith in our hearts and inspire us to work towards our own upliftment. One such saint I did have the good fortune to meet was Khaki Baba.

Khaki Baba said, "A saint who comes from a particular time and society is going to be like other people from that time and society." This made perfect sense to me. Sadhus do not fall out of the sky, so it is natural that the good and bad tendencies seen in society are very likely to be present in them as well. However, some sages arrive at a place where they are full of love and wisdom. The deep and real knowledge they have about the workings of the universe cannot be matched even by reading many libraries full of books.

One morning, we woke up early and went for a walk on a mountain that seemed to be made of granite rock. It was a bit misty. We sat under a cedar tree and talked about a few things. As the mist cleared, I happened to notice a small structure on a hill far in the distance. I asked one of my companions, who was a sadhu, "Is that a temple or ashram I can see in the distance?"

The sadhu replied, "That is the place of Khaki Baba. We'll go there later in the afternoon. He is a divine being. I go visit him often. On the day of *ekadashi* (the eleventh lunar day of the bright or dark fortnight of every lunar month) an event for chanting is held at his ashram and it runs all night. A sadhu from Bengal also attends this event. He is a great devotee of Khaki Baba and sings wonderfully."

That afternoon, we walked downwards from Almora and headed to Khaki Baba's ashram. We arrived at a mountain stream along the way and refreshed ourselves by drinking the sweet, fresh water. Then we climbed up the mountain to arrive at Khaki Baba's ashram. The ashrams of saints are worth studying for their great organization and layout. They are a wonderful example of dwellings that can be made beautiful even without having modern conveniences.

Khaki Baba's own hut was octagonal in shape. It had a thatched roof, which looked worn on the outside from having faced a lot of rain, and also on the inside from smoke from the *dhuni* (sacred fire). In the center of the hut, a large dhuni was burning brightly. There were about three or four fire tongs made from iron in the dhuni, and a couple of tridents were planted in the ground next to it. Close to it was a large and heavy wooden seat, and Khaki Baba's large frame was seated on it. There were some local devotees sitting around Baba at the time. Some water was being heated in a small pot close by. We went into the hut, bowed respectfully to Baba with folded hands, and sat down.

Khaki Baba received us with great love and respect. The sadhu who was traveling with us introduced us to Baba. On hearing that I was from Belgaum, Khaki Baba asked: "Are you from Belgaum or Shahpur?" I was stunned. These two towns were hardly a mile away from each other. Most people had not even heard of Shahpur, yet this saint in the faraway reaches of the Himalayas knew about it! When I said that I was from Shahpur, Baba said, "Shahpur falls under the princely state of Sangli, which is not under British rule. Some people from the Marwadi community in Shahpur had started building a temple dedicated to Lord Balaji; has it been completed?" I told Baba everything of note that was going on in Shahpur at the time.

Later, he asked me where else I had traveled and what things I had experienced or done during my travels. Now, my travels were not inconsiderable by any stretch of the imagination, yet no matter what place I mentioned, this saint seemed to know a great deal about it. He would tell me so much about the place that it seemed he was a local resident there, and then proceed to ask me questions about what was going on there.

One of my companions, Mardhekar Baba, belonged to a particular sect called Ramdasis. Khaki Baba proceeded to talk about the history of this sect, and then asked some more questions. This saint demonstrated that even without any formal education, his knowledge of geography, current affairs, and history far exceeded ours. When it became obvious that we were reaching the limits of our knowledge, he stopped asking questions so as to not embarrass us.

We wished to travel to spiritual places such as Gangotri, Yamnotri, Kedarnath and Badrinath. The sadhu who was with us wished to travel further to Mount Kailash. We asked Khaki Baba for some information about these places. Baba then proceeded to tell us about many such spots in the Himalayas. On seeing that we looked a little lost, he picked up a wooden stick and drew a map for us on the ground so we could understand better. He told us about four ways we could get to Badrinath. By taking the first option, a large portion of the journey could be covered by rail to minimize walking. The second option was better if we wanted plenty to eat and drink along the way. The third option was best to get there in the shortest amount of time. But, he said we'd have to take along a lot of coins if we decided to take the third option, because the people in the area were very poor and would not have change for even small currency notes. The fourth road he told us about was his favorite; he called it "Khaki Baba's path." It was the most scenic and beautiful of all the options, passing through many forests. However, it was very sparsely populated, with a minimum distance of forty miles between any two settlements.

On hearing him give such detailed information, I asked "Maharaj, how many times have you been to Badrinath?"

He replied: "Seventeen times."

The sadhu who was accompanying us asked about directions to Mount Kailash, and I quipped in: "Maharaj, I am guessing you have been to Kailash also!" to which Khaki Baba replied: "Yes, eight times!" and then he went on to describe the way in great detail, as if he were seeing it with his own eyes at that very moment. He then went on to tell us about a saint called Morpankhi Baba, who visited Mount Kailash every year. We also asked Khaki Baba about other saints who lived in the area close to his ashram, one of whom was the great sage Sombari Baba.

Khaki Baba then went on to talk to us about the people, food, and social situations in various areas of the country. He praised the people of Gujarat for their faith and the people of Maharashtra for their hospitality (these states are in the West of the country). He talked about how the people of Bengal (in the East) did not respect the Ganga, other rivers and lakes in the area, polluting these water bodies with garbage. He talked about how arrangements at the shrines in Rameshwaram (in South India) could be improved.

After this, Khaki Baba offered us tea. The tea in the Himalayas is grown locally, and the local people say it is quite useful for the severe winters there. We said we did not want any, so Baba asked one of the devotees present there to give us some sweets. I told Baba that I did not take any sugar (in those days, the British forced Indians to buy sugar made in Britain, and this was one of the ways freedom fighters like the author protested), and he said I should not worry as this sugar was locally made in India. I had made a vow to not eat sugar for six years, and when I told Baba this, he gave me some almonds and other dried fruits instead, and then we started talking again.

Baba took some hot water from the pot to drink, but before drinking any himself, he offered a few drops to the fire. I was a little surprised to see this, and seeing my surprise, the sadhu who was traveling with us mentioned that Khaki Baba always offered food and drink to the fire before taking any himself. Then Khaki Baba spoke: *"Apne Ram toh din mein ek hi baar bati banakar paa lete hain. Aaj dopahar ko jo paya so phir kal dopahar ko payenge."* ["I eat once a day—preparing small *chapatis*. What I got today (in the afternoon), so now I'll eat next afternoon, i.e. tomorrow."]

I thought to myself: *So the sweets, almonds, and other things are just for visitors, and he does not take any himself. What a wonderful being!* I could see that in his room there was a thick rope used to hang clothes, and all it held was a small loincloth. Baba's entire body was smeared with ash, and his long beard and mustache were reddish in color, like fire.

We then proceeded to talk about modern-day sadhus. Some people who had studied English became sadhus, then went on to write books in English, give lectures, and talk about doing social work. On hearing about this, Khaki Baba burst out laughing. He said, "These English-speaking sadhus, how are they serving the poor? How are they helping those who are in pain?" Then he suddenly became serious, and looking at the *dharamshala* (a hostel for the pilgrims to stay in while on pilgrimage), he said, "They just talk. They do not have the capacity to become like Swami Vivekananda. They just translate books. They should chant the name of the Lord and perform some penance. If possible, they should also feed the hungry. What is the point of empty talk?"

The sadhu who was with us asked, "Are you going to Badrinath this year, Maharaj?" Baba replied, pointing to the soles of his feet that had large cracks: "God has given me this punishment. This child had become a great lover of travel, so He thought He needed to tie this child down to one place and did this to my feet. Now if I wish to travel I will have to wear shoes made of jute."

It's impossible to know how many people Khaki Baba served. He administered medicines and treatments to those who were sick, advised and inspired people who were lost and confused, fed the hungry people who turned up at his ashram, and resolved disputes between friends and family members. He was a great yogi. Even though he had no responsibilities or attachments, he was detached from the world in a positive way. He was truly like a lotus that is not affected by the water it resides in (the lotus is considered a symbol of yoga because even though it grows in water, its leaves or petals do not get wet; this represents the philosophy of living in the world without being affected by it).

The wonderful *lok-sahitya* (folk literature) of India is still alive and vibrant due to these sadhus and their ashrams. They help to protect and spread the spiritual riches of our culture. It is a progressive, economical, and trustworthy system that has been working for untold millennia.

Academic studies can take the support of history or geographical and archeological evidence to talk about the unity of India as a nation, but in reality, it is these sadhus who have created the feeling of oneness and connection in society. In the old days, a king would receive any sadhus who came to the kingdom and find out about faraway kingdoms: how people lived there, what things were good or bad there, and so on. When leaving the kingdom, the sadhus would bless the kings and advise them about any social ills or problems that they had observed in the kingdom during their stay there. In this way, information about the real situation on the ground and the problems of the common man were presented to the king by a highly respected, kind, and neutral person. At the same time, kings who wanted the approval of these respected sadhus were motivated to serve their subjects well.

When a sadhu turned up in a village, he would usually set up his fire near the local temple or under a tree. His arrival brought great benefits to the village. The children of the village learned a lot about the world and about life simply by listening to his stories. Businessmen got information on how to run their businesses, and what was going on in the world outside their area. Brave soldiers could find out where their services were required and appreciated. The healers in the village got new knowledge of herbs and treatments. Sick people were also healed by these sadhus. Often, the people of the village would be inspired to carry out much-needed refurbishment work for temples and dharamshalas and to undertake other works of charity. Just like a butterfly goes from one flower to another pollinating them, these sadhus traveled from place to place facilitating cultural exchanges.

Unfortunately, since society as a whole has now degraded, the sadhu community is not immune to those changes. Many people therefore spend time trying to criticize and undermine this group of people without considering the importance of their role in society. The old societies of Egypt, Rome, and Greece are all gone now; but India's cultural prowess remains. With these thoughts in my mind, we bid goodbye to Khaki Baba and continued on our journey.

PART III
SOMBARI BABA MAHARAJJI

Early Days

Another famous sage is Sombari Baba, so named because he used to feed whoever came to see him on Mondays (*Sombari* means Monday). He arrived in the Kumaon in the late 1800s and stayed until he left his body in 1919.

PIND DADAN KHAN'S IMPORTANCE IN HISTORY

(Contributed by Dhanilal Sah)

I was told that Baba was born in Pind Dadankhan in Punjab, in about 1824 or 1825. *Pind* means village, and *Dadankhan* is "the saint who lived here," thus the name Pind Dadankhan. Some people say Baba was born around 1815. It's hard to say for sure when it comes to

Sombari Baba

sages because their physical appearance may bear no relation to the age of their body.

Pind Dadankhan and the surrounding area has long been a part of India's centuries-old spiritual and historic inheritance. The town of Pind Dadankhan is situated on the banks of the mighty river Jhelum. It is a beautiful spot towards the west of Lahore (in present day west Pakistan). Many people travel there to enjoy the beauty of nature and to restore their health. A little distance from Pind Dadankhan, across the river Jhelum, Alexander the Great fought a great battle with the Indian King Puru. A little north of Pind Dadankhan is a salt mine known as the Khewra (or Mayo) salt mine, which provided salt to northern India from the time of the Mughal kings. (These are the oldest salt mines in Pakistan and the second largest in the world. Alexander's troops came across these mines in 320 BC.)

In the area of the mine is a very important lake called Katas, and the area is called Katas Raj. The lake is at a height of around 2000 feet above sea level. It is written in the *puranas* (ancient Sanskrit texts) that when Lord Shiva's wife Sati died, he walked around the world in inconsolable pain. The tears that fell from his eyes formed lakes in two places: one is Lake Pushkar, located at Ajmer, and the other is Lake Katas, located near Pind Dadankhan. Thousands of devotees come to bathe in the lake every year. Around this lake is a complex of twelve temples and there is also an old fort nearby. It is said that the Pandavas (five brothers from the Indian epic, the Mahabharata) lived near Katas Raj for seven years.

Close to Katas Raj is a place called Choa Saidanshah where beautiful varieties of roses are grown, and rose essence is manufactured from these. A few miles away is another important place called Nandanashah where remains of old temples and an old fort called Nandana fort can be found. Mehmood Ghaznavi attacked this place around the year 1004 to try and destroy the temples there. The style of the temples there is similar to those found in Kashmir. The ruins of the famous historical university of Takshashila were also found in the area.

PIND DADAN KHAN

(Contributed by Shri Surendranath Jauhar (Fakir), Sri Aurobindo Ashram, Nainital)

Pind Dadan Khan is a town situated on the bank of the mighty river Jhelum, in the Jhelum district of West Pakistan. My birth place was Vahalee, a village in the same Tehsil. *Pind* means village. Dadan Khan was a *fakir* (Muslim ascetic) after whose name this village was established, which gradually grew and developed into a town and *mandi* (wholesale market).

The nearest school from our village was at Bhera, a town on the other side of the Jhelum river, just a few miles away from Pind Dadan Khan. My father used to cross the Jhelum from Pind Dadan Khan every week for several years, until he passed his matriculation examination from Punjab University. Many other members of my family, such as my paternal uncle and several cousins, also traveled to and from Bhera for their education.

Our village Vahalee was only served by a single shop that sold provisions. There were no other shops within a radius of ten to twelve miles. This shop supplied the villagers with all sorts of goods, such as provisions, groceries, cloth, shoes, soap, educational material, herbal medicines, spices, and so on. The shop probably had around a thousand different types of items for sale. It was a small shop where items were placed on shelves in an apparently hodge-podge manner, but the owner, Hukum Chand, knew the location and price of every single item in the shop. He never had to refer to any notes. His hand would automatically and spontaneously reach the articles that a customer asked for. Hukum Chand had to go to Pind Dadan Khan every month to purchase all the items for his shop.

So the name of Pind Dadan Khan was deeply engraved in our hearts.

THE INCIDENT WITH THE STICK

(Contributed by Hira Vallabh Pant)

One day, when he was a boy, Baba was walking with the help of a walking stick on the uneven terrain. It started to rain, and he found shelter in a small cave. As soon as he entered the cave, someone called out and said, "*Oye* you, come out of that cave!"

The boy replied: "Dear Sir, I am just a small boy, and have entered this cave to save myself from the rain. Please come in; there is enough space for both of us."

On hearing this, the man lost his temper, entered the cave, snatched the stick from the boy's hand and started hitting him with it. After this unpleasant experience, the boy left his walking stick in the cave and went on his way, having learned the important lesson that possessing certain objects can cause problems. From that day onwards, he never used a walking stick.

BABA'S FIRST MEETING WITH HIS GURU

(Contributed by Shri Govindram Kala, Ex-Deputy Collector)

My friend Lala Radheshyam from Kashipur was a great devotee of Sombari Baba. He told me that Baba's Guru was a Muslim saint. Baba met his guru on the banks of the river Raavi (this river flows by the modern-day border of India and Pakistan). It was the month of May or June in the summer, and the sand on the banks was very hot. Baba was walking by the river bank, and due to the intense heat, he had to resort to laying his *angocha* (cloth used to cover the upper body) on the ground, walking on it, and then repeating the process. He happened upon a saint walking very fast along the way. Baba tried to keep up with the saint, and eventually they reached a small hillock. The saint pointed at a particular spot on the hillock and said, "Sombari, there is a treasure buried at this spot. Dig it up, take it and go."

Baba replied: "Maharaj, why don't you take it?"

The saint replied: "I do not want it."

Baba said, "I do not want it either."

Baba was very impressed with this saint, and later on became his disciple.

AS A POLICEMAN!

(Contributed by Shri Shankar Lal Sah)

Baba was born in a village called Pind Dadankhan in Punjab, in about 1824 or 1825. Some people say he was born around 1815. We cannot really say for sure when it comes to sages, as their physical appearance may bear no relation to the age of their body.

Baba liked *satsang* (sitting together with a guru and/or spiritual seekers) of *sant mahatmas* from childhood. A sant mahatma is a great soul who knows the truth. He once mentioned that he used to work in the police force. Once, while he was on duty, he went to some saints and enjoyed their company tremendously. As it happened, his superior officer visited that day; noticing that several policemen were absent without permission, he dismissed all those who were not present on duty. Baba was not dismissed though. Baba had always been very truthful from his childhood. He thought it must have been an oversight on the part of the superior that he was not dismissed, so he asked to be dismissed, saying he had also been absent without permission at the time. However, the superior told him that he was present at that time. Baba was taken aback. He realized that this was the grace of the saints that he had been with. He was deeply affected by this incident. He left job and became a *sanyasi* (renunciate).

Descriptions of Sombari Baba

Sombari Baba

SOMBARI BABA

(Contributed by I.L. Sah)

Baba lived a selfless life. He had no ego. His wants were few. For raiment he had two strips of cotton cloth, one to cover his loins and the other for the upper part of the body. A deerskin was his seat and bed, and a small wood fire his companion. Serenity and goodness beamed from his face. His was a radiant life. He made no demands of anybody. He claimed no scholarship, he never preached, he never wrote books, but he was a living religion and what he practiced was a lesson for others. He never instructed anyone directly. Every week Monday was Shiva's day and prasad was distributed to all who came from around the countryside. On all auspicious days of the Hindu calendar, there was puja and worship. Thus his teaching was indirect and silent. He preached the Hindu way of life by his own example.

SHORT DESCRIPTION OF BABA'S LIFE

(Contributed by Dhanilal Sah)

I was not able to meet Sombari Baba in person as I was very young when he left his body. However, my father and grandfather went to meet him whenever possible, and I heard a lot of stories from them about their experiences with Baba. My grandfather was a devotee of Lord Shiva and liked to serve sadhus. I also had the good fortune to meet many other people who had met Baba in person many times and had sought his guidance through their lives. Many of these people were wise men, doctors, lawyers, and successful businessmen who had spent a lot of time with Baba. They were kind enough to share their personal experiences with me. I am writing about their experiences from memory.

On hearing these stories, I felt a deep connection with Baba, and it kindled in me a love for the spiritual life and for sadhus. I traveled to places like Kakrighat, Kainchi, Khairna, Haldwani, Dwarahat, Sitlakhet, Dronagiri, and Padampuri quite regularly to take in the vibrations of these wonderful places that had been frequented by Sombari Baba and other great beings. I remember that as student I had passed close to Pind Dadan Khan, which is Baba's birthplace. It is in a beautiful area close to Rawalpindi and people travel to the area to benefit from its fresh air and water. The ancient city of Taxila Ewtabad is close to Pind Dadankhan, and that is where I was traveling. This city is a living example of India's great and ancient culture.

Baba consciously stayed away from crowds and ashrams. He always stayed away from villages. Despite this, people would seek him out and visit him for darshan. Baba would sometimes say that if people bothered him too much, he'd leave. That is one of the reasons he spent the summer months in Kakrighat and the winter months in Padampuri, which gets so cold in the winter that the snow piles as high as the bamboo trees! A little higher up from the ashram is a pond that remains frozen through most of the winter. Because of the location of the ashram in a deep valley, there isn't much sunlight. And at that time, Padampuri was surrounded by dense forests. Baba stayed in a small cave close to the the confluence of two small mountain streams.

Baba was a great lover of cleanliness. All the spots he stayed in were beautiful and clean. He never stayed in any one spot for very long. He said that staying too long in one place can result in attachment.

Baba had some very strict practices, which he always observed. He bathed in the river three times a day. His only clothing was a simple loincloth. Regardless of the season or weather, his daily schedule never changed. Women were not allowed in Baba's ashram. This does not mean he did not respect women. He considered women to be an embodiment of *Mahashakti*, the great divine feminine. It is believed that his personal deity was Goddess Bhagavati. He always respected women, and if any women passed close to the ashram, Baba would have prasad sent to them. Baba had great love for Lord Shiva in the form of Kashi Vishwanath and Goddess Annapurna, the goddess of plentiful food.

Baba's only possessions were very objects that he used every day: his kamandalu, *jhola* (small cloth pouch), a tiger skin, *chimta* (fire tongs), and *chillum* (pipe for smoking ganja/marijuana or charas/hash). There were no facilities in his ashrams for guests to stay. Baba considered guests to be God in human form. On any day, anywhere between ten and fifty people would come to the ashram to see him. When devotees came by, they were fed whatever was available at the time. Many people who were present for these impromptu bhandaras with Baba describe them with great joy and affection. Baba himself would never eat anything cooked for the bhandaras.

Baba was also a strict disciplinarian. If anyone displayed a lack of discipline, he never hesitated to let them know. When he was telling someone off, his words had an effect like an electric shock! In this way, Baba was like the great sage Sai Baba of Shirdi. Both these great sages liked to live alone, had the habit of smoking a chillum and were strict disciplinarians. Baba's words would guide people back to the right path. Being scolded by him was a form of blessing!

God comes to the Earth in the form of these great saints for the upliftment of mankind. Sombari Baba's life will always continue to inspire the people of Purvanchal. By the grace of Neem Karoli Baba, temples have been built in the places where Sombari Baba used to stay, such as Kainchi, Khairna, and Kakrighat. Visiting these places brings great peace to the heart.

DESCRIPTION OF BABA AND HIS LIFESTYLE

(Contributed by Pandit Devidutt Kabdwal)

The holy land of Uttarakhand has been blessed with the presence of great sages and siddhas throughout the ages. Jagadguru Adi Shankaracharya also left his body here.

One of the great siddhas who lived in Uttarakhand was Sombari

Baba. He was born in Pind Dadan Khan, in the Jhelum district of present day Pakistan. He was born in a well-to-do Saraswat *Brahmin* (priestly class) family. He left home at a very young age, without any sort of emotional upheaval or pain to himself or his family. He traveled to many spiritual places (called *tirth yatra*), learned several special vidyas (correct knowledge) and remained a pure *brahmachari* (a male who practices living according to Hindu Vedic scriptures) all his life. Sombari Baba lived in Uttarakhand for approximately 30 years. On January 2, 1919, at the age of about 70, he took maha-samadhi and left his body. During the cremation, there was a great crowd of people. Even animals gathered and did not move until the rites were complete.

Baba usually only wore a loincloth. Sometimes he would use an orange angocha to cover the upper body. He bathed three times a day and applied *vibhuti* (ash) all over his body after bathing. His daily schedule was as follows: Baba would get up in the early hours of the morning between 3 and 4 a.m., take a bath in the river, and then worship Lord Shiva. After this, he would sit in meditation until about 7 or 8 a.m. After this, he would be available to meet and bless anyone visiting the ashram until midday. At midday, he would take his second bath, perform a puja of Lord Shiva, and then sit in meditation until 3 or 4 in the afternoon. After this, he would again be available for visitors until the evening. Around dusk, he would take his third bath in the river, perform puja, and then remain available to visitors for darshan.

Prasad was distributed in the ashram all through the day, and devotees were also served lunch and dinner at the ashram. Baba looked after all the arrangements personally. Around 9 or 10 in the evening, after everyone had eaten, Baba would make a small *tikkar* (a bread cooked in fire) or *khichdi* (a one pot meal of rice and lentils) and eat himself. No one was allowed to remain the the ashram overnight; Baba sent them off to their homes or to the *dharamshala* across the river to spend the night, and he remained alone in his *kutiya*, which was open to the sky. Baba performed a *panchamahayagna* (five types of fire rituals) every day.

It seemed like Baba took on different *rupa* (look) during different parts of the day. In the mornings, he appeared fair and middle-aged, and there was a peaceful look on his face, like Lord Vishnu. Around midday, he looked old and appeared like Rudra (Shiva). Baba had long hair in dreadlocks, and kept a *shikha* (small lock of hair on the back of the head).

Baba's ashrams were usually close to a river bank; he would install a Shiva *lingam* (a stone symbol of Lord Shiva) first and then set up the ashram. Whenever someone visited the ashram, Baba made sure they had something to eat and drink. Then he would speak with them, ask them how they were, answer their questions, and resolve their problems. Before they left, Baba applied vibhuti to their forehead himself.

Baba was a siddha of the highest order. Such beings are free of all karma, and do not need to either participate in the world or renounce it. Yet, to show devotees the way, Baba lived as a total renunciate. Though he was himself free from all karma and did not need to do anything, he still performed karmas to guide devotees. He maintained all the practices that he undertook from the time people first saw him in Uttarakhand until he left his body decades later.

Even though a large number of visitors came to his ashrams every day, there were hardly any belongings kept in the ashrams. Baba did not want any large construction in the ashrams, though many devotees often wanted to build things. Once, when Baba was on a *yatra* (pilgrimage) to Badrinath, one devotee who had a great desire to do something for the ashram had a Shiva temple and two rooms built in the ashram. After his return, Baba simply continued to stay in his simple kuti, and the ashram's cooking also continued in the same place open to the sky. Devotees from faraway places like Bombay came to Baba for darshan and blessings, and they had the capacity (and desire) to spend large amounts of money for the ashram, but Baba would not allow this. Things were kept simple. Devotees would eat on plates made from leaves.

Many devotees had their wishes and dreams fulfilled by simply coming to the ashram for darshan. Once a man turned up at the ashram. He was despondent because his son had been lost. Baba asked the man to keep faith, saying that God removes all suffering. The man stayed at the ashram for a day, and the next morning his son turned up at the ashram. Both father and son happily went back to their home together. Policemen who were looking for culprits, such as thieves or murderers, and stopped over at the ashram for darshan would then come across the culprits on their way back. People who had lost their jobs often met their superiors on the way back after darshan and got their jobs back. There were many such incidents throughout Baba's life.

Baba lived the life of a total renunciate. He made all arrangements to feed devotees throughout the day, but would not eat himself until the night. He stayed in a very cold place like Padampuri in the winter, and in very hot places like Haldwani, Kakrighat, and Khairna in the summer.

Sombari Baba's countenance was divine and attractive, and his speech was also very sweet. A person who came in his presence did not wish to ever leave. Just by listening to his sweet speech, people would forget all the sorrows of the world. His face was always beaming with joy and love, and never angry. Whoever was fortunate enough to get darshan at his ashrams in places like Haldwani, Padampuri, Kakrighat, Badrinath, Kedarnath, and Khairna would forget all their sorrows, leave aside all negative emotions and thoughts in his presence, and be lost in the presence of the divine. This effect remained for a long time even after they went back home.

Devotees hardly ever needed to ask Baba a question. Without needing to speak, he resolved their doubts and problems in one way or another and removed their sorrows. Baba did not give any speeches. He gave simple examples or teachings in a way that the person got the meaning immediately.

He never sat idly, and also made all devotees perform some work in the ashram, according to their capacity. Devotees who came to the ashram automatically felt enthusiastic about doing some work. They forgot all idea of rank and position in the world and acted liked a family. Several people who had an outstanding argument for years found that their issues were permanently resolved when they met at the ashram. Baba also advised devotees on their work and family life. Devotees felt at peace and became fearless simply by receiving darshan. People of all religions: Christians, Muslims, Parsis, and Jains heard about him, came for darshan eagerly, and on receiving darshan, all felt blessed. Each devotee thought Baba loved him most of all. This was not surprising.

Mahatmas never have a problem with anyone, but even then, sometimes we see/hear of some bad people misbehaving with mahatmas. In the case of Sombari Baba, even bad people praised him. He did not leave someone because they were a bad person. Sometimes, thieves would come to the ashram late at night and quietly leave some offerings. To respect their feelings, Baba would use the offerings they left for a bhandara, and tell everyone who came there that the offerings were from people who wished to come back to the path of goodness. Baba did not like it if anyone brought offerings unhappily, with arrogance, or by undergoing suffering. He always said offerings should be made according to one's capacity, in a happy way. He instructed devotees to offer only that much that they did not even notice or need to think that they were taking something along as an offering.

All devotees found something attractive in Baba. Even those who did not know anything about the qualities of mahatmas loved him. Some people loved watching him, others were impressed by his words, yet others liked how disciplined he was in his daily schedule, yet others loved him for his kind behavior, and others were impressed by his renunciation and *tapas* (spiritual practices).

In one way or another, Baba always brought his devotees to the path of goodness. Baba used different ways to guide people based on the needs of their soul at that point in time. Many devotees were rid of their egos simply by taking darshan. He answered even the most complicated questions in simple terms and resolved them completely. He behaved with everyone depending on their nature and ability to grasp teachings. Though Baba had great powers, he hardly ever displayed them overtly; everything just seemed to automatically fall into place around him. Simply by the grace of darshan, many people had incurable diseases cured, childless couples were blessed with children, people with no job were able to secure jobs, those who were suffering materially became prosperous, and those who did not believe in God became believers.

Mahatmas often behave in different ways. Some behave with everyone according to their nature, some tend always to speak less with everyone, some are always lost in divine joy, some give lectures that normal people don't understand, some give guidance but are detached from people's worldly lives, some speak harshly, some act like they are crazy, some live in faraway places and are not accessible. Sombari Baba was different in that he was accessible to everyone, loved everyone, and was available to everyone who sought his guidance and blessings.

Some great beings come into this world just for the good of others and have no karmas of their own to fulfill. Baba spoke with everyone based on their needs and capacity, and brought them to the path of goodness. He was able to see life from the point of view of each devotee, and explain things in a way that made it easy for that person to understand. Regardless of whether a person was interested in the path of the world, renunciation, knowledge, yoga , bhakti, or anything else, Baba spoke with them in terms that appealed to them. Good people were, of course, attracted to Baba immediately. The interesting thing is that even bad people who initially saw a stern side to Baba and were afraid of him slowly got attracted to him and towards the righteous path. During festivals, Baba not only organized bhandaras to celebrate, but also explained the meaning and reasons behind the celebration to devotees. He often made everyone laugh with his wit, and when everyone was laughing, he simply smiled happily. Simply by having darshan, people became devotees.

Many devotees in different places, whether in the country or outside, reported meeting Baba in their hour of need, sometimes in dreams, sometimes through a vision, and sometimes even physically, when Baba was actually somewhere else! Baba had his own unique ways of warning devotees who were straying and bringing them back to the path. Almost every day, someone would relate such a tale at the ashram. Quite often, people present did not understand the meaning of Baba's words at that time, but realized the context much later. Even after Baba left the body, many devotees experienced his guidance directly.

GENERAL DESCRIPTION OF BABA'S LIFE

(Collected by Hira Vallabh Pant and K.K. Sah)

Baba always wore just a loincloth, never any clothes, even in the coldest weather. His needs were very simple. He did not drink milk or chai either. His kutiya did not even have a proper roof; it just had a couple of sheets of tin to protect the dhuni from rain and wind. He had a simple jute blanket and a deer or tiger skin to lay on the floor. Regardless of the weather or day, Baba's schedule never changed. He was totally selfless and treated everyone equally. No one was allowed to approach him without having a bath in the river. Although Baba was a strict brahmachari, occasionally he would allow a woman to come for darshan out of respect for the purity of her heart.

No one was allowed to touch Baba, and he did not usually touch anyone either. The only exception was that he always gave devotees prasad and applied *tika* on their forehead personally.

Baba was very active, and there was no hint of laziness in his being. Even while being completely lost in the Divine, he was also very alert and practical in the running of the ashram. For instance, if a cook ever forgot to add salt to a dish he was cooking, Baba would shout out from the kutiya to remind him to add salt.

In his youth, Sombari Baba had a practice of buying a couple of *sers* of vegetables, (one ser is a little under a kilo), making puris from a couple of sers of flour and then distributing the food among the sadhus and needy people. Apart from this, he would also make *atta* (dough) from 12 to 15 sers of whole wheat flour and distribute it too.

Sombari Baba had a very soft heart, but when it came to practical life, he was also very strict. Whenever he saw any personality faults in his devotees, he never hesitated to point them out honestly, with the intention to help them overcome these faults.

DESCRIPTION OF BABA'S LIFE

(Contributed by Shri Shankar Lal Sah)

It is estimated that Baba spent the last 40 years of life in Kumaon. Some of the noteworthy places associated with his stay are Kakrighat, Khairna, Kainchi and Padampuri. Of all these places, Padampuri was graced by Baba's presence most often. When Baba arrived at Padampuri the first time, there were no facilities there. The place was called Jhajjar earlier, and Baba gave it the name *Padampuri.* He would sit under a tree with just two tin sheets to offer shelter. The tree is still at the ashram at Padampuri. Baba also left his body at Padampuri.

Baba sometimes visited Laturiya Baba's ashram at Haldwani, and he also visited Katghariya, where Hairakhan Baba resided. However, no one knows where Baba did his sadhana as an aspirant. When he was first seen in these places, he was already a purna siddha. Baba could see the past, present, and future as clearly as an *amla* (round fruit about 1" in diameter) held in the palm of his hand. He would know of the problems of devotees before they spoke and would help them to get relief from their problems and pains.

Baba would wear just a kaupin and sit next to the dhuni with his chimta. Sometimes, a devotee would insist and offer Baba a *pashmina* shawl. To respect their feeling, Baba would accept the offering.

Baba had devotees from all religions. He would meet them in the lower part of the ashram. Women were not allowed to come into the storeroom or kitchen. Usually, no one was allowed to stay at Baba's ashram after midnight. He would say that he met other sages and beings at night, and they did not like anyone else being present.

Baba placed great emphasis on physical, mental and internal (spiritual) purity. He would say that karma can be overcome by cleanliness in thought, body, and habits. He was a great devotee of

Lord Shiva, and would hold a bhandara every Monday. Between 40 and 400 villagers would attend the bhandara.

DESCRIPTION OF BABA

(Contributed by Pandit Jagannath Joshi, ex-Municipal Commissioner, Nainital)

Close to Baba's *asana* (seat) was a place to receive guests. At Baba's lotus feet were some flowers offered by devotees. His arms and feet were thin, and he wore a kaupin on his waist. He wore a sacred thread and a necklace of rudraksha beads around his neck. His chin sported a small beard and his lips were closed lightly. His nose was slim, and his slightly lowered eyes were large and pinkish. A beautiful light burned in his eyes, which spoke of great patience and deep study. He had a broad forehead on which little dreadlocks fell lightly, and he also had long shikha. He was not too tall nor too short, and his body seemed wiry yet strong, like that of a great yogi. He had ash smeared all over his body, and where the skin could be seen, it was copper-colored. From the way he looked and behaved, he appeared to be a person who embodied all aspects of yoga.

Nobody knew his real name, but he would hold a bhandara at this spot on every Monday (*Sombar*), hence he came to be known as Sombari Baba. Between 100 and 400 villagers would attend the bhandara. Baba graced Kurmanchal with his presence and made it the place where he carried out his spiritual practices. A person whom Baba blessed was incredibly lucky. No enemy could harm them.

Baba was from a village in the Punjab region called Pind Dadankhan. It is the great fortune of Kurmanchal that Baba graced it with his presence and made it the place where he carried out his spiritual practices.

His family was prosperous, well-educated and highly-placed. His father was a judge; his brothers were lawyers and barristers. From his childhood, he liked to travel, and on reaching youth, he traveled to many spiritual spots. Baba talked of the villages of Pushkar and Katas as very powerful and pure spots on the earth, and described them as the eyes of the earth.

GENERAL DESCRIPTION OF BABA AND HIS ASHRAMS

(Contributed by Shri Tikaram Bhatt, Bhowali)

Some decades ago, sadhus were shown a great deal of respect and love by everyone. I feel that this is no longer the case today. At that time, having blind faith in a sadhu proved to be useful. But these days, having blind faith can be a cause of being misled or being taken advantage of! I have always believed that sadhus should be respected, but at the same time, I also believe that a person who is "in the world" should keep interactions with sadhus limited. Due to this belief, the time I spent with Sombari Baba was limited to as much as I felt was necessary for a householder.

I should also mention at this point that, in those days, devotees did not have a great deal of curiosity about the place of birth, social background, or religion of a saint. To listen to the pure and loving words of a sadhu and to follow their instructions was considered the righteous thing to do. I therefore do not know anything about Sombari Baba's background. I know a little bit about his life as a sadhu. He worshipped God in the form of murtis, meditated in the morning and evening, and followed the Hindu religion. He worshipped Lord Shiva.

Baba had mainly two ashrams—Padampuri and Kakrighat. (While traveling on foot, he would make a halt for a few days at

Khairna or Kainchi). Sometimes he used to go to Haldwani for a few days, staying at the Bareilly Road kuti.

I was fortunate enough to receive Baba's darshan at a very young age. It was the season of *shishir* (the winter months), and I was traveling to a place in the plains with my family. I was a child and could not understand much, but I could not resist trying to get darshan at every opportunity. Baba's speech, though unconventional and even confusing from a worldly perspective, was like nectar that felt wonderful to the ears.

Kakrighat

Old Shiva temple under banyan tree at Kakrighat

Kakrighat, by the banks of the Kosi River, is the gateway to the Almora region and has been frequented by great sages for many centuries. Many of them performed spiritual practices here. Until the end of the 19th century and even during the beginning of the 20th century, many great sages passed through this area.

KAKRIGHAT

(Contributed by Dhanilal Sah)

When the kings of the Chand dynasty came to the plains for the winter months, they would pass through Kakrighat. It was their practice to meet with the sages who stayed there and seek their advice and blessings.

Several sages have taken jeev samadhi at Kakrighat. (When a saint feels that their work in a particular body is done, they sometimes choose to be "buried alive" consciously. The saint enters a room and goes into a state of deep samadhi. The door to the room is then sealed. This practice is only undertaken by saints of the highest order, and their presence continues to bless anyone who comes to the area.) At this very spot on the banks of the Kosi river, Sombari Baba made his seat under a large banyan tree. He did not build any ashram, temple, or walls. He simply sat on the sand among the rocks that were naturally present at the spot.

DESCRIPTION OF KAKRIGHAT

(Contributed by Shri Badri Sah, Lawyer)

In old land records, Kakrighat is mentioned as Gudarmarhi.

About 25 miles away from Nainital, on the road to Almora via Garampani and Khairna, there is a village by the name of Naugaon. Close to the village is the confluence of two rivers, the Kosi and the Salmadhi, and a large temple is located close to this confluence. Yards upriver from the temple, along the right bank of the Kosi, is an area with five sacred trees known as *panch pallava*: banyan, peepul, *gular* (cluster fig), *aank* (crown flower) and *dhaank* (flame of the forest).

Also, a little distance away (about half a kilometer from Baba's asana), on the other side near the Shiva Temple, is the jeevit samadhi of three saints (on a wall in niche style). Most sages have a samadhi created in their honor after leaving the body, but a jeevit samadhi is different. When a sage asks to be buried while alive and fully conscious, this type of samadhi is considered to be a very auspicious event, and the sage continues to shower grace and blessings on anyone who visits the spot. At this place, the Kosi river flows at a peaceful and meandering pace. A person visiting this spot immediately feels relaxed, peaceful, and happy. The calm and peaceful vibrations of the sages still pervade at such places.

A short distance down from Gudariya Baba's cave is a spot with two large banyan trees, one located slightly higher than the other. Going back to the year 1914, under the lower banyan tree, there was a platform on which was located a small hut without a roof. Next to the hut there was a small temple. In the center of the hut was a fire pit where a fire was always kept burning. On one side of the hut, a *jyoti* (oil lamp) was kept lit in a niche. The flame of the lamp banishes darkness, and always moves upward, signifying the path of wisdom. The flame is also considered to be a form of Ma Durga. Where the jyoti lamp is lit daily, there can be no darkness or evil forces.

When I visited this spot, I noticed monkeys and cows near the ashram, and many beautiful birds, both local birds from the hills and migratory birds. All the birds and animals seemed to be content and peaceful, enjoying the vibrations of the ashram. Several leaves of the *bilva* tree were offered at the temple (the bilva, or "stone apple" tree, is sacred to Lord Shiva), and a faint smell of incense emanated from within.

BABA SENDS PRASAD FOR PRIYAJI

(Contributed by K.K. Sah)

When my sister Priyaji married, her home was in Almora. Once, she was passing by Kakrighat on the way to Almora. The road that passed close to the ashram was on the opposite side of the river, and as women were not allowed into Baba's ashram, she would have passed by from quite far, and would not have been visible from the ashram. Baba said to one of the devotees in the ashram: "The daughter of Inspector Bhawanidas Sah is coming. Go take this fruit as prasad for her," and he gave the man a guava to take for Priyaji. The man was quite surprised when Baba handed him a guava, as it was not the season for guavas at the time.

When Priyaji passed by the road across the river to the ashram, Baba stood on the bank of the river on the ashram side so she could have darshan, and blessed her from there. By this time, the devotee with whom Baba had sent the prasad arrived on her side of the river and gave her the guava. On seeing the guava, she was very moved at the love of this sage and tears started rolling down her cheeks. She had wished to have a guava earlier in the day, and wondered when she would be able to get one next since the season was a few months away.

MOONG ARRIVES FOR MAKING KHICHDI

(Contributed by Shri Dhanilal Sah)

Shri Sombari Baba could see the past and future like someone might watch a movie.

Pandit Bhairavdutt Bhandari, an advocate from Ranikhet, would visit Baba for darshan whenever he could. Once, in the month of *Jeth* (a month in the Hindu calendar that coincides with May/June in the Western calendar), he set off for Kakrighat late one evening on his bicycle.

He arrived at a village called Bazol on the way, gave his bicycle to the chief of the village for safekeeping, and continued to Kakrighat, arriving there in the morning. Baba had finished his morning practice and devotees had started gathering by the time Shri Bhandari arrived at the ashram. Baba looked at Shri Bhandari and said, "Ah, what can we say of these great people? He was there a little while ago, sat on an iron horse, and now he's here already! This evening he'll be back there!" Shri Bhandari was taken aback, because he had not told anyone of his plans. He usually stayed over at the ashram for a night, but during this particular visit, he needed to go back to Ranikhet the same evening.

That afternoon, Baba told a devotee, Hariduttji, to cook for Shri Bhandari. Hariduttji asked if he should make khichdi using *urad* (a lentil). On hearing this, Baba said, "It is the month of Jeth, it is terribly hot, and you're thinking of feeding him urad! (urad is usually eaten in winters). Make the khichdi from something that is cooling, like moong."

Haridutt muttered to Shri Bhandari: "If you had brought some moong along, it would have helped. This is an ashram, now where shall I get moong from?"

A little while later a man came by on horseback, and he called out to Hariduttji from the other bank of the river. So Hariduttji went across the river to meet the man, and the man gave him some bundles, saying that the grain wholesaler from a nearby village had sent them for the ashram. On opening the bundles, Hariduttji found moong, rice, butter and cabbage. Having learnt his lesson, he proceeded to make moong (yellow lentil) khichdi for Shri Bhandari as instructed by Baba.

Padampuri

Padampuri a few years after Sombari Baba's samadhi

A DESCRIPTION OF THE PADAMPURI ASHRAM

(Contributed by local person from Padampuri)

The venerable Sombari Baba was among the sages who made Uttarakhand their home in the early part of the 20th century. He was born in a village called Pind Dadan Khan in undivided India (this village lies is what is now Pakistan). After performing great spiritual practices in the areas of Kailash-Manasarovar, Badrinath, Kedarnath, Gangotri and Yamnotri, Baba arrived at a spot in the district of Nainital that he felt would be a good place to carry on his sadhana. He named the place Padampuri.

This place is located about forty kilometers from the town of Nainital, in a narrow valley that lies along the upper reaches of a small river called Kalsa. At this spot, two mountain streams merge to form the Kalsa river. Sombari Baba set up his ashram at the confluence of the two streams, amidst big rocks at the base of tall hills under a large banyan tree. This tree is still at the ashram at Padampuri. He did not build any ashram, temple, or walls. He simply sat on the sand among the rocks that were naturally present at the spot.

While Baba was living at Padampuri, stories of his spiritual prowess and his great powers spread far and wide. He was considered among the greatest sages to live in the Himalayas at that time. It is said that he had complete knowledge of past, present and future, and also that he was blessed with *Annapurna siddhi* (Goddess Annapurna is the presiding goddess of food. Siddhi means special achievement or blessing). He treated everyone equally. He was completely detached from the world and only wore a simple loincloth. He slept on the floor and has no possessions. Baba had a dhuni that was always kept lit. He spent most of his time in a natural cave under some large rocks, doing his spiritual practices.

People from all over the country came searching for him. People from abroad came seeking his blessings, as did some of the British administrators who were stationed in the country. Devotees came to Baba with their personal problems and Baba helped them all. Just seeing this great sage would bring peace to troubled minds and hearts. He looked upon everyone with great compassion. Even domesticated animals like cows and goats from the surrounding villages formed a habit of going to Baba's ashram after grazing in the forest. They would turn up at the ashram and be fed by him. Baba had great love for all of nature, including animals and trees. He asked people to stop the practice of killing the fish in the river.

It was not just devotees who visited Baba at the ashram. Very often, other great sages would come to Padampuri to visit him. Once, the great sage Sri Hairakhan Baba came to Padampuri to meet Sombari Baba, and spent some time with him. A platform was made at the place where Hairakhan Baba stayed in Padampuri. The famous Gandhian teacher Kaka Kalelkar wrote a book about his travels in the Himalayas and he dedicated a whole chapter in the book to Padampuri. Kakaji had heard about Sombari Baba, so he went to Padampuri to meet him. He stayed at Padampuri for some time and spent long hours with Baba.

Many years after Baba arrived at Padampuri, a small village formed there. One of Baba's great devotees, Shri Gulabsingh, had a small temple built there, and across the river, he had a small dharamshala built for sadhus and devotees to stay when they came to Padampuri. As far as Sombari Baba himself was concerned, he had no interest in temples and structures. He was a great renunciate and needed nothing. However, he did not oppose the building of the temple and the dharamshala for people who came to visit.

PADAMPURI

(Contributed by Shri Kaka Kalelkar)

There are two different philosophies that sadhus tend to follow. There are ones like Khaki Baba, who follow the philosophy of serving people in practical ways, such as healing those who are unwell, feeding the hungry, and clothing those who are in need of clothes.

Then there are those sadhus who follow a different kind of philosophy: they consider even this kind of work to be an obstruction on the spiritual path. They believe that a sadhu should remain in contemplation of the Divine and should not be attached even to social service. They believe that in order to donate anything, one first needs to create desire within oneself to attain something, attain it, and then donate it. They liken it to putting a hand in the mud, and then washing it clean, so they prefer to simply stay away from it all.

This does not mean that they are apathetic towards society or that they do not have compassion. They believe that the tendencies of the mind ought to be understood first. It is not the action, but the attachment and pride that go with an action that binds one down. The attachment arising from a so-called good action can be more binding because, when doing a good deed, it is much more difficult to identify that an attachment is being formed. They feel that even going to public events and giving discourses about good philosophies does not really serve because the speaker tends to get blinded to the fact that his words are not really having much of an effect on the listeners; he is just keen on saying what he wishes to say.

They believe that if someone is really in need of your guidance, they will find you one way or another. This is how the divine scheme of things works. Going around lecturing or trying to fix the world shows that you do not really have faith in the divine power that has been running the world since before the beginning of time. In case an occasion calls for you to share wisdom with someone or serve them in other ways, it is totally okay to do so in the moment and then be free of any attachment to the action. As long as you are still in the grasp of the three *gunas* (*sattva*, the quality of balance and harmony; *rajas*, the quality of passion and activity; and *tamas*, the quality of chaos and disorder) it is good to indulge in some sort of service to encourage the growth of compassion and love in the heart. However, it is important to remember that this is a tool for purifying your consciousness and it cannot free you from the clutches of attachment.

We had the good fortune of meeting a great sadhu who believed in this way of being.

Both Khaki Baba and Sombari Baba were similar in some ways. They both hardly ate and both wore hardly any clothes. Both were very wise and well traveled. But they were poles apart in terms of the philosophies by which they led their respective lives. Khaki Baba had an ashram, whereas Sombari Baba could not be found in any one place for more than a few days; he believed that by staying in a place for too long, one gets attached to the place and its surroundings. Khaki Baba collected many medicinal herbs and served anyone in need, whereas Sombari Baba did not collect anything. He chose to follow the path of the *virakta* (unattached).

When we had arrived at Khaki Baba's ashram, he offered us some sweets, and when I said I did not take sugar, he offered us *mewa* (dry fruits) instead. Sombari Baba, on the other hand, offered us a piece each from his own *baati* (a small thick piece of bread). It is a rare blessing to be served such pure food. I had never had such delicious food in my life. Baba had received some flour from the simple farmers near the ashram that very morning. He mixed it with some *ghee* (clarified butter) and fresh, pure water from the river, then cooked the baati himself using twigs from the forest. I cannot even begin to describe the sweetness and taste of the baati.

Khaki Baba would offer people things according to their taste, whereas Sombari Baba offered people a part of whatever he was having. Yet there were also striking similarities between these beings: Khaki Baba insisted on ordering Indian sugar specifically from a trader, and when we arrived at Sombari Baba's ashram, he was scolding a trader for using imported sugar that the British were trying to force upon the country.

We stayed in the region near Almora for a fortnight. We met a person with whom Swami Vivekananda had spent some time and were able to get a lot of information from him. After this, we planned to travel from Almora to Kathgodam and then to Haridwar, and from there we intended to make a journey into Garhwal. En route from Almora to Kathgodam, we decided to go via Mukteshwar, as we had heard of Sombari Baba who lived in that area.

Padampuri is blessed with great natural beauty. It is surrounded by tall peaks on all sides, and there are three small rivers flowing through the valley. If one looks up at the sky from this valley, it no longer appears as vast as it is; rather, it seems to be a small triangular roof. We arrived at Padampuri around dusk. Our guide, who was leading a horse that carried all our luggage, said, "Can you see that small temple across the river? Sombari Baba lives there." We first went to the dharamshala on our side of the river and arranged all our luggage. After this, we headed towards the ashram for darshan.

Baba had a rule that anyone coming for darshan should first clean themselves by washing their hands, feet, and face in the river. As he lived across the river, that rule was automatically implemented while crossing the river! As it was close to dusk, we sat on a big rock in the middle of the river and completed our practice. Then we carried on further to the ashram. Baba was totally in harmony with nature. His body was uncovered, except for a small loincloth. His hair had grown into dreadlocks that danced in front of his eyes and forehead. He held a chillum in one hand.

We bowed down and paid our respects. Baba bowed to us with equal respect, and proceeded to go sit by the temple. He invited us to go and sit close to him. Out of respect, we chose not to sit at the same level as this great sadhu, and decided to sit on the steps that led up to the small temple. Baba did not tolerate our mental attitude of "high and low." He came and sat next to us on the steps. On seeing this, we moved further down and sat on a mat that was kept on the ground. Baba would not be beaten. He came and sat on the bare ground next to the blanket. Now what else could we do? We removed the mat and sat on the bare ground too. On seeing this, Baba spoke, "I see the Divine in you. I have been waiting for you since the morning. You are like the divine trio of Brahma, Vishnu, and Mahesh who have come to bless me with your darshan."

On the face of it, Sombari Baba did not know who we were. No one had informed him of our arrival. No one could have because we had not informed anyone of our plans. We found out later that he had been telling people in the ashram since the morning, "Some people are coming to meet me. I am waiting for them." A farmer who had been there all day told us that since late afternoon, Baba had started getting up and looking towards the road to see if the visitors he was expecting had arrived. When he could not see us, he would mutter, "That cannot be. They have to arrive today." We informed Baba that our porter had arrived late, and that is why we were delayed. Had he arrived on time, we would have reached the ashram much earlier.

After this initial conversation, we told Baba about our journey. Sombari Baba had undertaken many yatras, so he was a living encyclopedia like Khaki Baba. No matter what area I spoke of, he described the area in great detail. He spoke pure Hindi, so we could not make out where he might have come from originally.

We mentioned Khaki Baba, and on hearing the name Sombari Baba immediately pranaamed respectfully. He said, "Khaki Baba is a great sadhu and renunciate. He serves a great number of people." Then he continued: "He is a great raj yogi, and gets involved with these things. I am a simple person—this tiger skin and kamandalu are my only possessions. If too many people start coming to see me here, I'm likely to disappear from here as well." After this, we talked about many other sadhus that Baba knew. Through this discussion, he also educated us about the different philosophies that each of the sadhus lived by.

I said to Baba: "You are teaching us about life. As a school teacher, I also teach my studcnts about life. The difference is that I speak of things I have read, whereas you speak of things from experience. Could you please give me some instructions on how to teach?"

Baba replied: "I know you teach your students the *Bhagavad Gita* and explain its meaning to them. But this is not appropriate. The detachment taught by the *Bhagavad Gita* is hard for even old and wise people to imbibe, so how can you expect young children to follow it?" He quoted a stanza from the Gita which speaks of action without desire or attachment, then continued, "How are they going to understand the meaning of something like this? First, let them learn to work and perform action with desire. Your teachings of *Vedanta* make them into useless people with no power or will. They are unable to complete the tasks that they wish to perform, and spend all their time talking about philosophy. The teachings of the Gita are for people who can understand and assimilate them."

This was a total revelation for me. I asked, "So I shouldn't teach them the Gita at all?"

Baba replied: "Sure, teach them some things from the Gita, but talk of desireless action is not for them at this stage in their lives."

After this, we asked Baba for information on our forthcoming travels in Uttarakhand. The more we spoke, the more we realized what a great authority this sadhu was on all kinds of matters. We stayed on for quite some time, then finally paid our respects to Baba and headed back to the dharamshala across the river. It was full by this time. Had we not arranged our luggage there earlier, we would probably not have found space to sleep there.

The next morning, we woke up early and went to meet Baba for darshan again and to say our farewells. Baba was finishing his meditation as we arrived. As we were talking, a mongoose came by. Baba said, "This is a blessing from the Divine, who is here to give you darshan in this form." Baba then offered us some chai. I mentioned that I did not take tea and Baba replied: "This is not like the chai you know. This is chai from the Himalayas. It has neither sugar nor milk. Drink up, it will help you during the journey." Along with the tea, Baba gave us three pieces from one single almond as prasad. He also added a special herb in the chai. After drinking the chai, we asked Baba for permission to carry on with our journey. He lovingly put his hands on our shoulders and blessed us saying, "The Divine is everywhere."

THE ASHRAM AT PADAMPURI

(Contributed by Pandit Jagannath Joshi, ex-Municipal Commissioner, Nainital)

Padampuri is a very cold place. In the winters, water left outside freezes into ice. Baba's ashram in Padampuri is located in a dense forest, at the foot of tall peaks, next to the confluence of three rain-fed rivers. A little higher up from the ashram is a pond which remains frozen through most of the winter. Because of the location of the ashram in a deep valley, there isn't much sunlight.

In the ashram, right next to the river, is a natural high ground. Simply by being in this place, one experiences an indescribable peace. The quality of the silence at the Padampuri ashram is quite different from that at the Kakrighat ashram. The silence at Padampuri is like a deep, meditative, and withdrawn silence, whereas that at Kakrighat, whilst equally deep, is engaged and celebratory.

Baba would say that Padampuri is a very holy place. One winter, on an unusually quiet and cold day, there was no movement even in the leaves of the trees, no sounds of birds or animals in the forest. The whole forest was covered with pure white snow that made night seem like day and day seem like night—the bright sky during the day made the valley seem dark in contrast, like the night; and at night, the light from the moon and stars reflecting off the snow made the valley seem bright like day. On this day, a great siddha who lived in the area blessed Baba with darshan, and also gave him food.

A certain tribe of people called the "Saun" lived in the area near Padampuri. Baba was very happy with these people. He said that they'd turn up with large logs for the dhuni and then leave quickly without expecting anything in return. They were known as simple, generous folk who guided lost travelers and always offered travelers food and shelter.

BABA'S USUAL SCHEDULE

(Contributed by Pandi Jagannath Joshi, ex-Municipal Commissioner, Nainital)

Sombari Baba's manner, his behavior, his countenance and the surroundings of his ashrams were very quiet, meditative and peaceful. He was like one of the great rishis of old as described in the scriptures. After his early morning practices, Baba would come out of his hut at eight in the morning. At about the same time, devotees and visitors would start coming to the ashram. Baba would distribute sweets to all visitors mixed with leaves of *tulsi* (holy basil). After this, tea would be served to all visitors. On some days, the tea would contain herbs based on Baba's instructions.

Then Baba would go to the dhuni at the lower level of the ashram closer to the river. There too, he would distribute fruits, sweets, and other prasad. If someone was on the way to the ashram, Baba would already know, and he would put aside some food for them in advance. Baba said, "Someone may bring an offering of pumpkins, someone may bring sweets. Mix it all in the prasad." Baba would mix everything together and distribute it as prasad. His teaching was that people make offerings according to their capacity. Everyone's offerings are accepted by the divine and treated alike. Once blessed, they become prasad and everything is equally beautiful, pure, and holy.

At around 10 or 11, the devotees present at the ashram would be asked to prepare lunch. While lunch was being prepared, Baba would go to the river bank, sit on his asana and do some japa. After this, he would go and perform *arti* at the dhuni, at the shrine of Lord Shiva and the samadhi of Gudaria Baba, which is on the ashram premises.

By then, it would be time for everyone to have lunch. Baba would ensure that everyone was fed, but he himself would not eat anything. He would not even drink water! At around 1:30 or so Baba would do his afternoon practices and then take some herbal tea. Visitors would relax, walk around, or engage in some work at the ashram.

Around dusk, everyone joined in for evening prayers. Baba would perform arti at the dhuni and at the Shiva shrine. After this, he would again go to the dhuni, speak with people for a little while, and distribute food and other prasad. Often Sombari would apply a *tilak* (mark on the forehead) using vibhuti, the sacred ash from the fire, to his devotees and thus prevent any danger or problems for them. That tilak would guarantee that the devotee would reach home safely. Baba would say that if someone traveled to him for darshan, it was his responsibility to see that they got there and returned home safely. After this, everyone would head home. No one was allowed to stay at the ashram after 8 p.m. Even other sadhus were not allowed to stay in the ashram after 8 p.m. He would say that he met other sages and beings at night, and they did not like anyone else being present.

After this, no one knows what Baba did; how much time he spent doing his practices, how long he rested, and so on. The next day's activities began as usual at 8 in the morning.

When Baba arrived at Padampuri the first time, there was nothing much there. He would sit under the banyan tree with just two tin sheets to offer shelter. Sombari never covered his kutir. Sometimes when it was raining, he slept under a roof. Padampuri was famous for very cold weather. He used to go there in the cold weather and go to Kakrighat when it was hot, which was very hot—the opposite of what we would do.

During the Holi festival, Baba would spend a week in a cave near a place called Khairna, across the river Kosi. He did this at the request of his devotees from the village of Majhera. The day after Holi, he would head back to the ashram at Kakrighat, where he would remain until the month of *Maghshirsha* (a month in the lunar Indian calendar, which usually falls between mid-October and mid-November). During the witer, Baba would move to his ashram back to Padampuri.

DAILY ACTIVITIES AT THE ASHRAM

(Contributed by Shri Ramlal Sah, Nainital)

There was a schedule at Baba's ashram. A group of cows would turn up in the morning and would be fed khichdi. After the cows left, it would be the turn of a group of mice. They would start making noises, be fed, and then leave. Towards evening, a group of monkeys would turn up, and they would be fed some chickpeas, fruits, and other things. One time when K.K.'s father, Shri Bhawanidas Sah, was present at the Padampuri ashram, there was a sack of *gram* (peas, lentils, or flour made from them) kept at the ashram, and Baba would give the people some every day to feed the monkeys.

He ate very little, only once a day, at night. The meal was very small, comprised of a small tikkar or sometimes a small amount of khichdi, about a handful. He would make a dish called batti from about the same quantity of flour. This he would divide in three equal parts. He would feed one part to the fish. Another part would be left aside, and no one knew whom this was for. The third part Baba would partake of himself. Apart from this little quantity, he never took anything else like tea, milk, or fruits.

LIVING AT THE ASHRAM

(Contributed by Hira Vallabh Lohni, Municipal Ranger, Retired, Nainital)

Many prominent and well-known people from the cities would visit the ashram. There was a small village called Khunigaad close by. People from this village would visit the ashram regularly. Shri Gopal Dutt Pandey, who was the local forester, was a great devotee of Baba and would visit the ashram frequently.

I started living at the ashram at Padampuri. I stayed there for three months and got used to all the customs at the ashram. I made acquaintance with all the people who stayed there and also the ones who visited frequently. Whenever Mohan Singh would come to pay respects, Baba would say, "What is the point of worshipping me like this? Serve the downtrodden, those in pain, and feed the hungry. That is the best seva you can do. You did a good thing by feeding the hungry Brahmin. Continue this practice."

Throughout my stay of three months at the ashram, I never once saw Baba eat or drink. All he would take is a quarter ratti of charas occasionally. He wore only a loincloth and had a shawl to cover his body. The shawl was full of small holes, probably from the sparks from his chillum. He only had a small pot of water with him, and a piece of wood nearby for his dhuni.

USED OFFERING

(Contributed by Pandit Khimanada Suyal, Kumaon)

Once in 1915, I went to visit Sombari Baba at the ashram in Padampuri. I had taken along one-and-a-quarter *tola* charas as an offering for Baba (a tola is about 11 grams. An offering of one-and-a-quarter units is considered auspicious). A sadhu was traveling along for Baba's darshan. On the way, the sadhu expressed a wish to smoke some of the charas that was meant for Baba. I declined, saying that it was a sealed packet and it would not be good to open it. It is a custom that anything offered to God or a holy person should be fresh and unused. For example, if it is a flower, it should not be smelled by anyone before it is offered; if it is an item of food, it should not be tasted by anyone else before it is offered.

The sadhu insisted, saying that there would be no problem. I eventually relented, and we smoked some of the charas. When we got to Padampuri, I prostrated to Baba and offered the charas. Baba looked at me and said, "So, you want to offer me an opened packet of charas! Don't you know you should not offer anything to God or a sadhu that had been used?" We thought Baba would not find out, but he knew everything!

CHILLUM

(Contributed by Shri Hira Vallabh Pant)

There was never any lack of anything at Baba's ashram; not just food, but also all other items were always available in abundance.

Some of the sadhus that visited would smoke between ten to fifteen grams of charas at a time. Even they got whatever they needed. Sometimes Baba would also smoke a chillum, but he never used a chillum that was used by the other sadhus. His chillum would always be prepared separately, with a very small quantity—about a quarter *ratti*. A ratti is a very small measure of weight, and a quarter ratti would be about the weight of a grain of mustard. There is a saying about sadhus and their use of charas to induce spiritually intoxicated states:

Jati ko ratti auron ko masha
Is se adhik peene par dekho tamasha

It means that for sadhus just starting the use of charas, one ratti is enough; for those who are used to it, a slightly larger quantity (called *masha*) is enough. If any more is used, then the whole thing is no longer about spirituality, and it is an entertaining drama for people to watch!

Baba was very particular about the amount: it would always be a quarter ratti, which is a very minuscule amount. Sometimes he would ask people to make it for him with this quantity, and sometimes he would give them the exact quantity to use for preparing his chillum. He would sometimes share his own chillum with others, but he was very particular not to use anyone else's chillum. His use of the chillum, just like his food, clothes and other necessities, was very minimal. His life was so simple, well-rounded, well-regulated, and pure that simply by having his darshan feelings of faith and devotion would rise in people's hearts. It was due to the simplicity and purity of Baba's life and daily routine that everyone would automatically be attracted to him.

SOME OF BABA'S ASANAS

(Contributed by Hiralal Sah, Hubbaji)

1. One of Baba's asanas is at Kakrighat. He would usually sit a little distance away from the ashram.
2. Kakrighat and Padampuri were the main places Sombari Baba stayed. He also had other places where he stopped along the road to Badrinath, such as Rudraprayag, Nandprayag, and Vishnuprayag. Close to Badrinath, there is a hot water spring called Tapta Kund. There are some steps that lead from this place towards Badrinath. There was a large rock here, with a hollow like a cave underneath. A structure has now been built there and it is used as a gathering place. Baba had an asana under this rock.
3. Close to Bareilly in Uttar Pradesh is a place called Soron, which is said to be the birth place of Tulsidas. In Soron, there is a *kund* (pond) of about 40 feet by 40 feet, close to a large tree. The ashes of great beings are immersed in the pond after their last rites. Sombari Baba had an asana under a tree close to this pond. About two miles away from the pond flows a river called the Bhagirathi Ganga. The water in the pond flows in from this river. The importance of this place has been mentioned in the Puranas. There is a story connected to Sagar Rishi, who has a hundred sons. Sombari Baba would say: *"Jab kabhi Ganga, Soron paar."* (You can get the same grace as from the Ganga at the Soron.)
4. On the Haldwani-Bareilly road is an orchard that was owned by a person called Bansidhar Seth. Baba had an asana there under a tree. And while traveling between Padampuri and Kakrighat, Baba would stop at Khairna and Kainchi (usually he would halt longer at Khairna). He had asanas in both these places also.

First Darshans with Baba

FIRST DARSHAN

(Contributed by Hiralal Sah, Hubbaji)

I first met Sombari Baba in November 1908. I was living in Mukteshwar at the time. I was supposed to go for the *chatti* function (ritual held on the sixth day after birth) for the son of my brother Joga Sah Kumaiiya. He was born on the 23rd of November 1908, so the function was being held on the 29th of November.

I left from Mukteshwar on a horse. I kept some pieces of almonds in one pocket of my coat and put some pistachios and raisins in the other pocket. I ate some of the nuts along the way and enjoyed doing so as they were very tasty. As I was quite young, around 20 years old, I was not very interested in spirituality and did not have any devotion towards saints.

I reached Padampuri along the way. There I crossed the river whilst still astride my horse and came to the road that led to Nainital. There was a shop on the road at that place. In those days, all material would be transported to shops in the area on horses from Haldwani. Close to the shop was a resting place where the owners of the horses could rest for the night and carry on with their journey the next day.

When I was on the road climbing up towards Nainital, my gaze fell to the left towards an ashram (I feel in hindsight that happening to look that way was an inspiration from Baba). I saw some people sitting there. I turned the horse downwards again and went close to the shop. I asked the shopkeeper to feed the horse some grains and look after him, saying that I would be back shortly. I pulled my trousers up to my knees, crossed the river, and arrived at the ashram. There were steps going up to the ashram from the river. I went up and saw a dhuni with wood burning. There was a structure like a shelf over the dhuni, on which was kept a copy of Tulsidas' *Ramayana*. A few feet away to the left was a temple of Goddess Annapurna. Between the dhuni and this temple, a staircase went upwards. At the top of the stairs was a small flat area. I found out later that this was Sombari Baba's place. He would sit there in the open, with no structure, no walls or roof, just his special dhuni.

A little above the Annapurna temple there was a small temple, and above that was a place called Swargashram. Whatever people brought along would be offered at the Annapurna temple. People would go to the temple upstairs using the staircase.

I was young, with no sense of devotion. I did not even have the experience of knowing how to behave in the presence of a saint, what to take as an offering, and so on. Somehow my eyes fell on the prasad offered at the Annapurna temple. I don't know what inspired me, but I emptied my pockets of whatever was left of the foodstuff I was carrying, put in all in a leaf and offered it all at the Annapurna temple.

From above, I heard the voice of Sombari Baba: "In the corner, there is a small bundle in a white cloth; pick it up." I picked up the bundle and touched it to try and see what was inside. I could make out that there were almonds inside. Without Baba asking me, I said, "This bundle has almonds in it."

Baba said "Shell the almonds and bring them to me. Go sit at the wall in the front."

I did as instructed and went to the wall to shell the almonds. On opening the bundle, I saw not just almonds, but also pistachios and raisins—all the same things that were in my pocket. Only the almonds were different, everything else was what I had offered. I went close to the wall, shelled the almonds, put them in the cloth, and went to the base of the staircase. I showed them to Baba and said, "Here it is, all of it. There are almonds, pistachios, and raisins." The items were in my hand, tied in a loose knot in the white cloth.

Baba said nothing about this, but asked, "Are you the brother of Joga Sah? He has sent a bunch of blankets. They will reach the people who are destined to have them." Then he said, "Open the bundle and fill in your pockets." I did as instructed, opened the small bundle and started to fill my pockets. Strangely, both coat pockets were filled, but the small bundle still had much left in it! Then Baba said, "Take the bundle, too. Now go." I bowed down, pranaamed Baba and left.

This was the first darshan. After this, I felt inspired to visit Baba over and over again. This was all due to Baba's compassion and inspiration. I did not have any karmas to receive such grace, but for some reason, Baba's grace surrounded me and increased day by day.

GRACE AND MALPUAS

(Contributed by Hira Vallabh Lohni, Municipal Ranger, Retired, Nainital)

In 1914 I was about 20 years old. I had just left my home in Satrali due to extreme poverty and I had come to Nainital in search of some work. Even though food was very cheap at the time, I had so little that many times I could not afford to eat. It was the winter season, and winters in Nainital are known to be very cold. Even in that weather, all I could afford to wear was a dhoti, a torn shirt and a *chola* (cloth wrapped around the body like a shawl). I had no shoes and had to walk barefoot in the bitter cold.

On reaching Nainital, I wandered around for a while in search of work. I heard about a place called Padampuri where a sage called Sombari Baba had an ashram. I heard that people were fed for free every day at the ashram, and on Mondays, a bhandara was held where tasty food and sweets were served to all in great quantities. On hearing this, I thought about going to the ashram, hoping that on getting there at least I would not have to worry about getting a meal. So the very next day, I set off for Padampuri.

Padampuri is a very cold place, colder than even Nainital. Even oil kept in a container thickens and turns solid in the winters there. I had no shoes on, and not enough clothes to keep out the cold. During the journey, I asked everyone I came across how far Padampuri was, and whether I was on the right road. There were no tea shops along the road as there are now. The only refreshment available was hot milk. It was very cheap, at about eight liters for a rupee, but I could not afford even that, so I simply kept walking.

At about 4 p.m., I reached a place called Matiyal. There was a solitary shop there, owned by Thakur Mohan Singh. The shop was quite busy, with lots of customers buying things. I waited for a while until the rush died down and then asked Mohan Singh how far Padampuri was. He asked me where I was going in Padampuri, and I said that I was going to Sombari Baba's ashram. He asked me if I had other travelers along. I said I was traveling alone. Mohan Singh advised me not to travel alone along that road as there was a tiger on the prowl and it was already starting to get late. There was a fire burning close to the shop, so I decided to sit next to it for a while to warm myself.

By now, I was very hungry. I had no money at all, not even a single *paisa*. I started to worry, thinking about my hunger, the cold, and the fact that I had no money. I had left Nainital thinking that I would reach Padampuri by the evening and would not have to worry about food. But here was a new problem that poured water on all my dreams: the presence of a tiger in the forest. The fear of death at the hands of the tiger stopped me from proceeding further after hearing the shopkeeper's warning.

To be perfectly honest, I had no faith and devotion towards Baba. I was simply thinking about the free food when I set out for Padampuri. Now I started to worry about where I could spend the night. In a little while, the shopkeeper started to shut his shop for the day. All sorts of questions started spinning in my mind: where could I go, how would I get food to eat, where could I spend the night, and so on.

Mohan Singhji asked me: "What community do you belong to?" I replied that I was a Brahmin, and he said, "There's a room upstairs, please go there." The room had a fire going inside, so I went in and sat there. I could see that food was being prepared in the house. Mohan Singh called out to someone in one of the inner rooms and said, "Don't add salt to the *subji* (vegetable dish). Our Brahmin guest will add salt to his taste, make himself some chapatis, and after he has had his fill, we will make food for ourselves."

I began to worry more, thinking that this person is a shopkeeper. If he's offering me food, surely he'll expect payment. I did not have any money, and I was also starving by now. I spoke up and told him that I did not have any money. Mohan Singh said, "Don't worry about that, Brahmin. Eat your fill." On hearing this, I went to the kitchen, made myself four rotis, and served myself some subji. On seeing this, Mohan Singh said, "That's not enough. Make four or five more." So I made four more chapatis, served myself more subji, and sat down in a corner to eat. Mohan Singh served me lovingly. He gave me a big glass of yoghurt, and also plenty of ghee.

After dinner was done and it was time to turn in for the night, Mohan Singh gave me some grass to make a bed and also a warm blanket for the night. By this time, I had totally forgotten about Baba. I had set out for Padampuri not out of love and devotion for Baba, but simply because I had heard I could get food there. Despite this, by Baba's grace, I got a hearty meal right at Mohan Singh's home. For me, this place was as good as Sombari Baba's ashram!

The next morning, after my ablutions, I went to Mohan Singh, thanked him profusely and asked for his permission to proceed to Padampuri. I thought that he had already fed me a hearty meal the previous night and I did not wish to take advantage of his generosity. I intended to have my next meal at Padampuri. However, Mohan Singh would have none of it. "No, Brahmin, eat and then go." He called out to the person inside, "Has the milk arrived yet? Heat it up, give some to our Brahmin guest. Give him some rice too so that he can make himself some *kheer* (rice pudding)."

What I did not know is that Mohan Singh was also a devotee of Baba and that he saw Baba in this penniless Brahmin traveler. For me, it was as if Baba brought his ashram to Matiyal! There is a saying in India that the servant of Rama is considered greater than Rama himself. I experienced this first hand: the devotee of Baba was greater than Baba for me at that moment.

I made myself some kheer, enjoyed it, and prepared to leave. I noticed that Mohan Singh was also getting ready. He gave a big tin of ghee to a porter to carry and then we all set off for Padampuri.

It is a short distance from Matiyal to Padampuri, just over a mile. We reached Padampuri quickly with no incident. On reaching the ashram, Mohan Singh asked me to wash my hands and feet in the Ganga (Baba used to call the river "Ganga"). I followed his instructions and then headed up to Baba's kutiya. A little distance below Baba's kutiya was a small hut, where a fire was lit. There were some people around the fire, smoking charas and tobacco. I sat there, too, taking in the warmth of the fire, and smoked some tobacco. I did not get Baba's darshan at the hut.

From the kutiya, Baba called out "Lohni, Lohni." I had just

arrived, and Baba did not know this, nor did he know me. So I did not respond, thinking that there must be another person in the ashram with the same name. A minute later, Baba's close devotee Shri Bageshwari came out of the kutiya, walked to the hut and asked, "Is there anyone called Lohni here?"

I replied: "I, too, am called Lohni," still thinking that Baba was looking for someone else with the same surname.

Shri Bageshwari said, "Father has been calling for you. Come up to the kutiya." (Shri Bageshwari used to address Baba as his father). I followed Shri Bageshwari up to the kutiya.

At the kutiya, I finally had darshan. I looked at Baba's thin frame and thought, *Is this Sombari Baba?* I did not bow down or pay respects.

Before I could say anything, Baba pushed a bag into my hand and said, "Take this, but don't fill your stomach like a donkey. Give some to Gangaji, some to the fish, and some to the dogs. After you're done, wash the bag and bring it back to me."

I headed to the Ganga. Putting my hand in the bag, I found that it contained four *malpuas* (sweet fried bread). I took out one, offered a part of it to the Ganga, another part to the fish, and yet another part to the dogs there. I ate the rest of it. I then proceeded to take out another malpua and eat it. After that, I was totally full. Usually, a grown man, especially one who had been hungry for a long time, can eat many malpuas. Yet here I was, totally full after having eaten less than two.

There were two more left in the bag. I didn't know what to do. I had nowhere to keep them as I had to wash and return the bag. I thought about this for a while, then finally offered the two remaining malpuas to the Ganga. I washed the bag and returned it to Baba. He did not speak.

Soon it was time for us to go rest. No one was allowed to stay at the ashram at night; they had to sleep in the dharamshala across the Ganga. As I was leaving, I overheard Baba speak with Mohan Singh: "You did a wonderful thing by feeding a hungry man. It was I who ate it."

Mohan Singh said, "Baba, it is all your prasad."

THE FIRST MEETING

(Contributed by Shri Girwan Dutt Joshi, Nainital)

In the year 1910, I was a little boy. My teacher, Shri Indra Lal Sah, had admitted me into the tenth grade in the Humphrey Mission School. Before that, I went to the smaller schools in the area. At this young age, a person does not have much need or desire for material things.

In those days, the sweet and cultured people of Nainital would speak of the miracles of Sombari Baba. That year, during the winter holidays, I set off for Kakrighat on foot along with my older brother and another relative. We stopped over at Garmpani at night. At about 7 the next morning, we arrived at the river opposite to where Baba's ashram was located. We were trying to cross the river by stepping on small rocks. None of us had taken a bath that morning. We had hardly gone a few yards when we heard a voice that seemed to come from the sky: "Do not come near Baba without having a bath." It was very cold at the time but, as instructed, we had a bath in the river and then proceeded for darshan. I bowed before Baba and offered a small copy of the *Bhagavad Gita* as a gift. Baba was pleased and blessed me, saying, "You will become a wise and learned man." Baba gave us a drink with tulsi, chili, and jaggery. He would often give us this drink during future visits. This was my first meeting with Baba.

MEETING BABA

(Contributed by Shri Krishnananda Shastri, Education Superintendent, Municipal Board, Nainital)

I was only able to meet Sombari Baba once, in 1918. I was traveling from a village called Lohali to Almora and, as the road passed by Kakrighat, I decided to meet Baba. My father had passed away recently. Baba talked about my father and asked me to continue his traditions and to live my life the way my father had lived his. Like everyone who came to visit Baba, I had also brought along some food as an offering. Baba would accept offerings from all devotees, mix them all together and then distribute it to all present. Somehow, this prasad always tasted wonderful! Those who have been fortunate enough to receive this prasad will understand what I mean. I find myself unable to either describe or write about the taste.

Baba was considered an avatar of Lord Shiva. He would know what was going on in the minds of people without them having to speak. Several well-known people who visited Nainital and the surrounding areas would come to the ashram to meet Baba. Some of them were Shri Mahamana Malviya, Shri Adityanath Jha, and Shri Krishna Joshi.

FIRST MEETING WITH BABA

(Contributed by Shri Badri Dutt Lohani, Translated by Wing Commander H C Pant)

From time immemorial, many divine souls have chosen Kurmanchal as their abode. One of the greatly revered saints among them was Sombari Baba. I witnessed many miracles and supernatural events during Baba's journey in the human body, and also saw his prophecies prove true. I am writing these down after being inspired by his other devotees to do so.

This event occurred around the year 1910, at the ashram of Padampuri. At the time, I was a teacher in a primary school in a village called Jamradi. I had the minimum qualifications required for the post. After the holidays, I was returning to Jamradi via Padampuri. I had heard about Sombari Baba and some of his miracles, so I wished to have darshan of this great sage.

As I approached the ashram, I saw Baba standing with a shawl over his shoulders, his hands folded behind his back. I was just 17 years old at the time and had never imagined I would be able to meet a real sage. There were a large number of devotees around at the time waiting to meet Baba. I folded my hands and paid my respects.

Looking at me, Baba said, "Lohni, you haven't eaten, and must be very hungry. Have some food and then carry on with your journey to your school." I was stunned. I had never met Baba before and yet he knew my name. Baba then spoke to a devotee who was nearby and said, "Listen, three devotees from Haldwani are coming and they will also be hungry. Arrange for some rice, pulses, salt and condiments, enough for four people. Prepare khichdi for all four, including Lohni."

I was surprised to hear this and moved forward towards the cord of devotees. They were sorting out fruits, milk, yoghurt, and vegetables. The fruits and vegetables were being cut into pieces, mixed up in large pans, and served as prasad. Inside and outside the temple, large heaps of assorted fruits, vegetables, and grains were being stacked. Devotees were chanting "Sombari Maharaj *ki Jai*" (glory to Sombari Maharaj), and their chants were being echoed back by the hills around the area, as if they too were paying tribute to this great sage.

In the meantime, a devotee appeared and announced that

khichdi was ready. I followed him to the place where we were supposed to eat. Baba was standing in the same position that I had first seen him in, with his hands folded behind his back. He asked me to take off my shirt and vest (it was common practice in those days to take clothes off the upper body while cooking or eating). The container in which the khichdi had been prepared was barely large enough to hold about a quarter kilo of food. Baba asked me to take the pot off the fire. He instructed me to put about half a kilo of food in the river for the fish and I did as instructed, wondering how such a small pot could contain such a large quantity of khichdi.

I then served the khichdi into three plates for the devotees who were expected to arrive from Haldwani. I remember serving about a quarter kilo in each plate, still quite unsure about how this much food was held in such a small container. Baba then asked me to serve myself, which I did. He then asked me to serve myself some more, which I also did. Then Baba asked me to serve some yoghurt, radish, and pickles. I followed his instructions.

Baba glanced towards the road. I followed his gaze and saw three people arriving—two businessmen and one cloth merchant. Baba said to them: "Food is ready for you. Please have it." The three men paid their respects to Baba and then we all ate. The khichdi was exceptionally tasty. Baba asked me to take the container over to the men, which I did. They served themselves some more and ate till they were full. Baba then walked towards the temple. I followed him and sought his permission to leave. Baba gave me some fruits and sweets as prasad and bid me goodbye. This was my first personal meeting with Sombari Baba.

Annapurna Siddhi

Devotees visiting for bhandara of Brahmachari Maharajji at Padampuri in 1959 or '60

One miracle that consistently occurred around Baba had to do with food. Often there were twenty or more people in the ashram and food or tea needed to be prepared for them all. The pot in which food would be prepared would be large enough to hold just enough food for all those who were present at that time. Suddenly some forty more people would turn up, but the food never ran out no matter how much each person ate. Baba never asked anyone to bring anything. Whatever was needed somehow seemed to arrive miraculously.

FOOD AT BABA'S ASHRAM

(Contributed by Pandit Devidutt Kabdwal)

When devotees came to visit, somehow it always happened

that some of them would bring along all the things needed for that day's meal, including the correct amount of ingredients, pots, pans, and utensils for all who were present that day. It would also invariably turn out that one of the devotees would be an expert in cooking something from the ingredients that had been brought! Baba would instruct this particular person to cook that day, without ever needing to inquire about their cooking skills or the ingredients that were available that day. If it was ever raining when the time came to cook, the rains would automatically stop. This was specially apparent during the monsoons, when it usually rains most of the day through the entire season.

Though large numbers of devotees visited the ashram every day, Baba preferred the ashram to remain empty like the sky. Whatever turned up was used up that very day. Somehow it always came to be that if more food arrived, more devotees would turn up to be fed, and if more devotees turned up, more food would automatically arrive! Also, the ingredients that were brought always turned out to be perfect to feed the type of people who were coming to visit, in accordance with their likings. No special arrangements ever needed to be made for this, it all came together naturally with no effort.

There was something else quite magical related to food at Sombari Baba's ashrams. Often, food would be cooked for the five or ten people who were at the ashram at the time of cooking, and then later, hundreds more people would come for darshan. Yet somehow, the same food would suffice for all devotees and enough would be left over to feed the birds and animals at the ashram.

It was often seen that even when Baba was deep in meditation and seemingly unaware of events, the purity of the ashram was always protected automatically. For instance, if someone bought an offering that was considered impure, it fell from their hands when they offered it, or someone sneezed into the plate so it could not be offered. The devotee would realize that it was not meant to be offered. If someone deliberately tried to offer something that was impure, they would get hurt and some drops of blood would fall into the offering, but the moment that person received Baba's darshan, the pain would vanish. In this way, they learned their lesson, and everyone else was protected from their bad intentions. If anyone had bad thoughts at the ashram, they got a very clear sign and realized they had done wrong. All this happened without Baba having to say or do anything overtly.

UNLIMITED FOOD FROM SMALL POT

(Contributed by Pandit Khimananda Suyal, Kumaon)

This is a miraculous incident that I witnessed with my own eyes. In 1912, I went to Kakrighat for darshan. Prasad was made in a small pot that could have held hardly half a kilo of food. Suddenly, many devotees turned up. The person distributing prasad hesitated, as he was sure it could not be enough for all these people. However, Baba told him not to worry and to serve everyone generously. As it turned out, there as enough prasad for everyone—all from that one small pot. There would be a bhandara at the ashram every Monday, and lots of devotees would get fed. There was never any scarcity of food at Baba's ashram.

MULTIPLE MEALS AND TIGER SIGHTING

(Contributed by Shri Hira Vallabh Pant)

Sometime during the period of the First World War, some people from Nainital who wished to have darshan of Sombari Baba left home, heading for Baba's ashram at Padampuri. In those days, there were no motorable roads in the area, so the entire journey of fifteen to sixteen miles would have to be made on foot. The last part of the journey from the village of Champhi to Padampuri was about four miles, of which three miles involved a very steep climb. The journey was a difficult one at the best of times, but during the monsoon season and winter it was even more taxing.

Of the group of people who had set out from Nainital, three people were from the Rais hotel in Tallital, who, after receiving darshan of Sombari Baba, wished to travel to the village of Khunigaad, four miles beyond Padampuri. They wanted to meet the forester at Khunigaad, Shri Gopal Dutta Pandey, about a personal matter.

When the group arrived in Padampuri and met Baba, he asked the three men from the Rais hotel to go where food was being served next to the river and eat some khichdi. The three men had already eaten before setting off from Nainital, so they told Baba they had already eaten. They said they wanted to travel further to Khunigaad and that they planned to have dinner at the village on arriving there. Baba smiled and said, "You will have your dinner at night; that is still many hours away. There's a lot of food here, go and eat." So they went to the area of the ashram where food was being served and ate the khichdi that they were served.

After lunch, they rested well, and then approached Baba to seek his permission to travel to Khunigaad. Baba said, "Wait a while, eat, and then go." The three people were taken aback, since they had already eaten before leaving Nainital, then Baba had asked them to eat just a little while ago. Now he was asking them to eat yet again! He had also said that they would have their dinner at night and they knew that the words spoken by great sages are never amiss, so it was not as if he was asking them to eat thinking they might miss dinner. They wondered what leela was at play.

There was no question of not following Baba's instructions, as doing so would mean bringing trouble upon themselves. It was late afternoon, and they were keen to start their journey as it was a four mile walk through thick forests known to be frequented by tigers and other wild animals. It was also a new moon day, so there would be no moonlight to guide them after dark; they were afraid to delay their journey any further. Sensing what was going on in their minds, Baba said, "Food is ready, so have some *halwa* (sweet confection) and puri, and then you can go." He added, "As you know, the road goes through thick jungle, and it is full of wild animals. If you hear or see any animals, don't stop or turn back, just keep walking. Take some *chir* (pine) torchwood and matches along for when it gets dark."

Following Baba's instructions, the three men ate well. After this, Baba gave them some sweets and tea. He then applied vibhuti to their foreheads. As they were leaving, they bowed down to Baba, and he reminded them: "Eat well tonight!" It was getting close to sunset by the time the men left Padampuri.

By the time they had walked a couple of miles towards Khunigaad, it was very dark and difficult to see. The men used the torchwood that Baba had asked them to take along. They had traveled about half a mile further, when about fifty yards to their left they saw a pair of eyes glowing in the light of the torches. They immediately realized these were the eyes of a tiger! Since Baba had already given them an indication of what was to come, they followed his instructions and continued to walk on. The men were very afraid now and lost their bearings. They could not remember how far Khungaad village was or whether they were heading in the right direction. They reached a rocky area and could not see a path ahead in any direction. They had also almost run out of torchwood, so they collected some pine needles and lit a fire. The light assured them somewhat and their fear of being attacked by the tiger subsided a little.

One of them had lost a shoe along the path, and another had lost the dhoti that was tied to his waist; it had probably been stuck in a thorny bush along the way. None of the men wanted to go back to find these items. They also remembered Baba had told them not to turn back. They sat there wondering what to do next. After about fifteen minutes, they heard faint voices. They also noticed a light shining on the mountain some distance below where they were, which reassured them.

The people lower down on the mountain saw the light from the fire that the travelers had lit and were quite surprised. They shouted out, "Are you travelers?" The travelers explained their predicament and that they had almost run out of torchwood. They pleaded with the locals for help and guidance. The local people asked the travelers to stay where they were and came for them with lanterns. The travelers prayed to Baba and thanked him for his grace. Shortly there-after, the local people reached them and took them to their homes and offered them tea. Then they escorted the travelers to the forester's house.

On meeting with the forester, the travelers told him the story of their journey. While they were talking, dinner was being prepared at the forester's house—dal, rice, chapatis, and *pakoras* (fried snack). When the guests arrived, the forester asked the cook to prepare some halva as well. The forester had no idea that Baba had told the travelers that they would have a hearty meal at night!

The travelers noticed two piles of fresh *neebus* (large lemons) in the room where they were meeting with the forester. The neebu fruit is used to make a local delicacy, which is prepared by peeling and chopping the large lemons and mixing the fruit with honey, yoghurt, and black salt. As they talked with the forester, their gaze kept falling on the neebus. The forester asked if they would like to try some, and also take some back to Nainital. The travelers were delighted. There was plenty of it, made with top quality honey. They had some before dinner, some along with dinner, and some more after dinner! So all in all, the travelers had four full meals that day, yet they were able to digest all that food easily.

The next day, the travelers had lunch and then set out for Nainital. They each took along two big neebus that the forester gave them. The journey on the way back (via Champhi) was uneventful and they reached Nainital before sunset.

THE GIFT OF POTATOES

(Contributed by Shri Hira Vallabh Pant)

In India, it is a tradition to take gifts when visiting holy men. What the gift is does not really matter; people take whatever they can afford. What counts is the intention behind the gift. Once some devotees from a nearby village had brought some high quality potatoes and offered them to Baba. Another devotee who had come for darshan thought, "Perhaps I could ask Baba for a few of these excellent potatoes so that I can plant them in my field." Baba could read what the man was thinking, but he did not say anything. Finally, the man spoke up and said, "Baba, could I take some of these potatoes so that I may plant them in my field to grow more?"

Baba said gently, "My son, what better use of these potatoes than to feed sadhus, Brahmans, devotees and guests who come here? What will grow from the blessings of hungry people is much better than what can possibly grow in your field. The blessings will also reach the person who has donated these potatoes with such love."

OFFERING FROM GODDESS ANNAPURNA

(Contributed by Pandit Jagannath Joshi, ex-Municipal Commissioner, Nainital)

As Baba was a celibate yogi, women were usually not allowed to visit his ashram; they were allowed to take darshan from afar. One day, a woman came to the ashram carrying a basket of rice as an offering. She walked straight to Baba's hut and stood in front of the door. Baba came out and accepted her offering with great love and respect. The woman circumambulated the hut, then went away. The other devotees were a little surprised at this incident and wondered who this woman might be, why Baba had allowed her to come to the ashram, and why he treated her with such reverence. They soon realized that she was probably the Goddess Annapurna (the goddess of good nourishment). Everyone knew that Baba had the power of Annapurna Siddhi. A yogi with this power never lacks any food. The food never ran out and no one ever went hungry. Even travelers who passed along the path close by were sent food from the ashram.

GETTING FOOD THAT ONE DESIRED

(Contributed by Pandit Jagannath Joshi, ex-Municipal Commissioner, Nainital)

Sometimes up to 400 devotees would arrive at the ashram, but somehow everyone would get whatever food they desired to eat. One day, a devotee wished to eat an orange. There was no chance of finding oranges in the forest, but when he reached the ashram, he saw a basket of oranges. Another time a devotee felt like having kheer, but he did not say anything as he did not want to ask. A few minutes later, someone brought out a big pot of kheer. Baba said, "Old man, your karma has brought you the kheer you wished for.

Enjoy it!"

Once, a well-known pandit from the area was preparing food at the ashram. As part of his spiritual practice, the pandit would only take rock salt. Knowing this, Baba pulled out a pinch of rock salt from the wall of his hut and sent it for the pandit.

Whenever a traveler would set out thinking that they would like to stop at the ashram for darshan on their way somewhere, they would invariably find food ready for them when they arrived. Those arriving in the early morning would find tea and sweets ready, while those arriving in the afternoon would find khichdi and chapatis, and those arriving in the evening would find sweets and tea waiting.

One day, four travelers arrived at the ashram at Kakrighat. One of the travelers was a good cook, and volunteered to cook for everyone. Baba sent ingredients from the ashram storehouse to make the food. However, it was much more than would be needed for the few people who were there at the time. Baba instructed the devotee to give it all to the cook and not bring anything back. When the cook protested, Baba called out from within his hut: "Don't worry, just cook it all. I will have the rest." The cook did as instructed. Just as the cooking finished, several more travelers arrived. Everyone ate well and no food was left over.

BABA'S COOKING

(Contributed by Pandit Jagannath Joshi, ex-Municipal Commissioner, Nainital)

Baba was also an excellent cook. Sometimes he would make food for the guests with his own hands. The dishes he conjured up were always very tasty. Once Baba made a chutney from potatoes, and on trying it, a person who was usually very reserved and respectful literally exclaimed out in delight! Baba knew many styles of cooking and he would often employ different styles to make food for guests.

From the incidents above, it is clear that Baba was graced with Annapurna Siddhi, but it is also important to consider what else was really being received by the guests who took food at the ashram. There were many devotees who were well-to-do, and had good meals at home every day. Quite a few wealthy people would also arrange for people to be fed as a form of charity. Baba used the power of his tapasya to feed people, while the wealthy people used the power of money to serve people. Both these things are commendable. What made taking food at Baba's ashram so special was that whoever took prasad there would not only have their hunger satiated and taste buds satisfied, but they also experienced great peace and happiness. This was the primary thing people were being "fed" at the ashram; the food was secondary.

FRYING PURIS IN WATER

(Contributed by Shri Ramlal Sah, Nainital)

Baba was blessed by Goddess Annapurna, and the storeroom at the ashram was always filled with all kinds food items.

A bhandara was held at Baba's ashrams every Monday. During one of the Monday bhandaras, there wasn't enough ghee to fry the puris so the cook went to Baba to ask what should be done. Baba asked him to fill a pot with water from the river and add it to the ghee in the frying pan. The devotee did as instructed. As soon as the water hit the pan, it turned into ghee!

The next day at about ten in the morning, a man came from Shri Jagatchand's house with a tin containing ghee. Baba instructed a devotee to pour this ghee into the river to return what had been taken from the river the previous day. A *naga* (naked) sadhu who had come to the ashram from a place called Mirzapur made an excuse about needing to go to the bathroom and went to the river to try and collect the ghee that had been poured in by the devotee on Baba's instructions. Baba was aware of what the sadhu was trying to do by the riverside and said to one of the devotees present: "Go tell the sadhu that if he wishes to have ghee, he should go to the city; this is an ashram."

BABA'S PREDICTION: DROPPING "HUNGER IN THE MIND"

(Contributed by Shri Hira Vallabh Pant)

Haridutt Bhagat hailed from a village called Maharagaon near Bhimtal. Baba would sometimes allow him to stay at the ashram in Padampuri for four to six months, and would ask him to perform puja at the shrine of Lord Shiva. Shri Hariduttji was a very simple man who wore simple clothes—a small dhoti that hardly reached his knees, and a simple small top made of a rough cloth. Regardless of the season or weather, he always took a bath at 4 a.m., after which he would perform puja of Lord Shiva with great love and devotion.

Sombari Baba had great affection for Shri Hariduttji. He talked about how Shri Hariduttji performed puja with such love and devotion, how he always took a bath in the river early in the morning regardless of the cold, how he wore very few clothes, and how even in a cold place like Padampuri Baba had never seen his nose watering, even in the winters, when he was offering cold water at the shrine of Lord Shiva.

Shri Hariduttji had just one personality trait for which Baba would often tell him off: he had a great fear that there would not be enough food left for him! This fear always played on in his mind, even though he had often seen hundreds of people being fed at the ashram with no one ever having to go hungry, and even when he could see that there was enough food in the kitchen to feed many people.

Hariduttji still worried about food even after seeing that there was always enough, so Baba criticized him for his lack of faith. Baba said to him, "Every day you see that hundreds of people are fed here and they also take food home as prasad for their families. You can also see that there is plenty more in the storeroom. You have been eating well, without ever having to go hungry. Despite all this, why do you not believe that you will get enough? If someone is really hungry in the stomach, the space that can usually be filled with half a *ser* can be filled by giving him more, say one ser or one-and-quarter sers. But how can one fill the stomach of someone who is hungry in the mind?" Baba would scold Hariduttji about this almost on a daily basis.

One day, he said, "Your hunger will only be satisfied when you are in charge of food storage at an ashram, feed many people, and feed yourself." Some time later, Hariduttji traveled to Mumbai, and started living in a math there. After two or three years, the mahant who was the head of the math passed away and, by the grace of Sombari Baba, Hariduttji was made the head of the math. As predicted by Baba, Hariduttji then went on to have control of the food store at the math and fed lots of people who came to visit. Eventually, his deep fear of not having enough to eat dropped away. Once this fear was gone, it made a marked difference in Shri Hariduttji's personality. Just as the sun can be hidden behind clouds and, when the clouds disperse, the sun shines through in all its glory, so too when bad traits drop away, the good traits of a person really shine through.

Hariduttji (Budju) spent most of his life together with Bageshwariji at Sombari Baba's ashram until Baba's samadhi

GRATING COCONUTS

(Contributed by Shri Tikaram Bhatt, Bhowali)

Baba never imparted any formal teachings or talks. He would not speak directly; one had to try hard to interpret and understand his words. It is clear from my experience in Nepal that he knew of things even before they occurred.

One day, he gave me two coconuts at the Padampuri ashram and asked me to grate them. I took the grater and sat down, thinking that there were just two coconuts and I'd be done soon. Then a strange thing happened: several visitors started coming and whoever came brought along two more coconuts! Soon there was a big pile of coconuts in front of me. By the afternoon I was still grating, and the pile of coconuts was still growing. Baba called out to me, "Are you still grating two coconuts? Get up now, you must be tired." The ways of the sages are unfathomable!

SWEETS FOR THE MAN FROM RAMNAGAR

(Contributed by Shri Tikaram Bhatt, Bhowali)

One day, at the Padampuri ashram, Baba expressed a wish that some sweets should be prepared. A little while later, people started coming to the ashram and each person brought along a different kind of offering, like sugar, milk, and so on. Eventually, there was enough to make a fairly large quantity of sweets, about 40 kilos! We prepared the sweets and Baba asked me to distribute them among all who were present.

Just two pieces were left. I said to Baba, "Maharaj, these two pieces are left."

Baba replied, "He's coming, bringing along 25 rupees from the person from Ramnagar. For 25 rupees, what more can he get? Keep them for him." Some fifteen minutes later, a person arrived at the ashram and offered 25 rupees at Baba's feet, saying that they had been sent by a person in Ramnagar.

AN UNENDING SUPPLY OF FOOD

(Contributed by Shri Tikaram Bhatt, Bhowali)

One particular miracle that always occurred around Baba was to do with food. Often there were some 20 or more people in the ashram and food or tea needed to be prepared for them all. The pot in which food would be prepared would be large enough to hold just enough food for all those who were present at that time. But then, suddenly some 40 more people would turn up, but the food always sufficed and never ran out, no matter how much each person ate. I never heard Baba ask anyone to bring anything. Whatever was needed somehow seemed to arrive miraculously.

Baba knew about the past, present and future. He never gave structured talks at any time. When he did speak, his words were often confusing and ambiguous, but he always resolved any questions or problems that devotees had.

Sometimes, Baba would go to the plains. Baba had a small hut about a mile away from Haldwani, in the direction of Lal Kuan, on the road to Bareilly (these days there is an ashram of Laturia Baba close by, Sombari Baba's hut is under a tree nearby). No one was allowed into Baba's ashram before 8 in the morning. He left his body at Padampuri. He had started speaking of changing the body some months prior to this.

I pay deep heartfelt homage to Sombari Maharaj.

SENDING GHEE FOR THE TEHSILDAR

(Contributed by Shri Girwan Dutt Joshi, Nainital)

Once, there were quite a few people at the ashram. It was evening, and it was starting to get dark. One of my friends from school, Shri Durga Singhji, who was an important government official holding the post of *Tehsildar* (tax collector), was visiting Padampuri that day. No one at the ashram had seen him or knew that he was in Padampuri at the time. There were some shops about 600 yards away from the ashram. Baba called out to one of the people present and gave him a small pot of ghee, saying, "Go, give this to the Tehsildar. The poor fellow is looking for some ghee but is unable to find any."

BHANDARAS AT THE ASHRAM

(Contributed By Shri Krishnananda Shastri, Education Superintendent, Municipal Board, Nainital)

Food was prepared at Baba's ashram every day and a large bhandara was held on Mondays. Arrangements to cook for the bhandara would usually be made by Shri Bholadutt Pande from the village of Champanola. Shri Pande was himself a person who believed in simple living, and he was unaffected by the world. There was a fairly small pot at the ashram, which was always kept covered, that would be used to serve food. No one was ever able to correctly fathom the capacity of this pot. It seemed that Goddess Annapurna herself remained present in it. Many devotees who have experienced the magic of this pot will confirm this. Baba would already know in advance how many devotees were arriving for a meal that day, and he would instruct the devotees who were preparing food. Yet, very often, more people would turn up at the last minute. They were all served out of the same little pot and yet the food never ran out.

SAVING MILK FOR CHANDRA LAL

(Contributed by Shri Dhanilal Sah)

One day, several devotees including Shri Kabdwal were at the ashram. Tea was prepared and served. A little while earlier, a devotee had brought a container of milk and Baba had asked him to keep it aside. When the tea was served, one of the people sitting there thought, "Baba is not entirely free of possessiveness. He asked for the milk to be kept aside and served us tea with no milk."

Baba looked straight at the man and said, "So, how many cows and buffaloes do you have at home? Are you used to having your tea with milk all the time?"

The man felt ashamed, and said, "Baba, I am very poor and hardly get enough to eat, never mind having milk with my tea every day."

Later that evening, a devotee by the name of Shri Chandra Lal arrived from Nainital. He had forgotten to bring milk, which he needed in order to take his medicines. Baba had kept the milk aside for him. Sages want nothing for themselves, and yet they take care of their devotees' every little need.

"HE IS GOING TO BE YOUR RELATIVE"

(Contributed by Shri Dhanilal Sah)

Pandeji was very particular about the food he ate. He would not cook food cooked by just anyone. Very often, he would make the food himself. One day, when he as at the ashram, Baba told him to go to the kitchen and eat what had already been cooked by someone else, saying, "It's okay, the man who has cooked the food is going to be your relative soon." Pandeji followed Baba's instructions and ate the food that had been prepared by someone called Shri Joshi. As it turned out, one year later Pandeji's sister-in-law got married to Shri Joshi. When Baba made the prediction, no one knew this would happen, as they were not even looking for a groom for Pandeji's sister-in-law at the time.

PRACTICAL SKILLS

(Contributed by Hira Vallabh Pant)

It would often be the case that hundreds of devotees ate at Baba's ashram at any given meal. However, there were very limited utensils and pots in the ashram: two or three large iron *kadhais*, two or three large brass platters, four or five brass pots and pans, and some cups and bowls. Many devotees wanted to bring more things for the ashram's kitchen, but Baba did not allow it.

Most of the cooking, such as making halwa, puris, and vegetables, was done in the large iron kadhais. When more food needed to be prepared and served, Baba would give practical ideas on what to do. For example, he would ask someone to make a hole in the ground, cover it with leaves, and then store the prepared food such as halwa and puris on it while the next batch was being cooked. He would laugh and say, *"Yukti se hi mukti hoti hai,"* which loosely translated means "*mukti* (liberation) is achieved by using your intelligence."

The khichdi at the ashram used to be a little soft and slightly wet. Baba called it *siddha khichdi* and said that by eating this type of khichdi, one can remain free of all disease. The khichdi would be very tasty; people who have had the good fortune to taste it still talk about it to this day.

PANDIT JAIDUTT AND THE TIKKAD

(Contributed by Hira Vallabh Pant)

At one time, Shri Jaidutt, a devotee of Baba who worked in Nainital, was at the ashram and Baba sent him a small piece of his own tikkar with another devotee. Shri Jaidutt sat beside the river to eat. It was wonderfully tasty and, in a daze, he sat there taking pieces from the tikkar and eating them. After a while, he stopped when he realized that his stomach was full. When he looked at the piece left over in his hand, he realized that it was still the same size as the original piece that Baba had sent him! He decided to keep it in his pocket to eat later. A few moments later, he put his hand in the pocket again, only to find that the piece of tikkar was gone. He looked in every pocket wondering if he had put it in a different pocket, but try as he might, he could not find it again. Baba always taught devotees to rely on grace and not to hoard.

THE COOK GOES HUNGRY

(Contributed by Pandit Devidutt Kabdwal)

Once an elder devotee came to the ashram at Kakrighat for darshan. He was from a good family and everyone could eat food that he had cooked, so Baba asked him to make some khichdi in a large kadhai. He made enough for the number of people who were in the ashram at the time, about twenty-five or so. A bit later in the afternoon, around thirty or forty more devotees arrived. The old devotee who was cooking that day asked Baba is he should cook some more. Baba replied that there was not enough time and, if God wished, the amount that had already been cooked would be enough for all. So the cook asked everyone to sit in a queue and started serving them. About sixty or seventy people ate to their heart's content that day from khichdi that was originally meant for about twenty-five people.

By the evening, about an hour before sunset, everyone had eaten except for the cook. There was just enough khichdi left for him. Before eating, he went to the river to wash his hands. On returning, he had hardly walked a few steps when he came across a tall man dressed like a lama. The man looked weak and said, "I have gone hungry for many days. Please give me something to eat."

The old cook had not eaten all day and was very hungry himself. He knew that there was enough khichdi left for himself, so he told the lama that it was not possible to get any food at that time. The cook was a good man, but in that moment his hunger made him selfish and he forgot that no one ever left Baba's ashram hungry. He forgot that he had just seen sixty or seventy people eat from food meant for twenty-five, and there was still enough left over for him. After brushing off the lama, he went to the kadhai to eat and found that the kadhai was totally empty.

On seeing this, he suddenly realized his mistake, remembered the hungry lama, and went looking for him. But try as he might he could not find the lama, who seemed to have disappeared. Dejected, the cook sat down with his head in his hands and decided that he would not get up from the spot until Baba said something. Baba let him repent for about half an hour, saying nothing. Then he called the cook over and asked him, "What is food for the cow, and what is food for man?"

The cook replied, "The cow eats grass, and the man eats grain." After this, Baba remained quiet and said nothing else.

The cook realized the khichdi had disappeared because of his selfishness. He quietly went to kitchen and started cleaning the kadhai. A few minute later, Baba sent some other devotees to make sure he was fed. From this incident, everyone learned it is not good to refuse food to a hungry person. They realized that it is important to keep selfishness in check because, when a person thinks selfishly, their intellect does not work well and they end up performing some actions that they are likely to regret later.

THE MILK AND THE TEA

(Contributed by Pandit Devidutt Kabdwal)

Once a devotee reached the Padampuri ashram in the evening. He had a horse on which he could have gone to the ashram, yet he was very respectful and so decided to leave the horse at home and walk all the way to the ashram for darshan. By the time he arrived at the ashram, he had been walking the entire day and was very tired and hungry. He was a well-to-do man, and had a habit of drinking three or four sers of milk every day. When he arrived, Baba asked a devotee if there was any milk in the ashram; there was about one ser left. Baba instructed him to give it to the visitor who had just arrived. The visitor gratefully accepted the milk and went to the river to rest and drink the milk.

As it happened, the other devotees had been served chai and sweets, but had not been given any milk that day. On seeing this incident, a man who was sitting by the dhuni in the lower part of the ashram thought to himself, "I thought that at the ashram everyone is treated equally. Then how come we were served chai with no milk, while this rich man gets all the milk?"

Immediately Baba's voice boomed out: "So, how many cows do you have at home, and how much milk do you drink every day?"

The man replied: "Baba, I do not have any cows and do not drink milk every day."

Baba went on to explain: "The man who had just been given milk is rich; he has four cows at home. He does not drink chai at all and is used to drinking three of four sers of milk every single day. He has a horse, yet he walked all the way to the ashram and did not eat anything along the way. He was given milk to take care of his bodily needs; your body is okay with chai, but his body needs milk. Does that seem like a problem to you?"

For mahatmas, everyone is the same; they do not differentiate between one person and another. However, people are different: some are healthy while others are sick, some are rich while others are poor, some are happy while others are miserable, some are intelligent while others are not, some are interested in the world while others are interested in renunciation. All of them are created by God and behave according to their nature, so they cannot be blamed for what they are. From the point of view of the soul, everyone is alike, including animals, but from the point of view of practical life, each one is different, so each person needs to be treated differently according to his or her nature and needs. It would be foolish to treat everyone in the same way when their nature is completely different. Baba taught this important lesson to the devotees present there that day, in his normal style of speaking less and instead demonstrating how to be.

BABA FEEDS DEVOTEES PERSONALLY ON THE LAST DIWALI

(Contributed by Pandit Devidutt Kabdwal)

Baba left his body in early January 1919. About two months earlier, a large number of devotees had gathered at the ashram for Mahalakshmi Puja during the festival of Diwali. Somehow that year the number of people who turned up was much larger than usual. No one realized at that time why this was so, but they understood when Baba left his body.

It was the custom ever year to distribute puris and sweets to all devotees who came to the ashram during Diwali. Since many devotees had gathered, there was also a lot of *mithai* (sweets) since no one came empty-handed. Around 3 or 4 in the afternoon many more devotees turned up and brought along more sweets. Eventually there was so much mithai that despite hundreds of devotees being present, it was more than enough to feed them all. Then more passersby started coming into the ashram. Next, people from nearby villages also arrived. Baba said, "By God's wish, there is so much mithai today that there is no need to cook; the mithai can be had for dinner." In an unlikely development, Baba said he would distribute mithai himself that day. All devotees were very happy to hear this.

Around sunset, everyone did their evening prayers and Baba also had his evening bath, followed by his practice. Then Baba asked everyone to sit in a queue with a large leaf plate in front of each one. Everyone was eager to receive prasad from Baba's hands. Love always shone from all of Baba's actions, but being served food by Baba himself was a new and different blessing, and the devotees were delighted. Some devotees worried about Baba holding the heavy platters, thinking his hands might hurt from holding them. Without them having to express this, Baba said, "Don't worry, the platters do not feel heavy at all. It makes me happy to serve you prasad. I'm doing it at God's inspiration and by my own wish. You have come so far, leaving behind celebrations in your own homes to spend time with me. If I take a little effort to distribute mithai to you, where is the problem?" Everyone was moved by Baba's love.

Then Baba placed mithai in every plate himself. It was all done so quickly and efficiently that people did not have to wait long. The amazing thing was that everyone got the exact kind of mithai that they loved, and also got the exact amount that was perfect for them. Baba did not have to think about this while serving; somehow it seemed that the right kind and amount of mithai automatically came into his hand as he was about to serve each person.

When everyone had eaten, they all felt felt happy, full, satisfied, and nourished. Looking around they saw that all plates were totally empty. Some people wondered, "I am perfectly full, but how come all the plates around me are empty? Did they get enough?" When they talked to each other, it turned out that everyone was perfectly satisfied and realized that no one else but Baba could have done this.

Baba watched all this, smiling. Then he said, "Actually, there is quite a lot of mithai left, why don't you all take a little more?" On hearing this, everyone thought, "Oh goodness, I simply cannot eat any more!" But out of love and respect for Baba, they did not say anything out loud. Baba distributed sweets again, about the same quantity as before. Magically, everyone was able to finish everything on their plate again, surprising themselves! They wondered what other miracle Baba was going to perform next. They felt sure that if Baba served them again, they'd be able to eat it all once again.

Baba smiled and said, "Oh, so now you want even more. But I won't give you any more because I have to keep some for myself!" Everyone laughed at this beautiful light-hearted fun with the sage, knowing full well he never ate more than a few bites of food.

FOOD APPEARS MAGICALLY IN THE ASHRAM STORE

(Contributed by Pandit Jagannath Joshi, Ex-Municipal Commissioner, Nainital)

On 20th May, 1916, I had the good fortune to meet Sombari Baba due to the insistence of a dear friend of mine, who was a judge by profession. In those days, travel was not as easy as it is now, so we left Almora at around 3 in the afternoon. On arriving at the river Kosi, we saw some horses available for rent. My friend was somewhat tired so we decided to rent a horse for him. There were a couple of other people along with us, and also a porter who was carrying a covered basket of fruits. We left from the spot at about 4:30 or 5 in the evening.

An hour later, the skies turned very dark and we were all completely drenched from the storm. The path was very rough and the horse lost its footing. My friend fell to the ground, but thankfully he was not hurt. It had turned so dark that continuing the journey would have been dangerous, so we decided to stay put. At around 8 p.m., we saw a light in the distance, approaching us. It turned out to be Dharam Singh, one of the assistants from Sombari Baba's ashram.

Baba had sent him to find us and lead us to the ashram. He told us the ashram was about two miles further. He also said Baba had told him four people were heading towards the ashram but were unable to find their way in the dark. We felt relieved on hearing these words.

Before leaving Almora I had told my friend that I did not have much time for saints. They performed severe penances for twelve years or more and received supernatural powers, but did not use them for the good of the common people. Instead they simply offered the powers to the Divine. What use are such people to the common man? When we reached the ashram, Baba greeted us warmly and received us respectfully. Then he lifted a finger and admonished me, "Why were you saying you don't believe in mahatmas?"

Baba then turned to Dharam Singh and said, "Dharmiya (an affectionate way for addressing Dharam Singh), these people are tired and wet. Quickly feed them some warm *sooji* (a dish made from semolina), and then make some puris for them. Go bring all the material from the ashram store and turn up the fire to start cooking."

Dharam Singh went to the ashram store and found it completely empty. He came back and said, "Baba, there is no food to cook and there is no wood, either."

Baba turned to another assistant and said, "Oh Khemanand, this Dharmiya cannot see any more, and he can't even sense anything by touch. You go to the store and check. First make sooji, feed it to the guests to warm them up, and then make food." We were shivering with the cold by now.

When Khemanand came back from the store, he reported: "Maharaj, the store is filled with 15 sacks of sugar, rice, and flour. The pots are full and overflowing with milk and yoghurt."

Baba turned to us and said, "Go to the store, see for yourself what is there and choose what you would like to have for dinner.

Whatever you would like to have will be prepared for dinner." Within minutes, the ashram was filled with the wonderful smell of *kachoris* (deep-fried puff pastry with spicy moong dal stuffing) and puris being prepared. The meal also included basmati rice and a special breed of rice called Jamoli. We ate to our hearts' content.

It was our good fortune to meet Baba, see two great demonstrations of grace, and to have this amazing meal at his ashram. The taste of the wonderful meal still lingers in my memory.

SENDING FOOD IN ADVANCE

(Contributed by Shri Govindram Kala, Ex-Deputy Collector)

Pandit Urvadutt Naithani worked in the village of Okhalkhada. His daughter was to be married to the son of the Deputy Collector who lived in the region of Tehri. The wedding procession was to set out from Kathgodam and reach Tehri over a period of three days. Pandit Urvadutt had made very good arrangements for food, but the groom's party was not eating much. We noticed that they had brought along a large trunkful of *laddoos* (ball-shaped sweets) and they enjoyed eating those at night, thereby not leaving much space in their bellies to eat much else.

The procession passed by Baba's ashram along the way. I went to meet Baba to seek his blessings. He gave me about four kilos of *panjeri* (a local sweet dish that is very nutritious and is usually fed to pregnant women) and asked me to take it along. I said, "Baba, they will not eat it. They're not eating anything we have prepared for them." I did not mention anything about the laddoos.

Baba spoke: "The laddoos are over. On the hard climb to Mornala, they will feel hungry and this will help."

Exactly as Baba had predicted, the groom's party felt very hungry during the climb to Mornala and they finished the panjeri.

THE THREE POTATOES

(Contributed by Shri Govindram Kala, Ex-Deputy Collector)

Once, Shri Govindram Kala went to visit Baba at the ashram in Padampuri. Baba gave him three freshly roasted potatoes from the dhuni, saying, "Here, eat these potatoes. They are meant for you, so don't give them to anyone else!" Govindramji nodded and proceeded to the river with the three potatoes. He sat by the river in silence and ate the first potato. By the time he started eating the second potato, he noticed something strange: he was feeling lost in otherworldly bliss. He was losing awareness of the world and his body and all he could feel was pure bliss. He was lost in joy, above the cares and worries of the world. As he looked at the third potato, a thought crossed his mind: "If I eat this one, I'm going to completely lose all interest in the world. God knows what will happen to me then."

Suddenly a sadhu turned up from nowhere and asked Govindramji: "What are you eating?" When he replied he was eating potatoes, the sadhu said, "I am very hungry. Could you please spare one for me?" Without thinking, Govindramji offered the third potato to the sadhu, who accepted it gratefully.

Later, Govindramji remembered Baba had instructed him not to give the potatoes to anyone else. Feeling bad, he went to Baba and narrated the entire story. He said, "Baba, I don't know if I would have been able to digest the joy. That third potato would probably have sent me over the edge!" Baba said nothing, and smiled sweetly. Govindramji realized that the sadhu was either Baba in a different form or someone that Baba had sent!

Pilgrimage

BABA'S TRAVELS

(Contributed by Dhanilal Sah)

Baba traveled all over India and there is probably no spiritually important spot that he did not visit. He was very well versed in the geography of the country and would share useful information with devotees and travelers. It is rare to find sadhus who stay away from settlements and choose to live in caves and by rivers. He would go to Badrinath via Kakrighat and Sitlakhet, then further on to Khairna and Karnaprayag, and then to Badrinath. He would travel alone with just a kamandalu, his chimta, a tiger skin (*vyaghcharm*), jhola, and his chillum, preferring to spend nights under trees close to a river, far away from villages and settlements. If a devotee arranged for wood to make a dhuni, he would accept it.

BADRINATH

(Collected by Shri Shankar Lal Sah)

Baba visited many pilgrimage spots all around India. He was seen around the holy shrine of Badrinath several times. Baba would often say that in the mountains near Badrinath thousands of yogis are undertaking tapasya.

SPIRITUAL TRAVELS

(Contributed by Pandit Jagannath Joshi, ex-Municipal Commissioner, Nainital)

During his pilgrimages, Baba also came to Nainital and Almora. In Almora, he would visit the Vishwanath temple every day for darshan and also take a holy bath. For the first few days, he would forget the way to the Vishwanath temple and a lady would guide him every time. One day the lady asked him, "What is the matter, Baba? How come you forget the way every day?" After this incident, Baba remembered the way correctly.

When Baba went to Kashi (Banaras), the same thing would happen. He visited the Vishwanath temple every day at midnight, but he would forget the way to the temple every day. An extremely beautiful woman would find him and guide him to the temple. She appeared to be a devotee, as she would be carrying flowers, incense, and sandalwood paste for puja. When Baba arrived at the Vishwanath temple at midnight, he would find the doors mysteriously open.

After completing his pilgrimage, Baba came to Kurmanchal and continued his spiritual practices. Once, he traveled to the holy shrine of Badrinath where he met the king of the local area, Maharaj Harihar, who was also a great yogi. During his pilgrimage, Baba treated and healed many sick people. Later, he stopped treating people for medical conditions per se, but if someone who came to the ashram was unwell, Baba would simply give them *prasad* and by having it, they would be healed.

THE MEETING BETWEEN BABA AND HIS FATHER

(Contributed by Pandit Devidutt Kabdwal)

Once Baba set off from Kakrighat for a yatra to Badrinath. Usually Baba went on a yatra alone, but he occasionally made an exception for someone who had a strong desire to go and could manage the difficult journey. The usual schedule of travel was as follows: wake before dawn, take his morning bath, do his practices, and then leave around 8 a.m. After walking till midday or 1p.m., he would set up camp in the forest, somewhere close to a river. There he would take his midday bath, meet people, talk to them, and distribute prasad until dusk, when he would take his evening bath, do his meditation, and then feed everyone who was present. After everyone had eaten, he would make for himself a small portion of khichdi or a tikkar, of which he shared three quarters and only took one quarter himself.

The fortunate ones who were able to join Baba on yatras to holy places like Badrinath and Amarnath reported that, on both the outward and return journeys, a crowd of village folk would gather every day before Baba arrived. No one came empty-handed; everyone brought along some offerings, according to their capacity, out of their love for this great sage. Some people brought milk, others yoghurt, sweets, fresh rice from the fields, fresh flour, fruits, flowers, and so on. Those who felt that Baba would pass by their village that year did not use that year's harvest, waiting to offer it to him first before using it themselves. If Baba did not travel that year, they first offered some of the harvest in his name and sent it to the ashram where Baba was at the time.

Whenever a crowd of people collected for darshan, Baba respected their love and stopped there for a while. At all times the crowd was full of people of all ages and all dispositions. Baba spent some time with them, spoke with everyone, distributed prasad, and sent them home happy, then he moved on. As people left, they could turn back over and over again for darshan as long as they could see him. Everyone loved Baba and thought that Baba loved him or her the most. Baba was so loving that even wicked people loved and praised him. Baba always made sure everyone was happy and then moved on. Those traveling with him reported that this took place every time Baba traveled anywhere.

On this particular yatra, after some days of traveling Baba

and his companions reached Badrinath. They went to a place called Garud Gufa and spent some time there, where Baba gave darshan to pilgrims. They then went to a place called Joshimath and stayed there for a few days. The special thing about that year's yatra was that Baba's father had also set out from Punjab for a yatra to Badrinath. He traveled from Haridwar to Joshimath and then reached Badrinath, by which time Baba had returned from Badrinath and was in Joshimath. On his return journey, Baba's father stopped over in Joshimath for a day. He heard that a great sage was staying there, so with great respect and love he set off for darshan, taking along offerings of fruit and flowers. He had no idea that the sage was actually his son because Baba had left home at a very young age and his father had not seen him since then.

Baba's father was a wise and pious person and he belonged to a wealthy family. On arriving at the spot where Baba was, he tried to prostrate before Baba, but Baba stood up and moved back because he knew this was his father and that it would not be appropriate for him to prostrate before his son. Baba's father had not recognized him and was surprised at this reaction from a sadhu. He felt bad and looked at Baba, wondering why he had acted in this way. Without saying a word, Baba simply looked at his father very lovingly, in the process opening the petals of his heart.

Without a word being said, the father realized this was his son and he started crying out of love. Without thinking, he hugged Baba out of love as a father and then fell at Baba's feet out of respect for a great soul after realizing Baba's divine nature. He said, "You have caused the upliftment of seven generations in our family. I have no regrets or pain about the fact that you left home; in fact, I consider myself blessed to have a son like you." This time, Baba did not stop him from prostrating.

When Baba's father offered a sum of 100 rupees, Baba said, "This gift of love from you has reached me and I accept it. Now use the money for a bhandara to feed sadhus, saints, and Brahmins." When Baba's father left after this darshan, the sight was incredible to behold: his countenance was beaming and he was lost in love and joy. In accordance with Baba's wishes, his father stayed in Joshimath for three nights, added some more money to the hundred rupees and conducted several bhandaras.

When Baba's father passed away in Punjab, Baba was at the ashram in Kakrighat. There was no chance of the news from Punjab reaching Kakrighat in time since there was no modern means of communication. No one knew what had come to pass, but when they saw Baba conducting specific rituals (*anjali*) that day, everyone realized that his father had left the body that day. After that, Baba continued to perform annual rites (tarpan) for his father every year. Despite being a completely free being, Baba still followed ideal code of conduct (*maryada*). Baba always fulfilled his duties on both the inner and outer planes of life, and showed devotees how to be in the outer world while also making progress in the inner world. This is the path of righteousness.

THE OFFICIAL AND THE AMARNATH YATRA

(Contributed by Pandit Devidutt Kabdwal)

Once Baba decided to go for a pilgrimage to Amarnath and left from Kakrighat about a week later. Some devotees wished to go along, but they did not have the good fortune to join him this particular time as they did not visit the ashram in the few days between Baba's decision and him setting out on the journey. This time, two devotees came to the ashram one day before Baba left, all prepared for a pilgrimage. They did not know that Baba was planning to go to Amarnath that year, but they had set out from their homes hoping that he would. When they expressed this wish, Baba asked them: "How did you know I am thinking of going to Amarnath?"

They replied: "Baba, we did not know. We just had a feeling that this year you might go to Amarnath. So we set out from home and came here."

Baba said, "Love is such a powerful force that nothing can remain hidden from it." Because of their love, Baba gave them permission to join him on the journey. The devotees rested at the dharamshala that night, and set off on the yatra with Baba the next day.

Along the way, the party had to travel by train for part of the journey. In one place, there were so many passengers in the compartment that even Baba had to stand. The two devotees accompanying Baba felt very bad, not for themselves, but about the fact that Baba had to stand. It was so cramped, with so many people standing, that they could not even ask anyone to make some space for Baba to sit.

Thinking about this, the two men felt sad. Though Baba had no problem standing, he felt bad on seeing their pain and that made them feel even worse. After this, Baba smiled and said, "If you wish that there should be no one else in this compartment apart from us, then God can do this too. But don't be sad because of me having to stand. I have no problem with it."

On hearing Baba's words the men felt a little better. They still hoped that Baba would not have to stand. Devotees have strong emotions for God. They know that God is above happiness and sorrow, and yet seeing God going through any "pain" from a practical point of view hurts them. For instance, in the case of Lord Rama, everyone knew that he was an incarnation, and yet Lakshman and others around him cried when he underwent any pain. Because of the love of devotees, God also listens to their desires.

As it happened, at the next station, all other passengers from that compartment got off the train and no one else got into the compartment for the rest of the journey, though they traveled several stops further and other compartments were crammed. On seeing this, the devotees realized it was Baba's grace that he was fulfilling their wish.

A little further in the journey, the train arrived at a station, and the two men with Baba saw a great crowd gathered there. It was the station where they had to change trains. On getting off, they found out that the Amarnath yatra had been closed that year on official instructions and no one was getting tickets to go further, which is why there were so many people at the station.

On asking around, they found out that a certain officer was in charge. Baba went to officer himself and spoke to the officer: "All these people have come from so far, leaving behind their work and homes, hoping to get darshan. Can you imagine how they are going to feel if they have to go back without darshan?"

On hearing this, the officer felt sorry, but was also worried about losing his job if he allowed them to continue on the journey. He said, "Baba, I have no problem giving permission for them to proceed, but I will be fired from my job and may have to face great problems later."

Baba replied, "If you help these pilgrims to complete their pilgrimage and have darshan, Lord Amarnathji will definitely help you and you will face no problems in your job. Helping any being is like serving God."

On hearing this, the officer's fear left and he decided to give the pilgrims permission to proceed. All the pilgrims were very happy. Those who were listening to the conversation chanted *"Shri*

Amarnathji ki jai!" and set off.

A few days later, it turned out that the reasons why the administration had stopped the yatra that year resolved themselves. The administrators also felt bad they had stopped the yatra that year. When they found out that the yatra had gone ahead as planned, they were not angry with the officer, but very happy with him for having chosen to give the pilgrims the go-ahead. His senior officers congratulated him on making the right decision. Everyone in the department where he worked found out about how he had given the go-ahead for the yatra without caring about his own job, and looked at him with great respect. The officer realized that God always lends a helping hand when one does something selflessly and with faith.

THE SADHU WITH THE SECRET OF MAKING GOLD

(Contributed by Pandit Devidutt Kabdwal)

Further during this yatra, a sadhu from the plains who was going to Amarnath by himself also joined the party. Having met Baba en route, he wished to travel together and Baba was happy for him to join the party. Of the people who had come with Baba from Kakrighat, one was quite intelligent. He had traveled the country and was a good businessman, who loved the company of sadhus and mahatmas. Throughout the journey to Amarnath, he served this sadhu well. Sombari Baba usually did not allow anyone to serve him, as he never needed it. On the return journey as well, this man served the sadhu well.

One day the party stopped at a certain place in the afternoon, deciding to spend the night there. The sadhu said to the others in the party, "This is where our paths separate. I shall rest here a little and then be on my way." After a short rest and some food and water, he said to the others, "You should rest; I shall take Baba's permission and leave." Saying this, he went to Baba, who was sitting a little distance away in a shady spot. The sadhu sat next to Baba for a while, paid his respects, and came back to the main party. As he prepared to leave, he told the man who had served him: "I am very happy with your service; if you have a wish, you can ask for it now."

The man was very content and had no desires. He replied, "By God's grace I have everything I need. Money is required for helping others and, if this is done without any ego, having more money than you need is not a bad thing. It is important to have discernment, otherwise normal people become egoistic and everything is spoiled. I do not need extra money right now. If God wishes, He decides to help some people through others, but I do not consider myself particularly worthy. I am happy with just remembering God."

On hearing his reply, the sadhu felt very happy and said, "Very good, come walk with me for a while." When they had walked a few feet, he said to the man: "I know a process by which you can make as much gold as you want using a certain herb. The herb is in a place not very far from here; I will show it to you."

The man had realized earlier that this was not a normal sadhu. Though he thought he was contented, a subtle desire was present in him. The desire for gold arose from within suddenly and he started seeing gold everywhere. He thought, "Perhaps God wishes to do some good work through me."

After they had walked a few more feet, Sombari Baba called out to him, "Come here." On hearing Baba call him, he felt worried about losing the chance to find the magic herb, so he said, "Coming, Baba," and started walking faster, hoping to find out where the herb was before going back to Baba.

Baba roared: "Come back immediately without taking another

step!" On hearing these words, the man immediately came to his senses. He realized his mind had become greedy. He felt bad about what had happened and turned back immediately, not even waiting to pay respects to the sadhu. Later, he realized that perhaps the sadhu knew about his weakness and had created the entire scene to free him from the subtle desire for money and gold.

The man came back to Baba. For some time, Baba said nothing, but the man realized Baba was angry. Then Baba spoke: "Now you cannot stay with me any longer. Go home. You will learn how to make gold and help the world. If you don't, how will the world work?" The man felt very bad about his mistake. There were tears in his eyes, not so much because of what Baba had said, but because he could not bear to be separated from Baba.

For some time, Baba remained quiet, allowing him to feel repentant. Then he spoke gently, "If you promise that you will not try to learn such things, even in your dreams, then you can stay with me." The man prostrated, made three lines on the ground with his nose and promised not even to dream of such a thing ever again. On hearing this, Baba's countenance became soft once more, and he sweetly explained to the man how desires can lead one astray.

Healing

HEALING COUGH AND ASTHMA WITH COLD MILK IN WINTER

(Contributed by Pandit Jagannath Joshi, ex-Municipal Commissioner, Nainital)

Once, two men came to the ashram at Padampuri for Baba's darshan during the winter season. Both were suffering from a severe cough. As they were about to go home, Baba gave them some cold milk and prasad. They were a little hesitant to take the cold milk as it was the middle of winter and they were already suffering from cough, but owing to their faith in Baba they drank the milk anyway. Within a few minutes, their cough was gone.

Around the same time, Sombari Baba sent the same prasad to Baba Ramji who was living at the Ramakrishna Math in a place called Chilkapat. Baba Ramji was suffering from acute asthma at that time. On taking the prasad sent by Sombari Baba, he was healed of the asthma completely.

Sombari Baba added sugar candy, black pepper, and Kashmiri saffron to milk. These ingredients by themselves are not used in healing any diseases. No one knew what else he added to the milk apart from these simple ingredients. It is said that it is important for yogis to know the art of healing because serving the sick is considered to be a great social service. This is a wonderful concept, but in recent times practicing medicine without certificates and degrees has become problematic. Because of this, Baba stopped treating people formally for ailments. He did continue to heal them with prasad.

LALA RADHESHYAM GETS CURED OF TB

(Contributed by Hira Vallabh Pant)

Lala Radheshamji from Kashipur was a very good man. He came from a very rich family of cloth merchants. He was affected by tuberculosis, for which he was undergoing treatment with a doctor. The doctor's treatments came with many restrictions, and he followed them all diligently in the hope that it would help with his healing. However, with the passage of time, the disease progressed further, and Radheshyam started losing hope. On the one hand, the disease troubled him and, on the other, the restrictions imposed by the treatment also bothered him.

At one point, he gave up all hope and started thinking he was going to die. At that time, someone told him about Sombari Baba and suggested that he should go for darshan. He thought it would be a good idea. He was so sick that he had to be carried there on a stretcher. When the party reached the ashram, Baba sent a message for him to take a bath in the river before coming to the ashram. Radheshyamji was worried and thought he would try to talk to Baba about the bath after meeting him. He took off his shoes and started going towards the ashram, when Baba shouted out from across the river: "Take a bath in the river before coming here."

Radheshyamji said, "Baba, I am unwell and undergoing treatment with a doctor; I am not even allowed to remove my clothes or wash my hands and face with cold water. How can I take a bath in this cold river?" He had not taken a bath for months by this time.

Baba scolded him and sent two people across, instructing them to take his clothes off carefully, make him take dips in the Ganga, wipe his body, and then bring him across. They did as instructed. Before the first dip, Radheshyamji was very afraid for his well-being. But after the first dip, he felt a bit fresh and strong, so he tried more and had five dips altogether. After the bath, he felt strong; it seemed like half the disease was gone!

When he reached the ashram for darshan, Baba gave him prasad and chai. It was evening by then and dinner was ready. Baba instructed him to eat khichdi. Radheshyamji had not eaten in six months and was afraid to eat all of a sudden, but he did not dare to speak up in Baba's presence, so he sat quietly in the queue to eat. Baba also instructed that he should be given cold water to drink!

Radheshyamji ate khichdi and drank the cold water according to Baba's instructions. By the time he completed the meal, he realized that the disease was completely gone and he felt very healthy, with a just little weakness. When he returned back to Kashipur, people were shocked to see the change in his health. He paid off the doctor and never needed to see him again. Simply receiving darshan and prasad had fixed a seemingly incurable disease.

Radheshyamji lived to be over 80 and even got to see his grandchildren growing up. He became a great devotee of Baba and visited the ashram regularly for darshan. He would often send sweets to the ashram. Baba also always treated him with great love.

HEALING THE COMPOUNDER NATHA SINGH

(Contributed by Shri Dhanilal Sah)

One day Baba slipped on some smooth rocks in the river and hurt his foot. The wound was quite deep and he was running a fever. Dr. Jha heard about this and decided to go to Padampuri to see Sombari Baba. However, just as he was about to set off, a team of officers from the central government arrived at Mukteshwar for an inspection, so he could not leave. Instead, he sent his compounder, Natha Singh, to see Baba.

Natha Singh arrived at Padampuri, where he washed and dressed Baba's wound. Baba gave him some prasad and said, "Wash your hands well in the river." Natha Singh did as instructed and, after a while, he set out for Mukteshwar. On arriving there, he noticed a miracle. Natha Singh had many *muskut* (warts) on his hands for many years, which would often cause patients to hesitate to accept treatment from him. With Baba's blessing, the muskuts had completely disappeared by the time he arrived in Mukteshwar.

BABA TAKES ON RADHESHYAM'S FEVER

(Contributed by Shri Dhanilal Sah)

Once Baba was at the ashram and one of his dear devotees, Shri Devidutt Kabdwal, was with him. A postman approached with a letter for Baba, which he asked Shri Kabdwal to read. It was from a devotee called Radheshyam from Kashipur. He wrote that he had traveled to Prayag (Allahabad) to attend a court case. While in Allahabad, he developed a fever, and even after undertaking much treatment the fever had not abated. His health continued to deteriorate day by day and it looked like he would die soon. Dejected, and finished with doctors, he decided to write to Baba for help.

On hearing the contents of the letter, Baba did not say anything. He went to his cave. Shri Kabdwal waited outside. Baba called, "Devidutt, could you please light the dhuni and put the blanket around me?" Deviduttji did as instructed. Some time later, Baba asked him to put out the dhuni and remove the blanket. When he did, he noticed that Baba was running a high fever. For several days, Baba remained in this condition. Hundreds of miles away, Radheshyam began to recover and, in a few days, his heath was fully restored.

BABA PROTECTS PANDEJI'S FEET

(Contributed by Shri Dhanilal Sah)

One day, one of Laxmidutt Pande's clients who lived in Champawat had a beautiful and expensive pairs of velvet slippers made for Pandeji as a gift. Pandeji loved the slippers. He wore them and headed to Padampuri. On coming close to the ashram, he hid the slippers in a bush near by, as footwear was not allowed into the ashram. On leaving the ashram, he went to the bush and looked for the slippers, but could not find them. After much searching, he still could not find the slippers and concluded that they must have been stolen. He started walking towards Almora with bare feet. The road was full of sharp stones and thorns, yet, when he arrived in Almora, his feet were totally unhurt, owing to Baba's grace.

THE IMPORTANCE OF TAKING A BATH

(Contributed by Pandit Devidutt Kabdwal)

A young devotee once reached Baba's ashram in Haldwani around sunrise. He was not well and, owing to the fear of his health going further downhill, he had not had a bath in many days. That day, too, he did not have a bath. He took some offerings of flowers and fruit to the Shiva temple. Baba was in meditation at the time. When the youth was about to offer the flowers and fruits, the platter in his hands suddenly felt very heavy and he experienced great fear, so he turned back immediately.

By this time, Baba had completed his meditation. Baba told the devotee that nothing should be offered in a temple without first taking a bath. On hearing Baba's words, the youth lost his fear of the illness and went for a bath. After the bath, he felt light and fresh and went to the temple again. He picked up the platter of offerings, which he had left outside the temple, and this time it felt very light. He offered the fruits and flowers with a happy heart.

After this day, the man always took a bath before going to the temple. He tried to test the theory once more when he was alone in a different place, and when his experience was the same as before he was fully convinced that Baba's guidance was right.

BABA SAVES A DYING WOMAN

(Contributed by Pandit Devidutt Kabdwal)

Once a well-respected man decided to go to to Badrinath for

a yatra. He planned on taking many members of his extended family along, young and old. When the news of his planned journey spread, several neighbors approached him asking if they could join the yatra. The man considered that taking so many people along might present him with some problems since the journey was long and arduous, but it did not feel right to refuse people when they asked to join a pilgrimage, so he agreed.

A few days before starting the yatra, he went to Padampuri for darshan, thinking that it would be a good idea to seek Baba's blessings for the journey. He stayed there for a night, and the next day, before setting off to return home, he told Baba about his plans for the yatra and sought Baba's blessings. Baba said, "You are traveling with many people, some very young and some very old; who knows if all of them will return with you."

On hearing this, the man thought, "Baba is warning me about some ill occurrences. However, if I postpone the yatra after all this preparation, people will be disappointed. If I tell the others that I would like to go with just my family, they will feel bad that I changed my mind after agreeing at first. That said, if someone dies during the trip, it will also present a major problem." Thinking thus, he remained quiet.

Then Baba said, "Okay, go for the yatra, and don't think so much. If God wishes, all will be well and everyone will return safely." The man felt reassured on hearing these words from Baba and he returned home happily.

On the day of departure, the man thought that he should have asked Baba before making plans for the yatra. "It seems that one of the people must be in trouble, otherwise Baba would not say what he did. Now it seems that Baba will definitely have to undergo some trouble on our behalf, owing to my stupidity."

The journey to Badrinath was uneventful. However, on the day of arrival, one woman in the party became very ill. Three days later, it seemed that she was on death's door, and the party even started making funeral arrangements. This man was very worried because the woman was from a very well-respected family; if she passed, many people would be affected and thinking this, he became very sad. Suddenly, he remembered Baba and prayed for help. A little later, news arrived that an old mahatma had left his body suddenly in his cave close to Badrinath temple, without any particular illness. This news spread very quickly as there were always crowds of visitors in his cave. Strangely, as soon as they heard this news, the woman who was ill recovered suddenly and stood up by herself. The man realized that Baba must have communicated with the old mahatma and made some kind of arrangement.

The woman who recovered from her acute illness said that when she was lying on the bed, she was delirious and semi-conscious. She had a vision of Baba, who told her that an old mahatma had agreed to take on her death. "After he leaves his body by his own free will, you will be fine," Baba told her.

On hearing this story, the man leading the yatra party understood what she meant, but the others in the party were surprised, as they did not know about the discussion he had with Baba at Padampuri. When he told them what had transpired, everyone was touched by how much Baba cared for his devotees.

After the yatra, the man went back to meet Baba at Padampuri. As soon as he appeared in front of Baba, Baba said, "Next time, don't decide to go on a yatra before asking first; the old mahatma had to give up his body due to the woman's illness." This confirmed that it was indeed Baba who had saved the woman's life.

BABA SENDS DOCTORS WHO HEAL MIRACULOUSLY

(Contributed by Pandit Devidutt Kabdwal)

A man from the hills, who had the good fortune to meet Baba twice or thrice, went to the plains for some work during the monsoon season. In the plains, he became quite ill. At first he developed malaria and then later he was unable to pass stools or urine. He went to see a doctor, who tried some treatment but it did not help. The doctor gave up and said he could not do anything. The man then went to a *vaidya* (an Ayurvedic doctor) who tried his own treatments, including giving the man a *jamalgota*, a strong purgative used for horses. There was no effect. The vaidya then tried other treatments, but none of them had any effect. By now, it had been 48 hours and the man had not passed any stools or urine. He lost faith in the vaidya, thought of Baba and decided to go back to the hills. He was in much pain, but believed that God does everything for our good. He bore the pain with fortitude.

On reaching the hills, he went to the hospital. The Assistant Civil Surgeon and the Civil Surgeon both examined him. They tried various treatments, and finally he was able to pass some urine, but no stools. At first, the doctors were happy that he had at least been able to pass urine, but when it was noticed that the urine had blood in it, they became somewhat worried. Eight or ten days passed. The man had stopped eating and had no hunger. He was very weak and in great pain. The Assistant Surgeon was a very kind man and decided to give the patient a morphine injection to relieve the pain. He said, "We will continue medication and treatment for your condition separately, but I shall also give you a morphine injection regularly till you are healed so that you do not have to undergo so much pain."

After the morphine injection the man did not feel any pain, which lifted his spirits. He had become very weak and lethargic, but felt better due to the lack of pain. He developed great faith in the morphine injection, and thought doctors were like God, having invented so many things that fix our pain so quickly. He said to the Assistant Civil Surgeon: "You saved me from more pain; you are like God for me."

The doctor, who was a wise man, replied: "We are not God. Medicines only work due to God's wish, and when a patient's *prarabdha* (that part of past karma that created the present body) is good. The intelligence that invented the injections was also given to doctors by God. Otherwise how could we have come up with these things?"

The patient thought: "I was praying to God for a long time, but still had the pain. It is the doctor who fixed it with one injection."

This situation continued for some time. It was now almost a month since he had initially developed the symptoms of the sickness. He had three or four morphine injections a day to keep pain in control, but there was no difference in his condition: he was still unable to pass stools, and there was blood in his urine. Having lost all hunger, he had become stick thin, and could not even get up easily. His face had shrunk. Both the surgeons finally said that they could not do anything for him, and that he should go home to spend his remaining time with his loved ones. On hearing this, the man was dejected but decided to spend some more days in the hospital due his attachment to the injections, which afforded him relief from the pain.

One afternoon he felt some pain and thought he should ask the doctor for another injection. Usually, he would get an injection in the morning and then there would be no pain until three of four p.m. In this way, he took three or four injections through the day. That day, the pain came back around midday, so he thought perhaps the doctor had used a milder dose in the morning. When the doctor came, he asked for another injection. The doctor said that the morning's injection had been the usual full-strength injection.

The doctor believed in God and that medicines were secondary, while grace was the primary factor in healing. We cannot understand God's ways: sometimes it may seem like we have to go through much trouble, but it is always for our own good. We usually think having our desires fulfilled is good for us, but we often wish for things that we do not really need and which can hinder our spiritual journey. Being a kind person, he decided to give the patient another full-strength injection.

When the pain increased even after the second injection, the patient felt worried, but he kept hoping that the injection would help. Around half an hour passed as he waited for the effect of the second injection. When there was no effect, he became very worried and called for the doctor again. He had now lost his last hope, the morphine, and he felt terribly weak.

When the doctor arrived, he said to the man: "What can I do now? Only grace can help you now." Worried on seeing the patient so weak, the doctor thought he might pass away, so he gave him another medicine for pain. Even that had no effect. By now, the patient was almost fainting with pain. The doctor gave up hope, and leaving a *compunder* (assistant) to look after the patient, he went on his rounds to treat other patients.

Now the patient finally put his faith in God. He called out to Baba from his heart, and soon fell asleep. He saw Baba come to him. Baba said, "Have faith in God; He can do anything."

The man started to cry, and said, "Where can I go now to find God, Baba? For me, you are God."

On hearing this, Baba's heart melted, and he said, "Okay, there is no cause for worry. I am sending you two doctors who will heal you." Still in the dream, the man saw two doctors come down from skies and sit close to him. They looked like Sikhs. They were tall and healthy, with black moustaches and beards. They wore white turbans, sky blue coats, white shirts, trousers, socks, and full length boots. They had medicine boxes in their hand. One of the doctors moved the man's shirt, applied a stethoscope, and tapped the patient's heart with his fingers for about two minutes. Then the doctors spoke to each other, saying their work was done and that they should go. Then without saying anything else, they went up into the sky.

Soon after, the man awoke. He felt like going to toilet. The staff came to help him, but he did not need their help. The pain was gone, and he felt energetic. He went to the toilet and all that had been stuck in his system for a month cleared out in one go. The man felt very hungry and asked for some food. When he was asked what he wanted to eat, he said he would like four sers of apples and cold water. The men brought him what he had asked for, thinking that he was not going to live and perhaps this was his last wish. The patient remembered Baba, ate all the apples, got up and started going home.

The man who was with him said, "What happened to you? You were already sick with one disease, now have you got a new disease of eating?"

The patient replied: "By Baba's grace, I am cured, so why stay in the hospital? I'll tell you the rest of the story at home. Let's go now." On hearing this, the people with him packed up his things in a hurry and started walking with him towards his home.

The man was not only healed of his physical sickness, but also his faith increased. When he got up from the bed he felt perfectly well, and his vitality now was even more than it was before he got sick. He wondered, "I am feeling totally well; why was I brought to the hospital?" About an hour later after leaving the hospital, he said to the people with him "I was never sick; why was I taken to the hospital?"

Some days later he went to Padampuri for darshan. On seeing him, Baba smiled: "Doctors are amazing. They can not only fix pain with a single injection, but they can even prevent death!"

On hearing this, the man remembered everything that had come to pass. He was deeply moved by Baba's love and said, "With your blessings, Baba, I have realized that God's grace is everything. Learning this through experience is very different than trying to understand it through thinking."

LIFTING OF GRIEF FROM THE HEART

(Contributed by Pandit Devidutt Kabdwal)

There was once a *tapasvi* (ascetic) who was always busy in worship and meditation. He had a young son who fell sick. He was an only son and much loved. The father sought help from many doctors and vaidyas; they all tried different treatments on the boy, but his illness did not abate. The doctors and vaidyas told the father: "Don't worry, we will heal your boy one way or another."

Someone had once asked Ramakrishna Paramahansa, "When does God laugh?" He replied, "When someone is not well and the doctors say don't worry, I will fix this."

The boy's illness raged on and the man eventually lost hope. One day, the son passed away. The doctors consoled him saying, "We tried everything we could, but perhaps it was God's wish and his time here was over." Twelve days after the cremation, the boy's last rites were completed.

It all happened so quickly that no one around the village knew about the boy's illness. When they found out the boy had passed, all the well-wishers came to console him. They felt bad about what had happened, but did not worry too much about the father as he was usually the one who consoled others during their time of grief. They said, "You always consoled us with your kind and wise words, quoting such beautiful things from the scriptures, helping us to overcome our grief. We are not as wise as you, and cannot speak as eloquently as you, so cannot explain things to you so well. Please try and give yourself the same advice now."

The taspasvi replied: "When I was advising you, it was happening to you, not to me. Now it is happening to me. It is easier to advise others, but not always easy to follow the advice yourself."

His sorrow increased day by day, but eventually he realized that so much attachment was not good. He started reading scriptures, like the Yoga Vashistha. Still, his heart did not find peace and he was constantly troubled by the memory of his son. Finally, he remembered Sombari Baba and went to meet him at the ashram in Haldwani. When he arrived, Baba spoke, "What is the matter? Grief seems to have gripped you completely, but no matter, from now on you will be free from it." As Baba spoke, the sadness lifted from the man's heart and he was free from the sorrow. He was moved by Baba's love.

Many years after the event, he continued to tell people how Baba had cleared the grief from his heart with a few simple words, and how he never again felt that sorrowful about his son's passing. Such is the power of love.

HEALING SHRI NAITHANI'S SON

(Contributed by Shri Badri Dutt Lohani, Translated by Wing Commander H C Pant)

Shri Urvadutt Naithani was a senior officer in the Gola Forest Range. In those days, he often visited a place called Khamsyum, one of the subdivisions of the forest department, where felling of trees and sawing of wood was in progress on a large scale. He was staying with his family in Nainital at the time and would travel from Nainital to the Gola Range on horseback, crossing Padampuri along the way.

Shri Naithani was a learned scholar and an experienced officer. He abhorred saffron-clad beggars who posed as sadhus. He did feel that Sombari Baba had some miraculous powers, based on stories he had heard and by watching so many devotees clamor to meet Baba. Despite this, while passing by the Padampuri ashram, he would shout out, "O Sombari Baba, why are you cheating all these innocent people!" and then carry on riding towards his destination.

One day, Shri Naithani's only son became seriously ill and his chances of survival were declared to be very low. In the dead of the night, some people were sent from Nainital to the Gola Range to inform Shri Naithani. At first light, Shri Naithani set out for Nainital with a heavy heart. He was understandably anxious about his son's condition. That day, as he was passing Padampuri, he did not call out and try to taunt Baba in his usual way.

Baba called out to him: "O Naithani, stop worrying about your son. He has been feeling better since the morning and is getting stronger by the minute. Come, take some vibhuti and prasad for your son." The seemingly simple items of vibhuti and prasad given by saints are known to bestow many boons, such as health, wealth, progeny, spiritual and worldly powers.

Shri Naithani disembarked from the horse, bowed to Baba, uttering incoherent words as he was choked with emotion and love. Finally being able to speak, he fell down at Baba's feet and said, "Baba, if what you have said comes to be true, then I, Naithani, will become your devoted disciple. Please forgive me."

Baba helped him up and said, "Proceed to your home."

Naithani wiped the tears from his eyes, and Baba grasped his hand, and along with two others, helped him to mount the horse. On arriving in Nainital, he found to his great joy that his son was hale and hearty. From that day, Naithani became like a loving and obedient son of Sombari Baba.

HEALING A LEPER

(Contributed by Shri Govindram Kala, Ex-Deputy Collector)

Baba told me that he preferred to set up his ashrams in places like Kakrighat and Padampuri because they were very quiet, peaceful spots, away from the hubbub of large populations. He also told me that he was from Punjab, and used to work for the government.

Baba was a saint of the highest caliber. He could read people's minds, and he healed many people of all sorts of afflictions. One day, a leper came to the ashram in Padampuri. Baba asked him to open a store and keep a profit margin of only two percent. The man did as instructed. By Baba's grace, he was soon healed of leprosy.

DIGESTIVE TROUBLES

(Contributed by I.L. Sah)

In about 1948, a businessman of Kashipur, who lived up to the ripe age of over 75 years, relayed to me that, when he was about twelve or thirteen years of age, he suffered from lung trouble for a long time and had the best material treatment, both allopathic and Ayurvedic. He had become very weak and his digestion was hopeless. His father, who knew Baba, ultimately decided to take the sick boy to him. When he arrived at the ashram, he related to Baba what had happened and entreated him to help. Baba told him that he was no doctor or physician and that if he could cure people he would not be living in caves and jungles.

To test his faith, Baba put him off for two or three days. At last one morning, when the father went to the ashram with the sick boy and repeated his entreaties, Baba said, "I have nothing except these ashes." Baba then gave him a pinch of ashes from the fire burning near him. "Just put a bit of it on his tongue and apply the rest to his forehead." The boy was cured and the father's faith and devotion had been tested.

Soon after, prasad was distributed to the people who had come as usual to see the Baba. The father and the boy were given equal shares. The father hesitated. His son had been on sick diet for months and his digestion had been deranged. The prasad was a wheat gruel rich in ghee. Baba, who could read minds through and through, told the father, "Don't be afraid of it. Let the boy have as much of the prasad as he likes." The boy gladly gulped the whole of it. There was no recurrence of the trouble afterwards.

The next day the father was told to go back and do his business. The father and son were ever after this grateful and devoted to Baba.

PREVENTING SUICIDE

(Contributed by I.L. Sah)

It was ten years after my first darshan before I had another occasion to see Baba. Monsoon was coming to an end. I was returning from Almora. After traveling several miles, I met an elderly *Shakta Brahmana* (one who worships the divine feminine) who was in service at Nainital. As evening approached, we decided to stop at Kartiagarh for the night. We were told Baba was in his ashram here across the river and we had better go and see him. We crossed a small bridge and went to the other side of the river. Baba was sitting near a fire below a wide-spreading small banyan tree. There was a cave, with a small lamp burning. There was a small Shiva temple also. Here one felt great peace and a sacred quiet.

After Baba had made the usual inquiries, my companion started relating his tale of woe, saying that he was so sick and broken in body and mind that he felt inclined to commit suicide unless he had the grace of Baba. Baba would not answer him directly, but addressed me and said that he was no doctor or physician, living in a solitary place without any knowledge and possessing little or no power and authority. He several times said that if he had any knowledge or power to intercede for others, he would use such knowledge or power for his own good in the first place instead of living in solitary wild places.

My companion paid no heed to what Baba said, but continued, "Baba, you are my all-in-all. You can do even what no god can do."

This continued for some time. To change the trend of the talk, after some time Baba asked my friend to prepare tobacco for him. He did so. Baba had the knack and power to read the minds and thoughts of people by a mere glance. As my companion was preparing the chillum, Baba addressed me again and said that smoking tobacco was a bad habit, but he had not been able to give it up. I had always considered this as a bad habit, but I was not then thinking so. He perhaps meant to say both to me and my companion that even he had a weakness that ordinary people have.

After the tobacco was handed to him, he asked my companion to go to the cave and bring a pot of prasad, which he gave to each of us and directed us to give some to the river and partake of it before we came to the fire again. We did so and then went back and sat with Baba near the fire for a little while. My companion went on repeating his woes and prayed to Baba to do something for him.

Ultimately Baba said, addressing me, "I have told him to simply give up the habit and that thereafter he would have peace." My companion said that he tried to do so many times and failed. Baba addressed him to try this again and then wait for the result. As it was already late, he asked us to leave the ashram and pass the night at the rest house.

On the occasion of my first darshan, I could not understand things. Twelve years later I could grasp things better. I was more reverent and could understand a little how the Baba was ministering to the moral and spiritual needs of the people for helping to spread good with all around.

DR. BHARGAVA BANDAGED BABA'S LEG

(Contributed by Dr. Manoharlal Bhargav)

There was a doctor called Manoharlal Bhargav from Ajmer in the state of Rajasthan. He was posted in Mukteshwar for work and would visit the ashram regularly. During the first World War, Dr. Bhargav was asked to report for war duty. Worried, he went to see Sombari Baba, who applied some vibhuti to his forehead and said, "Don't worry, you will be fine."

Just then he noticed a wound on Baba's leg. The wound had festered and he could even see some maggots in the wound. The doctor exclaimed, "Baba, this looks very serious. Please let me bandage your leg, otherwise it will only get worse and you won't be able to walk."

Baba replied, "Don't worry son, it is food for the maggots, that is their karma, let them be." The doctor insisted. Seeing his love and devotion, Baba relented.

At night, after the doctor left, Baba took off the bandages and simply rubbed some ash from the dhuni into the wound. By the next morning, the wound had healed completely. The doctor came by again the next day to check on Baba, and Baba exclaimed: "Oh doctor, look, your treatment has done wonders; my leg has healed completely!"

Dr. Bhargava was moved by the love with which Baba spoke, knowing full well that his treatment could not have been the cause of such immediate healing.

Animals

TIGERS AND COBRAS

(Contributed by Shri Hira Vallabh Pant)

Many people in the area knew that every night, two tigers would come to the ashram at night and go straight to the Shiva temple. After darshan, they would go to Baba for darshan and sit by his dhuni for a little while before walking off into the forest. This was their daily routine—they would take the same path as Hanumanji did: the Shiva shrine first and then Baba's dhuni. Apart from the tigers, people had also seen *nagraj* (king cobras) near Baba. Quite often, as Baba sat for his evening prayers on his seat, people would notice a cobra coiled under it. Sometimes Baba would talk about meeting tigers or cobras in the night. He would explain that sometimes great beings would come in the form of these animals to meet him.

THE BARASINGHA

(Collected by Shri Shankar Lal Sah)

Once a *barasingha* (a breed of deer with antlers) was being chased by dogs and hunters as part of a hunt and it ran into Baba's Padampuri ashram. On hearing the barasingha, Baba immediately left his dhuni and went to see the animal. Seeing that the animal had sought refuge in Baba's ashram, the hunters went away. Baba gave it some milk to drink. He then called a devotee, Shri Bageshwari, and said, "Bageshwari, who knows who has come in this form. He will only be here for two or three days. Look after him and make sure he is comfortable." As Baba had predicted, the animal died of its wounds in a few days. Baba sent a devotee to Haldwani to get a beautiful shawl, wrapped the barasingha's body in it, and performed the last rites of the animal himself. Baba's non-violence and love was the same for all, whether man or beast.

It is said sometimes tigers would visit the ashram. Baba would warn people in advance that a tiger was sitting in a particular spot and that they should avoid going there.

THE FOREST OFFICER AND THE SNAKES

(Contributed by Shri Shankar Lal Sah, as told by Shri Urbadutt Pande)

Shri Urbadutt Pande's father was working as a camp clerk with the forest department at the time. One day, he was traveling on horseback along with his British officer and the officer's wife and they passed by Baba's ashram at Padampuri. Shri Pande asked his officer for a few minutes so that he could go have darshan. The officer said it was quite late in the evening and they were quite reluctant to wait. However, they respected his feelings, and said, "Okay, we'll go ahead. Why don't you go to the ashram quickly and then catch up with us. Be aware though, we need to arrive in time, and if you are late you'll lose your job." Pandeji agreed. He tied up his horse outside the ashram and went to Baba for darshan.

On seeing him, Baba greeted him warmly. "Oh, here you are. Welcome, welcome. Come sit with me and smoke some ganja." Pandeji was concerned about catching up to the officers in time, but he did not wish to go against Baba's instructions, so he sat and smoked for a little while. Then Baba said, "Khichdi will be ready in half an hour, you should eat and then go." By now, Pande was nervous about his job, but he decided not to worry about it, owing to his faith in Baba. So he waited, had dinner as instructed by Baba, and then headed off. By then, an hour or so had passed from the time he arrived at the ashram. He was sure that he would be late and that the officers would probably suspend him from his job for the delay.

He passed a place called Champhi and was approaching a steep climb near the next place, called Matiyal, when all at once he saw the English officer and his wife. They were both still on their horses, and the horses were rearing up on their hind legs and neighing loudly. When he came closer, the officer saw him and exclaimed, "Oh, you have come! Help us!" Pandeji wondered what the matter was. Then he saw two large cobras were on the path, one in front of each horse, with their hoods raised. The horses were scared and refused to move ahead. The officer and his wife did not dare to get off the horses. They had been waiting at the spot for nearly an hour, unable to move ahead, and the cobras did not leave either. As soon as Shri Pande arrived, the cobras folded their hoods and slithered away. Far from reprimanding Shri Pande for being late, the officer thanked him for saving their lives, and awarded him a plot of land.

DR. JHA IS SAVED FROM A TIGER

(Contributed by Shri Dhanilal Sah)

Dr. Ayodhaprasad Jha, who lived in Mukteshwar, would often

have to travel to Bhimtal via Bhowali to meet his patients. It would sometimes be quite late at night when he returned. The road passed through thick jungle. Once he was passing through the forest late at night after seeing some patients in Bhimtal. He heard a tiger growling, and before he knew it the tiger within attacking distance. Somehow he managed to spur his horse on, with the tiger in hot pursuit. Dr. Jha prayed to Sombari Baba for help. All of a sudden, he saw Baba standing between the horse and the tiger, with a jhola over his shoulder, holding his chimta in one hand. The tiger immediately stopped chasing Dr. Jha and slinked away into the forest.

Dr. Jha continued to serve people until the very end of his life. He was quite successful in his career, and treated needy people without charging for his services. He left his body with a picture of Sombari Baba in front of his eyes.

GOPAL SAH'S HORSE AND THE TIGER

(Contributed by Shri Dhanilal Sah)

A student called Gopal Sah from the village of Gonda was once traveling on horseback to Nainital to meet his grandfather, who has asked him to come there. On the way, he decided to stop at Padampuri for Baba's darshan. As he was in a hurry, he did not wash his hands and feet, but went straight to see Baba. When he paid his respects, Baba first berated him for not washing his hands and feet, but then gave him prasad and asked him to hurry on to Nainital, saying that it was important for him to arrive by evening. Baba also said that his relative in Bhowali, Shri Mohanlal Sah, would insist for him to stay, and that he should ask to be excused and carry on to Nainital.

When Gopalji arrived at Bhowali, his relative insisted that he stay and rest for a while, exactly as Baba had predicted. Gopalji was tired after the long journey and decided to rest. The house servant took his horse to the stables, which were a little distance away from the house. The servant tied Gopalji's horse at the far end of the stables, some distance away from the other horses, locked the door, and then came back to the house. After dinner, the servant went to fetch Gopalji's horse and came back crying. A tiger had broken into the stables by tearing down the door. He had ignored all the other horses, crossed all the way across the stables and killed Gopalji's horse. The horse did not even belong to Gopalji; it was a special horse that belonged to his friend. The friend had lent him the horse as a favor since he needed to go to Nainital quickly. Gopalji learnt his lesson: to always follow Baba's instructions.

PURE OFFERINGS

(Contributed by Pandit Devidutt Kabdwal)

Once, during the Mahashivratri festival, many saints and devotees had gathered at the ashram at Kakrighat. A group of devotees were heading to the ashram with large platters full of sweets to offer at the ashram. The journey was long, so they had to leave early. Along the way, some of the devotees who were not very strong physically felt tired. Considering their condition, the group decided to take out some of the sweets they were carrying from one of the platters and give it to the people who were experiencing weakness. They took care when taking out the sweets to do it respectfully, as prescribed by their beliefs. Some sweets were removed from one platter, and the other platters were not disturbed.

When the devotees reached the ashram, Baba was just about to complete his afternoon meditation. The servant who was carrying the platter from which some sweets had been removed was at the end of the queue. When everyone else had set their platters down,

Baba spoke to him and asked him to leave his platter aside, as it had already been eaten from and could not be used in the ashram. He then asked the people who had brought the platter: "Why did you bring impure sweets to offer at the ashram on a day like Mahashivratri?"

The devotees were unsure what to say. In their minds, they had removed a small quantity in accordance to the practices that were taught to them, so how come the entire platter was now impure? To help them understand, Baba said, "Let's try something. Let us offer these sweets to some monkeys and see what happens."

Everyone agreed. The servant was asked to go and place the platter of sweets in a certain place close by, and he did as instructed. At the time there were no monkeys in sight, but soon after a large troupe of wild monkeys turned up. They found the platter and started picking up the sweets from it. Strangely though, they did not start to eat the sweets immediately. They broke the sweets into pieces, smelled them, and then threw them away. On seeing this, the devotees realized that Baba was right. A minute later though, they started doubting again, thinking that perhaps because the monkeys were wild, they did not know what sweets were, so they did not eat the sweets.

Sensing this, Baba deliberately asked the devotees: "Are you satisfied?" When they did not reply, Baba said, "If the same monkeys eat sweets from the other platters, will you still have any doubts?" The devotees agreed to this test.

Two more servants were sent to the same place with untouched platters of sweets: one held the same type of sweets as those that had been offered before, and one was a completely different type. By this time, the monkeys were at the riverbank. When the servants appeared carrying the two platters of sweets, the monkeys grabbed the sweets before the platters were even put on the ground and gobbled everything up immediately. This time, they did not smell or break any sweets, but simply started eating them immediately.

On seeing this, the devotees realized the truth of Baba's words. They were touched by his understanding of their minds' weaknesses, and by how he had so lovingly and patiently taught them an important lesson.

THE BRITISH COMMANDER AND THE FISH

(Contributed by Pandit Devidutt Kabdwal)

Once a British platoon commander came to Kakrighat to fish with his men. He was looking to set up his camp in the area. Someone told him that on the side of the river where the ashram was located, there were many large fish and that they were not afraid of humans, which meant it would be easy to fish there. The commander was a good man, and had he known the fish were fed at Baba's ashram, out of respect he would not have gone fishing there. However, in order to try to please him, his men hid this fact. So the party set up camp close to the river and rested there that night. The next day, after lunch, the commander crossed over to the side of the river where the ashram was and started fishing.

As he put his fishing rod in the water, the people in the ashram realized what he was trying to do. There were some naga sadhus and fakirs visiting the ashram at the time. The nagas often are known to be fierce in their behavior. On seeing that the commander meant to harm living beings, they became angry and started going down to the river, chimtas in hand, to attack him. Baba called out to them, "Stop, and sit down calmly. It is not the dharma of a sadhu to lose his peace. What can men do? It is God who protects everyone. If your desire to protect the fish is egoless, God will definitely answer and save the fish himself. Wait a while," Baba continued, "and see what happens. If required, someone who can speak English can explain things to the Englishman, and I'm sure he will understand."

The nagas knew of Baba's greatness, so they agreed; everyone waited to see what unfolded. The fish in the river were quite big, as they got fed prasad from the ashram every day. No one every fished or harmed them there in any way, so they never hesitated to eat anything offered by anyone from the ashram. The fish were so used to people from the ashram that the fish would come so close to the bank that, if anyone wished, they could simply catch the fish with their bare hands.

As the commander put his hook in with the bait attached, an amazing thing happened. The fish bit the hook and ate the bait, but did not get hooked. This happened many times. The commander was rather surprised and asked his servants to also put in their hooks. The same thing happened with them, too, again and again. The commander eventually tired of his efforts. Not a single fish was caught. Everyone in the ashram was watching this scene, and they appreciated not just Baba's way of handling the incident, but also Baba's patience and kindness towards the commander. The commander was dejected by then, so he stopped fishing and decided to hunt animals in the forest near the ashram. He saw a few small animals and tried to hunt them, but was unable to capture, hurt, or kill even one. By now, it was evening and the commander came back to his tent empty-handed.

The commander was a good man and he believed in God. All evening, he wondered about the fish, thinking that had they not taken the bait, it would have been a different thing. How come they ate the bait every time but were never hooked? Also, he had not been able to hunt a single animal in a forest that was teeming with wildlife. It was all very puzzling, so he asked his men what the deal was. The men then told him that a great mahatma lived there, and that no one fished or hunted near the ashram.

On hearing this, the commander realized that what had happened was because of Baba's presence. He told his men, "You made a grave mistake by not telling me about this before." The next morning, he went to ashram with his men for darshan. He asked one of the men to offer some money at Baba's feet as an offering. When the man was about to offer the money, Baba called a devotee who spoke English and asked him to translate so that the commander could understand what Baba was saying. Baba said to the man: "Tell the Englishman to ask his men to buy some sweets with this money and feed it to the fish." The devotee translated and accordingly the commander asked his servants to get sweets and other food for the fish from the shop. When the servants arrived with the food in large platters, he went to the river to feed the fish.

Now, another strange thing happened. The fish that had been eating the bait came to the bank, smelled the food he was offering, and swam away without eating it. The commander tried many times to feed them different types of food, but the same thing happened over and over. At the ashram, Baba said to a devotee: "Being a commander in the British army, he is used to ordering the public around, and thinks he can do the same with the fish. That won't work with them; only being polite and gentle and offering the food with love will work." Baba always advised devotees to do their duty sincerely, even if the British had enslaved them. "Right now, he thinks even the fish are his slaves," Baba laughed. He then had a devotee send a message to the commander to offer the food with love and respect.

The commander was a smart man and understood the purport of Baba's message. He went back to the bank to offer the food to the fish, this time with respect and love in his heart. A wonderful scene followed: as soon as the platters of food were put down near the bank, fish of all sizes, big and small, came to the bank from every direction with great speed. Before the commander could even put all the food into the river, they jumped out and started eating it from the platters. There were so many fish splashing about that it seemed the waters of the river had risen, and the platters became wet. Everyone watched this scene in wonder. Everything was finished very quickly and then the fish disappeared back into the river as quickly as they had appeared.

The commander came to Baba to pay his respects. He said to Baba (through a translator): "With your grace, I have understood what love really is, and now I have lost all desire to fish or hunt." Baba gave him some prasad, blessed him, and sent him on his way.

The devotees who were present for this incident realized the grace and effect of Baba's presence. With great joy, and without any pain to any being, he had demonstrated through this little drama what the grace of God is like. The devotees also realized how Baba was connected to everyone at the level of the soul, and could inspire people from within to come to the path of righteousness, as he had done with the commander. The nagas present also learned an important lesson in patience, love, their own dharma, and belief in the grace of God.

FISH AND MONKEYS

(Contributed by I.L. Sah)

The Baba silently helped people. Even wild animals, fish, and fowl in the neighborhood were fed day by day and it seems they were also grateful to the great yogi and obeyed him. Once the collector and district magistrate, who was a good angler, went fishing in Almora.

Opposite Baba's ashram at Kartigurh, he noticed shoals of fish playing in the water. He stopped and put his rod and line in the water. The fish would come to the line, but would not bite. Again and again the bait was changed, with the same result. This went on for nearly three quarters of an hour. When the Sahib was tired of this, one of his Indian assistants told him, "Sahib, you will not be able to catch any fish here, as the fish are the preserve of the Baba who lives in the ashram opposite. If we go downstream some two miles away from this place, you will be able to hook the fish."

The collector had the good sense to accept this advice, but before he did so, he asked his assistant if he could go and visit the Baba and express his regret for disturbing the fish in his area of influence. He did so and was glad to have blessings and prasad from the Baba. He made an offering of cash to the ashram also. Thereafter, whenever he happened to pass this place, he made it a point to pay his respects to the Baba.

On another occasion, some group of men from Nainital, including the son of one of the leading rich men of the town, planned to go on a Sunday for Baba's darshan. They were told that anything accepted for the bhandara of the ashram should be clean and packed and should not be put in any unclean place on the way. A basketful of sweets was prepared, packed, tied in a new sheet of cloth, and a good porter was engaged for the purpose. The party had to go some 13 miles on foot. It was warm and halfway there they felt thirsty and hungry as well, as they forgot to take anything beside what was in the basket.

Some of the party suggested that after washing his hands, one of them take some eatables from the basket and partake of these, and then drink water from a roadside spring. All of them agreed and saw no harm in doing so. On reaching the ashram, the storekeeper in the presence of the Baba was requested to take the basket to the bhandara. To the amazement of all, the Baba said that the sweets were contaminated; as such, they could not be offered to god and had better be left outside. Baba engaged in talk with other visitors for a long while. Then he said that prasad offering, which is made to a god, should be offered with a pure mind and body. He related how the boys had felt hungry and thirsty and in a hurry had taken a part of what they took as an offering. "You will see the truth of this just now," he said.

The basket was directed to the place some distance from the place and placed under a tree and its contents exposed. Apes and monkeys after a while came down the trees in the neighborhood. They would come along singly or in parties to the basket, look at the contents, and then go back without touching these. Everyone was astonished. And then the Baba directed that the basket should be emptied in the river and that the fish would eat up the sweets.

THE GREEDY BRAHMIN AND THE TIGER

(Contributed by Hira Vallabh Lohni, Municipal Ranger, Retired, Nainital)

There was a poor Brahmin called Chintamani in a village nearby. He collected wood and leaves of the *malu* tree from the forest and brought them to the ashram (malu leaves are large and broad, and they are often used as plates to eat on). Chintamani was very poor, and there would be no food in his house for half the days of the month, so he would come to the ashram to have a meal. One day Baba said to him: "Chintwa, I will make you rich. But *saale,* be sure to donate half of it." (*Saale* means "wife's brother" in Hindi, but it's also used as a light insult or expletive.)

By Baba's grace, Chintamani found a buried treasure close to his village. He took the treasure and reburied it close to his house.

He stopped visiting the ashram. The villagers came to know he had found treasure and someone reported this to the police. The police summoned him, and he went to the local police station.

One morning at about 5 a.m., Baba summoned me and said, "Lohni, go call Gopal Dutt, the forester." I had hardly walked a few steps when Baba called out, "Lohni, come here." I went back to him. He applied vibhuti to my forehead and said, "You may go now. The road goes through thick forest. This will take care of you."

I set out for Gopal Duttji's place. As I walked through the forest, I saw two small lights glowing like torches some distance away. I kept walking and the lights got closer. As I passed the spot, I saw that they were the eyes of a tiger. The tiger was sitting on a human corpse, eating it. I kept walking. A little distance away, I saw a *hadpiya* (wooden vessel used to store ghee) and a hat lying on the ground close to the path.

I approached a steep climb in the road toward Khunigaad. I heard the sounds of beating drums. This usually meant people were trying to scare off wild animals. As I continued on the path, I came across a large group of people who were making the noise. Forester Gopal Duttji was with them. He told me that a tiger had been prowling in the area over the last three days. He also told me that Chintamani had gone to the police station but did not return; perhaps the tiger had killed him. He asked me if I had seen a tiger on my way up, and if I had, how come I was okay? I told him what I had seen on the way.

We walked to the ashram together. We passed the half-eaten corpse again; it was Chintamani. The tiger had probably been scared away by all the noise, so it was not to be seen. I told Gopal Duttji that owing to Baba's vibhuti, I was safe.

Time has passed. By Baba's grace, today I have no fear. I have a well-to-do household. My children are well fed and well looked after.

It is all his prasad, and I know that he will continue to shower his grace on me in both worlds: the worldly and the spiritual. Glory to Baba. Glory to his devotees.

Ordinary Miracles

I.L. SAH SEES EXAM PAPER IN A DREAM

(Contributed by I.L. Sah)

I.L. Sah, along with some friends, was going to Almora for an exam in history. He was not very well prepared for the exam and was therefore worried about how things would turn out. On the way to Almora, the party stopped over at Khairna for darshan of Sombari Baba. During darshan, I.L. Sah silently prayed to Baba for help.

As he slept that night, he had a dream in which he saw an examination paper with a question on the topic of the "second war of Panipat." When he woke in the morning, he remembered the dream and read up on the historical war. When they neared Almora, he talked to his friends about the dream. The friends laughed, saying that he had wasted his time and that questions were always asked about the other two wars in Panipat—the first war and the third war—because they were considered historically far more significant.

But when the examination paper arrived, it turned out that there was indeed a question on the second war of Panipat! Shri Sah was overjoyed as he was well prepared for this question, and he passed the exam successfully!

STEPPING OVER THE LINE

(Contributed by I.L. Sah)

While in my teens, one early Spring afternoon I set out on foot with a couple of friends from Nainital and stopped in the evening at Khairna at a wayside shop for the night before going to Almora to sit at my High School exams. We were preparing to sleep when the keeper of the shop, an elderly person, came and suggested that we had better go and have darshan of a sadhu before going to Almora in the morning.

It was a dark night, spring was about and it was pleasantly cold. We accompanied our guide, crossed a hanging bridge and the sandy wash before reaching the cave where the sadhu stayed. The river was flowing nearby. A dim light was burning in the cave and there was a small fire burning in the front part of the cave. As we approached, someone in a gruff voice addressed our guide and told him that he was trespassing the boundary of the ashram with shoes on.

"I am sorry," the guide said. After asking us to retrace our steps back, he took off his shoes and asked us also to do so. In the dark none of us had noticed this line.

Then the Baba from the river bank directed our guide to sit near the fire with us and await his return. We were told by our guide that the Baba went to the river bank to feed the fish several times each day.

We had not long to wait before the Baba came and sat near the fire opposite to us. With matted locks and ash-smeared body, he was of short stature and of advanced age. He inquired of us about our parents and about some prominent men in the town. Then he related to us the story of a king who had everything to indulge in sense life, but never found real peace and joy. We were then given prasad. Before he bid us to leave the lovely ashram, our guide requested the Baba bless us so as to achieve success. The Baba said that one who works honestly and diligently is always successful.

We returned and had a sound sleep. The sacred peace and

quiet that pervaded the ashram was my first unforgettable experience before entering life.

THE MAN CARRYING ALCOHOL

(Contributed by Shri Tikaram Bhatt, Bhowali)

One day Baba was sitting at his asana. Suddenly he started speaking, "*Saale*! He's coming to my ashram with a bad thing in his pocket. He intends to make his wife drink it." We started looking around, but could not see anyone. A few minutes later we saw a man approaching the ashram, some 200 yards away. As he came closer, Baba shouted at him: "Don't come here with that bad thing! Break it!"

The person took out a bottle of alcohol from his pocket and was about to throw it on the ground when Baba said, "Not here! Throw it far, otherwise the glass might hurt someone." The man threw the bottle far away, took a bath in the river as instructed by Baba, and then came to sit next to Baba. At this time, Baba said, "You bad man! Making a woman drink alcohol! Here, take this vibhuti and apply it to her forehead; she will be fine."

THE MAN WITH THE BASKET OF BANANAS

(Contributed by Shri Tikaram Bhatt, Bhowali)

Baba would partake of charas. If someone was carrying some charas in their pocket, he would definitely take it from them! If someone fought at home to bring charas for Baba, he would know about it even before the man arrived. One day, a man was coming to the ashram with some bananas in a covered basket. On the way, another man met him and asked, "Are these fish for sale?"

The first man replied: "I have bananas in the basket, and no, they are not for sale."

When he arrived at the ashram, Baba asked: "Have you brought fish?" Before he could reply, Baba said, "Why did you keep the basket of bananas covered? That's why the other person thought you were bringing fish." The man did not have any words, and kept looking at Baba in amazement.

PANDIT MOTIRAM'S DRINKING

(Contributed by Hira Vallabh Pant)

A devotee of Sombari Baba's, called Pandit Motiramji, had a drinking habit. Even when going for darshan he would often drink beforehand, and also take two or three bottles of drink along. Baba was usually very strict. He would stop anyone who was carrying drinks before they even crossed the river to the ashram, and make them throw away the alcohol before they were allowed to cross. However, in the case of Pandit Motiramji, Baba never said a word.

One time Shri Motiramji came to the ashram badly drunk and sat at the dhuni. Some other sadhus and devotees were there. They could all tell he was drunk, but no one dared say anything to him in front of Sombari Baba. As usual, Baba was very kind and sweet to Shri Motiramji. That day, Motiramji threw up near the dhuni and yet Baba did not say anything to him; he simply instructed other devotees to clean the area with water. The devotees wondered what was going on. How come Baba was so lenient with this man?

Baba knew this question was playing on their minds; he simply smiled and said, "The pair of scales I use to measure someone are very different from yours." After that day, Shri Motiramji gave up alcohol completely. Who knows what past karmas were being cleared out in Baba's holy presence!

THAKUR JAGATCHAND GURKHA STOPS DRINKING

(Contributed by Hira Vallabh Pant)

Thakur Jagadchandji Gurkha owned the Hartola Estate between Ramgad and Mukteshwar; he spent his time between the Estate and Nainital. While traveling from one of these places to the other, he always made it a point to stop over at the ashram at Padampuri for darshan. In this way, he had visited the ashram hundreds of times. He would also often send fruits from the Estate to the ashram.

Shri Gurkha loved his drink, and also consumed a lot of meat. However, Baba never told him off about either of these things at any time and always spoke with him lovingly. At one time he left from Nainital with the intention to go to the Estate. He was already drunk by the time he left, and he took nineteen more bottles along, as he intended to spend a few days at the Estate. Initially, he had intended to go straight to his destination, but after walking along a bit, he decided to stop over at Padampuri for darshan.

On reaching the ashram, he felt very bad about having turned up drunk for darshan. He was also afraid that Baba would scold him. However, Baba did not mention anything about the drink, and spoke with him very lovingly, as usual. After a while, Baba sent him on his way. After leaving the ashram, Gurkhaji started thinking about his drinking. On the one hand, he felt like throwing away the bottles but, on the other hand, he had already spent a good amount of money on the drinks so he did not feel like wasting them. He felt he had to do something about it that very night, without waiting for the next day, so he drank all nineteen bottles that night. On reaching Hartola, he fell into his bed and got up two full days later.

After that day he never drank again, and also gave up consuming meat.

A GAMBLER GIVES UP HIS ADDICTION

(Contributed by Pandit Devidutt Kabdwal)

A devotee who visited the ashram regularly had a gambling habit. He was a good man, but gambled beyond his means, especially during the festival of Diwali. It is a popular custom in some areas of India to gamble on the day of Mahalakshmi puja during the Diwali festival, when the Goddess of wealth, Devi Mahalakshmi, is worshipped.

One year, a man came to the ashram at Padampuri for darshan during Diwali. Around dusk on Mahalakshmi puja day, he remembered his gambling habit. Though there was enough time for him to get home in time to gamble, Baba gave him prasad and sent him off. On thc way back, the man felt a little tired and somewhat sleepy. A few minutes later, he saw next to the road a small building two floors high, with shops on the bottom and some rooms above. The shops were closed for the evening. He saw a cot on the verandah in front of the shops and decided to rest there for a few minutes. Before he knew it, he had fallen asleep.

After a short snooze, he opened his eyes and realized that some people were gambling in the rooms above the shops. A minute later an argument broke out between the gamblers and soon after escalated into a fight. He heard voices saying something about a *khukri* (a large and dangerous knife) and realized the argument was serious, and that these men were probably brigands. He suddenly felt very worried about his own safety, thinking that if these people saw him, they might mistake him for an official or policeman who had turned up to investigate illegal gambling and kill him. He trembled in fear and prayed to Baba to protect him. On doing so, he heard Baba's voice: "If you promise never to gamble again, then your life can be saved."

Shaken from his experience and moved by Baba's love, he promised never to gamble again. As soon as he did this, the argument in the rooms above died down. A few minutes later, the gambling stopped, and one by one the gamblers left the building and went to their homes.

The man returned home happily and never gambled again. With this experience, his desire to gamble also went away. He realized that Baba had not only helped him to stop gambling by extracting a promise, but also helped him keep the promise by dissolving the desire altogether.

THE GAMBLER FROM BAREILLY

(Contributed by Pandit Devidutt Kabdwal)

A man from Bareilly had a gambling habit. He once wrote to his friend who had a shop close to the ashram, and said, "Can you ask Baba if I will win in gambling this Diwali?" His friend visited the ashram regularly, so on his next visit he read the letter to Baba and asked the question as requested by his friend. Baba replied, "I do not see him winning anything, but one day, everyone is going to surely die." The devotee wrote back to his friend in Bareilly with Baba's exact words. Some days later, the man from Bareilly came to the ashram and told devotees that on reading Baba's message his mind was completely cleared of all desire for gambling, and that he had totally given up gambling since.

GOVERNMENT ABOVE THE GOVERNMENT

(Contributed by Pandit Devidutt Kabdwal)

The residents of Kurmanchal (Kumaon) considered Sombari

Baba an avatar of Lord Shiva. A lot of people would visit Baba for darshan, and it was his habit that he would unfailingly tell each person something beneficial. Baba's guidance was specific to the person's needs, both worldly and spiritual, as he was able to see easily inside people's hearts and minds and knew what was going on in their lives. Devotees would quickly develop great faith in Baba.

Pandit Devidutt Kabdwal was a devotee of Baba who worked in a government office. He would visit Baba at the ashram in Padampuri every Saturday, and also on any other days whenever the office was closed.

One day he had a disagreement with a superior officer at work. The officer made some false allegations against Shri Kabdwal, as a result of which he was suspended from his job. He lodged an appeal, but the appeal was rejected.

One day, Baba asked him what was going on at work, and he related what had happened. Baba advised him to approach the superior of the officer who had rejected the appeal. On hearing this, Shri Kabdwal said that the officer who had rejected the appeal was at the highest post, so he could only appeal directly to the government. But according to the legal process, he was not allowed to appeal to the government either. Shri Kabdwal was quite disheartened. Baba reassured him saying, "Don't worry, there is another government above your government!"

After this, Baba did not speak but he inspired Shri Kabdwal from within to appeal to the government. Strengthened by Baba's words and owing to his devotion and faith towards Baba, Shri Kabdwal decided not to give in without making an appeal. He submitted an appeal, but unfortunately it was rejected. Baba did not raise the topic again for some time, so Shri Kabdwal did not say anything about it to Baba either. One day, Baba inspired him again from within, saying, "If something does not work the first time around, try again!" Knowing that the words of a great sage like Baba never prove false, he considered resubmitting his appeal. However, he was not sure how to go about it, since the officer against whose advice he had lodged the first appeal was sure to squash the second appeal as well.

Some days later, the officer in question was transferred to a different location. Shri Kabdwal decided to meet the new officer and speak with him. The new officer received Shri Kabdwal with respect and gave him a patient hearing. Once he understood the case well, he advised Shri Kabdwal to resubmit the appeal, assuring him of his personal support. This time around the government accepted the appeal and recorded it. After this, Shri Kabdwal carried out all the work required for the appeal with great diligence and fervor, and eventually he won the case and was reinstated. After this incident, his faith in Baba grew stronger. Every time he spoke of Baba's compassion and grace, he would become overwhelmed with emotion.

After winning the appeal, Shri Kabdwal continued in the government job for some years, but internally he underwent a great transformation. He started spending more and more time with Baba and devoted himself to the study of scriptures. In 1919, when Sombari Baba left his body, Shri Kabdwal felt very sad, but continued his work at the office somehow, though his heart was not in it at all.

Lessons and Grace

DARSHAN OF HANUMANJI

(Contributed by Shri Hira Vallabh Pant)

Once during monsoon season, Baba was at the ashram at Padampuri. It was raining very hard. Some sadhus and devotees were sitting around the dhuni at the lower level of the ashram, while Baba was sitting by the dhuni at the upper level. A broad-shouldered yogi arrived wearing nothing but a saffron loincloth. His skin had a reddish tone to it. The loincloth was soaked from the rain, but his body looked like not a drop of water had touched it.

When he arrived at the ashram, he looked at the people sitting around the lower dhuni, and they noticed him too. He did not sit with them or say anything but proceeded straight to the Shiva temple. After taking darshan at the temple, he went to meet Baba at the upper dhuni. A little while later, he came down to the lower dhuni, removed his wet loincloth, and sat near the dhuni totally naked. When he did this, the other people around the lower dhuni were taken aback because they found the act of sitting naked close to the dhuni offensive. Some sadhus even got up to hit him with their fire tongs. On seeing this, the yogi left his wet loincloth where it was and simply walked away.

When this happened, Baba called out from the dhuni above: "Hanumanji has just graced me with his darshan; you people must also have had darshan, yes?"

On hearing this, there was a big rush amongst the sadhus and devotees to try and find the yogi, but they could not find him. They tried searching for him around the ashram for a while, but Hanumanji, who just a few minutes ago wanted to come and sit with them, was nowhere to be found. The people came back to the lower dhuni and talked about how the yogi's skin had been of a reddish color (Hanuman's body is red), but that none of them had paid any attention to that fact. They realized that Hanumanji had probably used his *maya* (power of illusion) to ensure that they did not realize this at the time. They tried to find the loincloth that Hanumanji had left by the dhuni, but now even that had disappeared! At first, they thought that

Hanuman looking at K.K. at Vrindavan Ashram

one of the group must have kept it aside, but everyone said that they had seen the loincloth lying on the ground, and no one had kept it aside when they all went searching for Hanumanji. The loincloth was nowhere to be seen!

THE INCIDENT AT PADAMPURI ASHRAM AT NIGHT

(Contributed by Hiralal Sah)

Basanaat Babu and I arrived in Padampuri with the intention to stay there for a few days. No one was allowed to stay in the ashram at night, so we would have to sleep in the dharamshala across the river. Basanaat Babu was curious to find out what Baba does at night. When he told me this, it got me wondering, too. We made a plan not to sleep inside at the dharamshala that night, but on the verandah from where we could see the ashram across the river, and from there, watch the happenings in the ashram at night. We both set up our bed rolls on the verandah that night.

We had hardly put down our bed rolls and lay down when we immediately fell fast asleep. It was a deep sleep, much deeper than usual. We would usually wake up early, around 4 or 5 a.m., but the next morning it was 9 a.m. by the time we woke up. We felt very bad about what we had done. We got up, did our morning ablutions, and reached the ashram.

Baba was all-knowing, and knowing what was in our hearts was a little thing for him. As soon as we reached the ashram, he roared at us like an angry tiger: "Leave this place!" We had just arrived the previous day and Baba was asking us to leave. We felt very sad and afraid on seeing his anger, and we hesitated. Looking at us in this state, Baba said, "Listen, don't do it again." On hearing his words, we felt relieved and happy. Baba's was always generous and soft-hearted.

There were two lessons to be learnt from this incident. The first one is that one should never doubt or try to test a sadhu. Baba destroyed the ego that made us think we were qualified to test a saint; we fell asleep as soon as soon as we put heads on our pillows and we got up very late. Secondly, on seeing us repent for our act, he forgave us easily and just said "Don't do it again," teaching us about forgiveness and compassion.

HARIDUTTJI MEETS GHOSTS

(Told by Hariduttji, Budgi)

One of Baba's closest devotees, Hariduttji, was modern in his thinking. He once said to Baba, "Baba, all these people who talk of ghosts, I think they just make up stories. There is no such thing as a ghost."

On hearing this, Baba said, "Okay, Haridutt. Today you can see for yourself if the stories are true or false."

That evening, Hariduttji stayed at the dharamshala across from the ashram. He was alone in the room. The room was completely bare, except for a large container of drinking water. In the middle of the night, Hariduttji heard a loud voice calling his name and woke up. As his eyes adjusted to the darkness in the room, he saw that it was filled with dozens of ghostly apparitions—spirits! They started saying to him, "Give us meat, give us bones, give us meat, give us bones."

Hariduttji was a strong, fearless man. He said to them, "I have nothing for you," then he reached into the container, took out some water, and sprinkled it on the ghosts. One by one they disappeared, except the last one, who was not affected by the water. Finally Hariduttji asked, "What do you want?" The spirit asked Hariduttji to promise to perform a certain special rite. When Hariduttji promised to do so, the spirit gave him a gift and left.

The next morning, when Hariduttji went to the ashram, Baba asked, "So Haridutt, how was your night?" Hariduttji described what had transpired. The incident taught him that there was some truth behind what people said about ghosts.

SADHU RETURNS MONEY

(As heard by Lala Radheshyam)

A person from the Sah community of Nainital once went to the Padampuri ashram for darshan. When he arrived at the dharamshala across the river from the ashram, he saw that a dhuni was lit on the lower floor, so he went and sat next to it for warmth. At the time, a sadhu was sitting at the dhuni. It was daytime, so after warming up a bit, the visitor removed his coat, left it at the dharamshala and went to ashram for darshan. He stayed at the ashram for some time, then returned to the dharamshala in the evening. He remembered his coat. He had brought along 500 rupees in his pocket, which was a very large amount in those days. He checked the coat, and realized that the money was gone. He was very shocked on losing such a big amount of money, so he went and told Baba what had transpired.

At the time, a devotee of Baba called Mohan Singh was sitting with Baba. Mohan Singh hailed from a small village called Matiyal near Padampuri, and he had a shop in the village. Mohan Singh would come to visit Baba very often. Baba instructed Mohan Singh: "Go to Haldwani. Don't say anything to anyone. The sadhu has taken the money and gone there." Mohan Singh took along a friend and went to Haldwani. They found the sadhu the next morning. By then, he had already spent some 20 or 30 rupees on food, drink, and buying some things. Mohan Singh talked to the sadhu about the money.

The sadhu quietly gave the remaining money to Mohan Singh, and came back with them until Champhi. Then he said, "I need to go to the toilet." Mohan Singh and his friend waited for a long time, but the sadhu did not return. He had walked back with them all the way to Champhi when he did not need to, and he could easily have walked some more to Padampuri. Baba probably did not want people to say that one sadhu got another sadhu into trouble with the law, so he must have inspired the sadhu to run off.

Mohan Singh carried on to Padampuri and told Baba the whole story. Baba instructed Mohan Singh to give the remaining money back to the traveler from the Sah community. After that day, businessmen were not allowed to leave any belongings near the dhuni on the lower floor of the dharamshala. Baba instructed that businessmen should stay at the upper floor of the dharamshala and use their own locks for the doors, since businessmen usually carried something valuable with them.

THE STOLEN TWO RUPEES

(Contributed by Shri Girwan Dutt Joshi, Nainital)

Once I was at the Padampuri ashram to visit Baba with my elder brother, who was three years older than me. Baba gave my brother a small copper pot filled with urad lentils, rice, and ghee. He instructed him, "Take this and make some khichdi. Feed everyone who comes, and eat yourself, too." The khichdi was made from the contents of the small pot, everyone ate, and yet there was some left. We were quite surprised.

Suddenly, one of the men present exclaimed, "There were two rupees in my pocket; someone seems to have stolen my money!" Baba heard all this from inside his hut. He instructed one of the people: "Go to that servant who is sleeping under that tree over there, kick him, and ask him to return the money to his master!" The tree was over 150 yards away from Baba's hut and it was impossible to see money from that far. The servant returned the money quietly when challenged.

"YOUR BROTHER IS FINE"

(Contributed by Shri Dhanilal Sah)

A doctor from Mukteshwar, Ayodhaprasad Jha, was a great devotee of Sombari Baba. He considered Baba to be an avatar. Baba also loved him and would often send vibhuti and prasad for him with other devotees who would be passing by his village. During the first World War, Shri Jha had to go to Mesopotamia (the area now covered in parts by Iraq, Kuwait, Turkey, and Syria). Baba would have vibhuti sent to him by post even while he was there.

One day when Dr. Jha was at home in Mukteshwar, a telegram arrived for him from Kanpur notifying him of his brother's illness. He immediately arranged for a train ticket from Kathgodam to Kanpur and set off for Kathgodam on horseback. On the way, he stopped at Padampuri for darshan. Baba asked him not to worry and to go back to Mukteshwar, saying that his brother was okay now. Shri Jha did not want to go against Baba's instructions, so he headed back to Mukteshwar. On the way, he met a man who had been sent after him from Mukteshwar. The man was carrying a telegram that said his brother had recovered fully and there was no need to come to Kanpur. It also turned out that the train on which Dr. Jha was supposed to go to Kanpur met with an accident. Owing to high winds, the train fell off a bridge and all passengers in the carriage that Dr. Jha was supposed to travel in and a couple of adjacent carriages were killed. Baba saved Dr. Jha's life.

RESCUING KESHAVDUTT IN HEAVY RAIN

(Contributed by Shri Dhanilal Sah)

Shri Keshavdutt Karnatak was a devotee of Baba. Once he was returning to Mukteshwar from Kashipur. He was traveling alone, and no one was expecting him at the ashram. It was raining heavily and the gully near Champhi was flooded with very fast moving water, making it impossible to cross. It was about to get dark. That evening, Baba told four strong young devotees to go to Champhi. He said that Keshavduttji was stuck on the other shore of the gully and they should swim over to help him across. They arrived at the gully to find Keshavduttji as Baba had said. They helped him across and brought him back to the ashram.

THE BOTTLE OF GANGA WATER

(Contributed by Shri Dhanilal Sah)

In those days, the government of the state of Uttar Pradesh had a branch of the secretariat at Prayag (Allahabad). Two local employees from Almora, Shri Ramlal Sah Thulgariya and Shri Biharilal Sah, had gone to the secretariat at Prayag for some work. On the way back to Almora, they each collected one bottle of Ganga water to take along for Baba, as was their custom. En route, they stopped over for a night at Padampuri and handed the bottles of Ganga water to Sombari Baba. As Ramlalji was about to hand the bottle over to Baba, it slipped from his hand and fell on the ground, spilling some water.

Baba said, "Ramlal, it seems something is afoot. Pour that water out on the ground completely." Ramlalji did as instructed, but he felt very bad that after carrying the water carefully all the way from Prayag, he had dropped it at the last moment when handing it over to Baba. However, he was pleased that Baba did get the bottle that Biharilalji had brought along.

Later that evening, about four miles away from Padampuri, they met Ramlalji's relatives who had come to receive them. It is a custom in India for younger relatives to touch the feet of their elders as a greeting. However, this time none of the relatives touched Ramlalji's feet. On inquiring why, they gave him the news that one of his cousins had passed away. There is a custom for Hindus that when a close relative passes away, the family does not give food or water to anyone for a period of ten days. Ramlalji realized this was probably the reason why the bottle of Ganga water had dropped from his hands before he could give it to Baba.

BABA FULFILLS HARISH'S WISH TO SEE THE WORLD

(Contributed by Shri Dhanilal Sah)

The family of Shri Dhanilal Sah from Ranikhet were great devotees of Sombari Baba. Shri Sahs's oldest son. Harish Jagati, was deaf and dumb since birth. Ever since he was a child, he was very attracted to Baba's photos, and as he grew older he grew to love Baba very much. He always carried a small photo of Sombari Baba in his wallet wherever he went.

In the year 1965, an international games event was being organized in Washington for deaf/dumb participants from all over the world. India was invited to send attendees. Harish was a very good sportsman and he was shortlisted to go to Madurai in South India for a selection event. As always, he took Baba's photo along. He did very well in the event and was put on a short list of athletes to be sent to the U.S. However, there was some kind of argument during the final selection process, as two different teams wanted to send their own representatives. They could not reach an understanding and eventually decided that no one would go to attend the event.

Harish was disappointed, but he had faith in Baba. He came

back to Ranikhet. Four days before the event was due to start, news arrived by phone: Harish had to go to America. In those days, it would usually take months to get all the paperwork required for a trip like this: passport, plane ticket, visa, foreign exchange, and so on. With Baba's blessings, everything was arranged within four days and Harish set off for America. As always, he took Baba along in his wallet. Harish flew over the Atlantic Ocean to New York and then proceeded to Washington. Harish performed well at the event. His faith in Baba's grace helped him fulfill his dream of traveling around the world.

A SUFI LEARNS FROM BABA

(Contributed by Shri Dhanilal Sah)

A Sufi came to ashram. He had heard a lot about Baba and the tasty food at the ashram. He had heard that anyone who came to the ashram always left with a full stomach, and no one ever went hungry. The Sufi was a tall, strong man, wearing a black robe, and he carried a stick in one hand. He looked impressive. On arriving at the ashram, he called out from across the river, "I'm hungry, feed me."

Baba shouted back: "Don't cross, wait there." He asked a devotee to take a small pot of khichdi over for the Sufi. Baba had asked for a small portion of khichdi to be kept aside after the morning meal. There was hardly enough for one person, never mind a big strapping man like the Sufi.

The devotee went across the river and served the khichdi to the Sufi, along with some pickles and yoghurt. As soon as he had served the food, the Sufi gobbled it all up and asked for more. The devotee served the Sufi again, and the same thing happened. This went on for some time. The Sufi was served again and again, and he continued to eat. The pot with the khichdi was quite small, and there was no way it could hold the amount of khichdi that the Sufi ate. Despite serving him over and over, the amount of khichdi left in the pot remained the same. Finally, the Sufi had enough and his belly was protruding. Standing up with great difficulty, he said "My goodness, it is just as I had heard!" His ego was gone. The Sufi washed his hands, bowed reverently to Baba, and left.

TREATING ALL EQUALLY

(Contributed by Pandit Jagannath Joshi, ex-Municipal Commissioner, Nainital)

In Baba's ashram, everyone was treated with the same respect regardless of their wealth, position, education, and so on. Baba showered his grace equally on all. Everyone ate the same food and shared the work fairly. However, depending on their faith, a person would get different spiritual blessings and experiences. Everyone saw Baba differently according to their own faith. Yogis learned methods of yoga from Baba and devotees came back with their faith and love strengthened. Baba placed great emphasis on physical, mental, and spiritual purity. He would say that karma can be overcome by cleanliness in thought, body, and habits.

Wise men considered Baba a great accomplished soul. Those who were interested in the scriptures considered him a very knowledgeable yogi. Learned Sanskrit scholars considered him a sage blessed with the confidence of knowing the Self. Those who loved food considered him to be like a cow who provides tasty and healthy milk, like *Kamadhenu* (the "cow of plenty" who always provides the desired milk).

The simple village folk knew Baba as a saint who held bhandaras on every Monday; travelers spoke of him as "the saint of Kakrighat"; people who had no connection to spirituality would call him "the fakir who sits by the road"; and people who wanted to poke fun called him "the khichdi yogi." As there are all kinds of people in the world, so there were people who criticized even a generous, loving being like Baba. Depending on what is in the heart, two people can look at the same thing and see something completely differently. Regardless of what people thought or said about him, Baba always treated everyone with love.

Of course, treating everyone equally does not mean treating everyone the same regardless of their situation or constitution. It simply means considering everyone as a child of God, wishing everyone well, and treating everyone in the way that will best work for their growth. The food fed to an elephant is different from the food fed to the cow, which is in turn different from the food fed to a dog. All should be fed with the same emotion of love and kindness, and Baba treated everyone according to their needs with the same kindness.

Each person behaves according to their own nature. Regardless of the path they take, they all eventually reach God, just like a river eventually reaches the ocean regardless of whether it follows a relatively straight path or a path with many twists and turns.

RESPECT FOR ALL PATHS

(Contributed by Pandit Jagannath Joshi, ex-Municipal Commissioner, Nainital)

Though Baba was a great devotee of Lord Shiva, had a Shiva Lingam installed at the temple, and held a bhandara every Monday in the name of Lord Shiva, he also respected and loved other paths. The jyoti lamp was always kept burning in the ashram in the name of the Divine Mother. During *navratri* (a fall festival of nine days in the honor of the Mother Goddess), Baba would worship the Divine Mother. After having his bath every day, he would recite the name of Lord Rama. He also had great respect for Jesus Christ and the Prophet

Mohammed. Baba would also speak highly of the path of worshipping fire followed by the Parsi community.

Baba sometimes listened to the recitation of holy scriptures, but he did not encourage worship with too much external paraphernalia and rituals, or very loud incantations of holy scriptures. He focused more on the use of mantras and inner spiritual practices. The main principle of his teaching was that if the "diet" (of thoughts, speech and action) is pure and loving, then the essence gained from such a "diet" is automatically bound to be positive.

LESSONS IN HUMILITY

(Contributed by Pandit Jagannath Joshi, ex-Municipal Commissioner, Nainital)

Baba did not like people showing off; he considered it egoistic behavior. Once a wealthy person who liked to show off was visiting Baba at the ashram. He thought to himself, "At this ashram, I won't get great tea like I do at home." A few minutes later, Baba sent some tea for the guests, and it turned out to be tea of the highest quality; it even had saffron added. The wealthy person was humbled and learned his lesson.

A rich merchant came by bringing along a large plate of very good quality sweets as an offering. He did not take off his shoes and proceeded straight to the ashram. He imagined that Baba would be very pleased with the quality of his offering. However, Baba fed all the sweets to the fish in the Kosi river. The merchant realized that great yogis like Baba are pleased with even a small handful of grain that is given with love and devotion, and that they do not care for the greatest gifts if they are not offered with love.

Once, in the month of *Poush* (a month in the lunar Indian calendar, which usually falls between mid-November and mid-

December), Baba was at the ashram at Padampuri. At about seven in the evening, Baba said, "It is night time. They're walking through the forest talking loudly, and coming to the ashram at an ungodly hour." At the time, no one understood what Baba meant.

A couple of hours later a group of seven or eight people arrived at the ashram from the road to Ramgarh. They offered some nice apples to Baba, but with the egoistic belief that no one else could have offered such good apples in that season (the apple season is around July and August). Baba did not say anything. He simply gave them prasad and some vibhuti, and sent them on their way.

The next day, as the people in the ashram went about their daily tasks, Baba asked them to cut up the apples that had been offered the previous night. A little later, some monkeys arrived at the ashram and Baba fed all the apples to the monkeys. He then sent one of the devotees to the storeroom and instructed him to get an apple that was there. The devotee came back with a beautiful, large, tasty apple, much better than the ones that had been offered the previous night. It was cut up and served to those present, who realized that Baba was teaching them about humility.

LEARNED MEN ARGUE ABOUT GOD

(Contributed by Hira Vallabh Pant)

Though Baba did not portray himself as a learned man, he was incredibly wise and could explain the most involved philosophies in a simple and straightforward way. Many learned men who came to him with questions about complicated things were often taken aback on seeing the direct and simple explanations he provided.

Once, Baba was at the Padampuri ashram and many learned men had gathered for darshan. While sitting there, they started discussing Vedanta. At one point, a heated discussion about God started among them. A sadhu by the name of Swami Parmanand tried to explain something to them, but they started arguing with him, too.

On hearing this, Baba came of his kutiya and spoke to Swami Parmanand, "Swami, you are a detached being, why get involved in discussions with these clever learned people of the world?" Then addressing the others, Baba said, "I have been listening to you for some time, but none of you are able to make your point in the right way. Tell me, have any of you seen God?"

One by one, the men all replied "No Baba, we have not."

"So," Baba said, "When you haven't seen God, how can you say anything about him? How can you insist that your point of view is right?"

The men realized their mistake and said, "Sorry Baba, we got carried away and were being egoistic. We have questions and try to pretend we have the answers for each other, when in reality, we have no idea what we are talking about."

Baba then smiled and explained the point to them in such a simple way that even a child would have been able to make sense of it.

PROTECTING DEVOTEES

(Contributed by Hira Vallabh Pant)

Whenever someone came to the ashram for darshan, Baba took on the responsibility for feeding them and keeping them safe until they got home. When a devotee left the ashram after darshan, Baba would track them till they got home safely. Sometimes he would speak about this to other devotees at the ashram saying "such-and-such person has reached home now."

Devotees would not need to ask Baba how long they should

stay; he would himself tell them when to set off for their journey ahead. If someone was in a rush, Baba would know this and tell them to make some khichdi for themselves immediately or get someone else to feed them, and then send them on their way.

At one time, a group of devotees wished to leave the ashram to go on to their destination. They waited for a while, but Baba did not tell them to go on, so they went to Baba and said, "Baba, could you please apply a tika to our foreheads as we would like to travel to our destination?"

On hearing this, Baba said very clearly: "Your life is in danger, stay here tonight." When the devotees did not pay heed, Baba refused to apply tika, and they went on regardless. The next day, their bodies were found in the forest; they had been attacked by a tiger.

THE INSECTS IN THE GRAINS

(Contributed by Hira Vallabh Pant)

Baba did not usually talk about philosophy. Instead, he would just give simple, practical instructions to devotees, as it was much easier for them to follow direct instructions rather than grapple with the intricacies of complicated philosophies. Very occasionally, Baba would impart lofty knowledge, but again, this was done through a simple sentence or action.

One day, Baba asked a devotee to clean some lentils and rice for making khichdi. It was getting close to dusk, and after instructing the devotee thus, Baba went to the river for his bath. On coming back he asked if it was done, and the devotee replied, "It will be done shortly, Baba."

A little later, Baba asked again: "So, is it done now?"

The devotee replied: "I'm doing it, Baba. It should be done soon."

A little later, Baba spoke: "It must be done by now, yes?" It was getting dark, and it would be time for dinner soon.

The young devotee spoke in a timid voice: "Baba, I see some living insects in the rice. That is why it is taking me time."

Baba said, "Oh, is that the case? Can you bring the platter over and show me what kind of insects they are?"

The devotee took the platter over to Baba. What happened next shocked everyone who was there. Baba took the platter in his hand, did not even look at it, and simply emptied it into the pot of boiling water that had been prepared for making khichdi. The devotees wondered how Baba, who followed strict spiritual practices such as taking a bath three times a day, could indulge in what they saw as a cruel act. They were worried if he was angry with them because of the delay in cleaning the rice.

Baba then laughed and said, "Everything is a living being, is it not?" indicating that the rice itself that nourishes our body is also a living being. On hearing this, the devotees understood the wisdom he was trying to impart to them through this little leela.

PANDIT DEVIDUTT KABDWAL CHANGES

(Contributed by Hira Vallabh Pant)

Pandit Devidutt Kabdwal, a devotee of Baba, liked good food, drink, and fine clothes. Once, in the course of his career, he became the victim of false allegations. Someone suggested that he should visit Sombari Baba, and he thought that it would be a good idea. Initially Baba scolded him a bit, and then assured him that everything would be okay. After this, Pandit Kabdwal started visiting the ashram twice a week.

One day Baba asked him: "Before you had a problem with your job, how often did you come here?"

Shri Kabdwal replied honestly: "Baba, I had not visited even once." Shri Kabdwal lived in Bhowali just nine miles away and could have visited many times if he wished to.

Then Baba said, "I did this to bring you on the right path. Don't worry, all will be well."

Pandit Kabdwal had to lodge a couple of appeals, but after a period of three years he finally won the case and got his job back. By that time, he was visiting Baba often and was a changed man with very simple tastes. Baba had used the situation at work to make changes to Shri Kabdwal's lifestyle.

THE MAN WITH WET CLOTHES

(Contributed by Pandit Devidutt Kabdwal)

One year, in the month of January, some devotees had gathered at the ashram in Padampuri for darshan. It was time for the evening meal, and it was very cold that day. Many devotees had gathered there and the custom was for everyone to remain seated till everyone had finished eating, so everyone expected to sit for around half an hour. As was the custom, everyone took off their shirts and sat in the queue to eat. Everyone knew this custom, but because of the cold, some people who had woolen shawls wrapped them around their upper bodies, and those who had long dhotis used them to cover their upper body.

One man had nothing to cover himself; he was only wearing a short dhoti, so he could not use that to cover his upper body. When everyone sat to eat, this man kept his vest on and sat close to the dhuni.

Then Baba spoke: "There is no problem if someone wants to eat with their vest on!" The man realized Baba was being sarcastic and that he ought to remove the vest, but pretended to take Baba's words literally and sat down quickly to eat, hoping Baba did make his real meaning clear in direct words. Baba said nothing. The man finished his food and went to the river to wash his hands. He also had a small *lota* (open container) to carry water and wished to fill it up.

As he was filling up the lota a thought crossed his mind: "This water by the bank is probably not clean; let me get water from a little further." As he stretched to fill the lota, his foot slipped and he was completely soaked. The man regretted not having listened to Baba. He was afraid to go face Baba, but he had no choice but to go to the dhuni for some heat as he was shivering from the cold. Baba asked him to sit near the dhuni, but did not ask how he came to be wet, as the lesson had already been learned.

There are three important things to learn from this incident. First, when asking a great being for advice, it is important to remove all preconceived notions from our mind. Otherwise, the mind could mislead us into hearing what we wish to hear. Second, when the heart does not give permission to do a certain thing (in this case the man knew it was not right to sit for the meal with his vest on), then one should avoid doing such a thing as far as possible. Third, one must be ready to undergo difficulties on the path of righteousness. Trying to avoid difficulties out of selfish motives can result in more difficulties later!

THE THIN MAN AND THE LARGE LOG

(Contributed by Pandit Devidutt Kabdwal)

Once, at Baba's Padampuri ashram, some people from the Saun community brought a large log of wood for the dhuni. The log needed to be moved up the steps to the dhuni and the path was narrow. About ten or twelve strong men were needed to push the log up the steps. One person who was thin and weak also joined in. For one second, he thought that he would be of no help and, in fact, might cause inconvenience to the people actually doing the work. He suppressed the thought and joined in anyway.

There was a wall close to the dhuni, and the log was first placed on the wall and then some smaller logs and other implements were used to roll the big log over them into the dhuni. While this was being done, the thin person was last, nearest the wall. Suddenly, the log slipped and the entire weight of the log crashed down on this man's knees for a few seconds. Within those few seconds, a mad rush of thoughts came to his mind: "I knew I should not have joined in, and that I would be of no help, yet I was too egoistic to follow my common sense. If my knees do not stop this log, I will be crushed between the log and the wall. If I am saved, how will I show Baba my face again after doing such a stupid thing?"

Suddenly, he found himself lying down some feet away from wall. He had no idea how he escaped from the log and got there safely.

From this incident, he learned two things: first, not to try egoistically things that are outside of one's capacity and, second, that no matter where Baba and his devotees were physically, Baba could always protect them.

BABA TEACHES A DOCTOR THE IMPORTANCE OF CHARITY

(Contributed by Pandit Devidutt Kabdwal)

One evening, a doctor arrived at the ashram in Padampuri. Though he was quite well-to-do, he was somewhat stingy and not in the habit of doing any charity or lending a helping hand. Three or four other devotees also arrived at the same time and had all brought some offerings along, whereas he had come empty-handed. He felt a little ashamed on realizing this, and thought of offering some money. On checking his pocket, he found no change; there was only a ten rupee note in the pocket. It was a large amount of money in those days, but despite his usual tendency, he offered the note. Baba instructed a devotee to take the money and buy some more things for the kitchen, which were used for preparing dinner that day.

A little later, in a way that seemed totally unconnected, Baba said to a devotee: "No one can ever be at a loss by doing charity that is within their means." The doctor was within earshot and heard this and thought it was just a general teaching by Baba, with no connection to the day's events or to him personally.

After everyone ate, at around 10 or 11p.m., they went across the river to stay in the dharamshala. The next day, the doctor was to return home. As he was about to set out for his journey, he remembered that he had absolutely no money on his person for the journey home, and that worried him somewhat. Absent-mindedly, he put his hand into his pocket and lo! he found a ten rupee note in there. He was totally taken aback. He knew that there was only one note in his pocket before making the offering because he had checked and re-checked several times to find something smaller to offer.

He realized then that Baba had created this little experience for him to learn the truth about charity, and that Baba's words about charity the earlier evening were meant for him. He took the teaching to heart and, from day onwards, he donated generously towards good projects.

GIFTS

(Contributed by Shri Hira Vallabh Pant)

When Baba lived at Padampuri, there were no roads in the area. There were only small paths through the forest. Everything was carried by porters on their backs or on pack animals like horses and donkeys. Items that grew in the area, such as potatoes and fruits, were carried to Haldwani and exchanged for goods such as jaggery, oil, salt, grains, clothes, and so on. The main path passed close to the ashram, so the porters and horses would sometimes stop at the dharamshala and shops close to the ashram. The people would use this as an opportunity for darshan. Sometimes, it would be dark by the time they arrived at Padampuri. In this case, the porters would stop overnight near the ashram, take prasad, rest for the night, and leave after taking darshan.

Sometimes the porters would make offerings of some items from their load, which did not belong to them as they were transporting goods owned by someone else. Whenever that happened, Baba would usually scold them, saying that they cannot donate something without the permission of the owner. He would say that regardless of whether or not the owner is present, the good karma from the donation always goes to the rightful owner, not to the people making the donation without the owner's knowledge. However, sometimes Baba would accept gifts that were given by these people without the owner's permission or knowledge. Only he knew the reason why; the ways of great beings are not for common men to understand or judge!

THE JUDGE FROM PRAYAG

(Contributed by Pandit Devidutt Kabdwal)

One day, a judge from the city of Prayag (also known as Allahabad), who held a high post in the judicial system, arrived at the ashram in Padampuri around 10 p.m. at night. He was accompanied by a large retinue of servants. He had brought along many offerings, and also a bag of money. When everything was offered, Baba took out just one rupee from bag and asked him to take the rest back, saying that money earned by bad means cannot be used by the ashram. The judge tried to convince Baba by saying that it could be put to good use for the sadhus and saints who frequented the ashram. Baba replied that they don't have any bad habits, and they don't need a great deal of money.

On hearing this, the judge prostrated before Baba, and said, "I am sorry Baba, I will never do anything like this again."

Baba consoled him and said "Don't worry about past; just be careful not to do this in the future."

At the time, other devotees present there thought that Baba and the judge were talking about the offering. Later, the judge revealed that he took many bribes and the offerings had been purchased from bribe money. He also said that exactly one rupee had been put in the bag by his innocent daughter with great respect for Baba, and that is the rupee Baba had accepted. The judge made a promise in front of Baba and all devotees to give up taking bribes and also to stop drinking. After this incident, the the judge became a devotee of Baba and regularly visited the ashram for darshan.

The life of a siddha is only for others. It may seem that he or she is not doing anything; they may just be sitting or talking, they may or may not even look at a person, but simply by their presence the whole being of a person is changed. This is the miracle of a siddha's grace.

THE KSHATRIYA LEARNS A LESSON ABOUT STRENGTH

(Contributed by Pandit Devidutt Kabdwal)

Once a young *Kshatriya* (a person from a warrior caste) came to the ashram. He was proud of his strength and did not know about the greatness of mahatmas. As was his habit, he sat not doing anything useful, ordering everyone around to do this or that. Some devotees brought some sticks of wood and kept them near the dhuni. Other devotees who were near the dhuni started adding the sticks to the fire. On seeing this, the young man said, "Why are so many people needed to move such small sticks? I can do it alone, and in one go."

At this moment, Baba returned from his afternoon bath and spoke to the young man. "Some sticks are a little outside the dhuni. Could you move them into the dhuni properly?"

The young man tried to do as Baba asked, but try as he might, he was unable to budge even a small stick. Baba then moved the sticks into the dhuni easily with his chimta and said to the young man: "Is this the strength of a Kshatriya that you feel so proud of?"

The young man realized his mistake and his ego was wiped out. From then on he became humble and used his strength for the right purposes: he did all sorts of work at the ashram, such as carrying firewood, cleaning heavy kadhais in the kitchen, and so on.

BABA REVERSES TIME

(Contributed by Pandit Devidutt Kabdwal)

One morning, a devotee who lived about twenty miles away came to the ashram at Kakrighat for darshan. He had to reach home for some work that evening, so he thought he'd receive darshan, rest a little, take some prasad, and then set out on the journey home. When he had darshan, Baba said, "You have plenty of time, have food and then go."

The man agreed, thinking, "The food will be ready soon and I can set out in an hour or two."

A few minutes later, about fifty or sixty more devotees turned up and food had to be cooked for them, too. Then some more people arrived! By the time food was ready for everyone, it was about four in the afternoon. By the time everyone has eaten, it was close to sunset. The man realized it was quite late and thought that there was no point in heading home now as he was already late. He decided to stay in the shop across the river for the night and leave for his home before sunrise the next day. Just as he was heading to shop, Baba called out to him and said, "Okay, now that you have had food, you should head home."

The man felt bad, thinking that Baba, who had made him stay there the whole day, was asking him to go home now that it was already too late. He walked a few steps and then totally forgot about his intention to stay overnight at the shop. He started walking home. He walked the entire distance of about twenty miles and reached the fields near his home in a sort of daze, unaware of the journey.

At the time, it was the month of *Ashwin* (a month in the lunar calendar, which falls around October in the solar calendar). Women and children were harvesting in the fields. On seeing him from a distance, his children exclaimed in delight "Father is home!" This woke the man up from his daze and he realized he had reached home. However, what took him by surprise was that it was the same day, and around the same time as the time when he had left the ashram at Kakrighat (4 p.m. in the afternoon). He was lost in thought: "How did I get here? I can see that I walked. The journey usually takes six or seven hours, so it must have taken me that long. But the time is still the same as when I left the ashram!" He was greatly puzzled and could not work out what had happened, so he talked to the villagers and explained his dilemma. On hearing his story, the villagers realized that it was Baba's leela and shared their thoughts with him.

The man was moved by Baba's love and how Baba had taken care of his desire to reach home by sunset that day. He understood that when a siddha asks one to do something, one should follow instructions without any doubt regardless of how it feels at the time, because a siddha can easily do things that we think are impossible and always protects devotees.

DESTINY

(Contributed by Pandit Devidutt Kabdwal)

A man suddenly felt a strong pull to go to Haridwar to spend the rest of his days as a renunciate. He had an old mother, a wife, and a brother at home, and no children. On the way he decided to stop at the ashram at Padampuri for darshan. He stayed one night, and as he was about to set off for Haridwar the next day, Baba asked him, "Where are you headed?" He replied that he had lost all interest in the world and that he was going to Haridwar to spend the rest of his life in search of his spiritual calling.

Baba said, "According to your destiny, you are supposed to have some children. When the right time comes, by God's grace, the attachment to the world will fall away from your heart fully. If you go to Haridwar now, after some time your destiny will pull you back. Even after becoming a renunciate sanyasi you will have to come back into the world. Go home."

The man believed Baba and went home. In the next few years, he had five children: three boys and two girls. Two or three years after the fifth child was born, in a short period of three of four months, his mother, wife, and all five children passed away one by one. The only relative he had left was one brother, who was married and had no children. At this time, the man remembered Baba's words. He lost all interest in the world, gave his land and wealth to his brother and set off to Rishikesh. He stopped over at Padampuri on the way for darshan, but Baba had already left his body by that time. The man proceeded to Rishikesh and became a sanyasi.

From this incident, it can be seen that it is not easy to avoid destiny, and that it is difficult to achieve a particular aim before the right time comes. However, once the time has come, the aim is achieved easily and without any obstacles.

FAITH INSTILLED BY SIMPLE WORDS

(Contributed by Pandit Devidutt Kabdwal)

A man who lived in the area had heard about Sombari Baba from some devotees. One of his neighbors used to visit the ashram once a month and this person could have joined him at any time, but never felt like doing so. One day his neighbor was preparing to go to the ashram as usual and asked him, "Why don't you come along with me? You will be able to receive the benefit of darshan, and I will benefit from your company for the journey."

The man replied: "What benefit? Whatever is written in my destiny will happen. Sadhus can tell you what will happen, but they cannot change it. What is the use of such a thing?" The neighbor realized that there was no point in trying to convince him and thus remained quiet. He thought that if Baba wished for this person to come to the ashram, it would happen, so he prepared to travel by himself.

On arriving at the ashram in Padampuri he had darshan, but did not talk about his friend. Strangely enough, Baba also did not ask him anything about the friend (Baba always knew, even if someone did not say anything).

As it happened, the man who had refused to go to the ashram with his neighbor had some work in the village of Dhari, located about two miles away from the ashram. He set out for Dhari and reached Padampuri around 4 p.m. He was supposed to reach Dhari by the evening, so he thought: "I still have time. Now that I am here,

I might as well go for darshan. There may be no benefit, but there is certainly no loss either, so why not!" Thinking this way, he walked towards the ashram.

Now, this man was a good man who believed in God and in the goodness of sadhus and mahatmas, but he believed that mahatmas can tell a person about what might happen, but they are unable to change destiny or help in any other way. He felt strongly that whatever is written in a person's destiny is bound to happen anyway, so there was no point in going to mahatmas for advice. He felt mahatmas can advise one about the path of righteousness, but are unable to inspire one to make changes in their life and actually walk on that path. "Our parents, teachers, and friends already tell us about the path of righteousness. Apart from some guidance, mahatmas cannot do much, so what is the use of going to them?"

On arriving at the ashram, he had darshan. While he was there, Baba said, "Things will happen according to a person's destiny. I can tell you what is likely to happen, but I cannot do anything to change it." While these words exactly mirrored the man's thoughts, and on the surface Baba seemed to be agreeing with the man's thinking, the effect that Baba's words had on the man was completely the opposite. He realized that his belief was wrong and that Baba could do as he wished and, if needed, could even change someone's destiny. He also understood that Baba was easily able inspire a person to walk on the path of righteousness. From that day, the man changed his opinion about visiting mahatmas and started visiting the ashram for darshan regularly.

A MAN GETS CURED OF HIS PRIDE IN HIS SELF-CONTROL

(Contributed by Pandit Devidutt Kabdwal)

A young man who visited the ashram regularly had great faith in the Tulsidas *Ramayana* and studied it whenever he had free time. He lived far from Nainital and visited the ashram three or four times a year when he could. With Baba's blessings, this man had great control over his emotions, thoughts, and base urges. He read the *Ramayana* regularly, practiced 100 malas of the Gayatri mantra every day, and also performed japa of *Ramnaam* whenever he could. He had maintained a separate room in his house for these spiritual activities and would lock the doors and do his practice privately every morning and evening. He had a wife and children.

Once, without any particular reason, he lost interest in his wife and children. He even stopped talking to his wife apart from things related to the running of the house. A year or so passed in this way, and one day he remembered a *shloka* (couplet) from the Tulsidas *Ramayana* that talks about how the pull of maya is very strong. The man thought: "I have no sensual desire now. Either Tulsidas is wrong or I have gained control over a great and powerful enemy—lust." This thought remained in his mind for the next few days and he became puffed up with pride thinking about his achievement. To cure him of this, Baba came up with an interesting solution.

One day this man was doing his japa of Ramnaam when he suddenly heard his wife's laughter. On hearing it, he got very excited; the mala fell from his hands and he went out of the room looking for his wife, with the intention to grab her hand and pull her into the bedroom. He had hardly walked four or five steps to look for her when the desire left him as suddenly as it had turned up. He became aware of what had happened and remained lost in thought for some time. For a whole year, he had no desire for women, and then suddenly it turned up in such a strong way that without thinking about the young children and elders in the house, in the middle of the day, he had set out to act on his lust. Had he continued with his intention, it would have been very difficult for him to face other people in the house later, out of shame.

He realized that he had become filled with pride about his false "achievement," and that Baba had taught him in a few seconds how strong lust can be, but in a way that did not cause him any trouble or shame in society. The other very important lesson Baba taught him through this incident was that egoistic thinking and false pride are likely to cause a downfall. A little later he found out that, during this incident, his wife was not even in the house; she had gone to the forest to cut grass, so he could not have heard her laughter. He realized that what is written in the Tulsidas *Ramayana* is very true.

Some days later this man went to Padampuri for darshan. As soon as he turned up at the ashram, Baba addressed him and said, "One should remain careful not to fall prey to pride." On hearing this, he realized the incident was all Baba's doing, and was touched by Baba's care and love and how he always protected his devotees. He spoke of his experience to other devotees and shared with them the lessons that he had learned from the incident.

PANDIT JAIDUTT AND THE GAZE OF GRACE

(Contributed by Pandit Devidutt Kabdwal)

Pandit Jaidutt, a devotee of Sombari Baba, worked in the court in Nainital. He would often visit the ashrams at Padampuri and Kakrighat for darshan. One day, while reading the *Ramayana,* he read a description about receiving a glance full of grace from God. He started to wonder what that might feel like. He wondered, "How must it feel to experience God's graceful gaze?" For several days afterwards, this thought remained in his mind. Eventually he decided to ask Baba about it.

The next time Shri Jaidutt visited the ashram at Padampuri, he found an opportunity. All the other devotees were busy and he was sitting cross-legged a few steps lower than Baba's asana. He somehow felt he should sit with his back to a wall for support. Having settled down thus, he felt now would be a good time to ask Baba his question.

No one was usually able to look at Baba directly because of his powerful presence. All of a sudden, Shri Jaidutt felt like looking at Baba and he saw Baba looking at him directly. He immediately experienced what it felt like to have God's eyes looking at him. He was transported into a deep, blissful state. His eyes closed. Had he not been inspired to sit with the support of the wall, he would probably have fallen down the steps.

A little while later, other devotees came close to Baba's asana for darshan, but no one noticed what had happened; they thought he was just sitting in meditation, despite the fact that his face was beaming with extraordinary bliss. But when he remained that way until evening, devotees started whispering between themselves that he looked like he was in samadhi. Then Baba spoke, "He seems to be in great joy, but he cannot sit like this forever. He'll have to get up soon."

A few moments after Baba said this, Shri Jaidutt opened his eyes, but did not say anything. He bowed to Baba and started going to the dharamshala across the river. Baba asked two strong devotees to take him to the dharamshala and make sure he sat down. He also told them not to try and make him talk. The men did as instructed. When they returned, Baba asked everyone to have dinner. He also told all devotees not to disturb Shri Jaidutt for dinner, saying that he would come for food if he felt like it.

After dinner, all devotees went to the dharamshala for the

night. Shri Jaidutt was still sitting in the same position. Everyone went to sleep, and the next morning, they went to the ashram for darshan after their routine morning bath. Baba asked them about Shri Jaidutt, and they replied he was still sitting in the same position as yesterday. Baba said there was nothing to worry about and that if Shri Jaidutt did not come by breakfast, they should go and check on him.

As instructed by Baba, some devotees went to check on Shri Jaidutt around 10 a.m. They found him still sitting in the same position, but he had opened his eyes by then. The devotees told him: "Baba is inquiring about you." On hearing this, he tried to get up, but could not. The other devotees slowly straightened his legs and helped him get up. He then had his bath, went to Baba for darshan, and had breakfast. After this, he went and sat in front of Baba again like the previous day.

A little later, it was time for Baba's afternoon *snan* (bath). Baba told him, "It is time for my afternoon snan. Why don't you get busy with some of the ashram work as usual?"

Shri Jaidutt did as instructed, but he was walking as if he was drunk. He remained in the ashram for seven days and slowly came back to normal from his state of being drunk with bliss. Then the other devotees were able to ask him how he managed to remain sitting for so long a week ago, when it was far outside anyone's normal capacity. He replied that he could not give them a reason, and they realized that it was Baba's grace.

Many days later, Shri Jaidutt talked about his experience to some close friends. He said that even thought the "drunken" state abated in a week or so, the feeling of bliss was never far from him and that he felt it all the time. He also mentioned that, after this experience, he never had any problems in his meditation practice and often lost track of time. When his friends asked him to describe how Baba had looked at him, he replied that there was no difference from Baba's normal gaze, and that the moment he thought of asking the question, even before he said a word, Baba had simply looked at him and lifted an eyebrow. His question was answered even without having to put it into words!

BABA REMOVES A DOUBT ABOUT THE SHRIMAD BHAGWATAM

(Contributed by Pandit Devidutt Kabdwal)

A pious old man who had faith in religious scriptures was a devotee of Sombari Baba, and he visited the ashrams at Haldwani, Kakrighat, Khairna, and Padampuri whenever he got an opportunity. Once he was listening to a recitation of the Indian scripture *Shrimad Bhagwatam*. In this book, there is a description of an event from Krishna's childhood. Krishna was playing around on the ground, and like any normal child he picked up some mud and stuffed it into his mouth. His older brother Balaram complained about this to their mother, Yashoda. Other people who had seen Krishna in the act confirmed that he had indeed done so.

Concerned, Yashoda asked Krishna: "Why did you put dirt into your mouth?"

Krishna replied: "I did not. These people are all lying. Check my mouth and you will see they are lying." He then opened his mouth and, on looking inside, Yashoda saw continents, oceans, planets, and the entire universe.

On hearing this description, a doubt crept up in the devotee's mind, "Hmmm. Krishna's mouth would have been small like any child's. So how can the entire universe fit inside? I understand that God can do anything, but there would not even have been enough time for Yashoda to see all these things in his mouth!"

A few seconds later, he felt bad about having such a doubt and tried to push it away. Many days later, despite much effort, he still could not get the thought out of his mind, so he decided to go to Baba and ask him. He traveled to the ashram at Kakrighat one day, arriving in the evening. After having some prasad and taking rest, he went to Baba to ask his question, but Baba stopped him saying: "Go and rest. You are tired and it is late. Tomorrow, come to me alone before sunrise."

Normally, Baba did not allow anyone to come to the ashram before sunrise. The man felt very happy that Baba had asked him to come over outside of normal hours, and felt confident that Baba was going solve his problem. He rested that night, woke up in the early hours of the morning, had a bath, and reached the ashram before sunrise as instructed. On reaching the ashram, he saw Baba standing in the clearing, with two small jholas in his hands. The jholas contained some sooji. Baba kept one jhola and gave the man the other one, saying, "I will feed everyone sooji from my jhola, and you do the same from yours."

The man was somewhat surprised, as he had never seen Baba do something like this before, and there was no one else close by to feed the sooji to. However, knowing Baba would have his reasons, he waited patiently. Within moments, he began to see large numbers of all manner of beings in Baba's body, hugging Baba lovingly. Baba was feeding them sooji from the jhola. There were animals, such as cows, horses, elephants, lions, tigers, panthers, dogs, and many other animals that he had never seen before. There was a big queue; many animals were eating, others were going, and more were coming. On seeing this sight, the man's mind went blank and he remained motionless like a statue, completely forgetting Baba's instructions to feed them sooji. He did not know how long he remained in that state, but later he recollected that it felt like it must have been about an hour or so. He remembered seeing all the animals in Baba's body, but also that Baba's body was the same size as normal. Yet all these animals, big and small, seemed to fit inside Baba's body!

The next moment he found himself back in the place where he had gone to rest at night. He had no idea how he arrived back there. The time was around sunrise, and his body was bathed and his clothes were the fresh ones he had worn, so he knew the experience was not just his imagination. He was delighted and touched that Baba had resolved his doubt about how the entire universe could fit in the small space inside Krishna's mouth. What he had witnessed with his own eyes was hard to believe himself, let alone explain to others, but the experience made him realize that nothing is impossible. God can do what was not going to be, and stop what was going to be.

He did not speak of his experience to anyone that day, but only shared it with some close friends much later. Baba taught people in the way that would help them understand best, and in the case of this man, it was best to have him experience it directly, rather than explain through any long-winded theories.

Before airplanes became a reality in modern times, people thought that the description of flying machines described in our old scriptures were just figments of someone's imagination. Today, everyone accepts them as commonplace reality. When this is the situation with simple worldly things like airplanes, how can we claim to know everything there is to know about God?

A man who thought he knew everything about God once said to the great sage Ramakrishna Paramahansa: "Even God has to follow rules," he said, pointing to a plant outside that had white hibiscus flowers. "He cannot make white flowers red, because He set the rules and even He cannot break them!" Ramakrishna laughed and said nothing. Some days later, the man returned to the Dakshineshwar temple, where Ramakrishna lived. On the same plant, he saw two flowers growing out of the same stem: one red, one white. He realized the lesson: nothing is impossible for God.

THE EXPERIENCE OF SPONTANEOUS SAMADHI

(Contributed by Pandit Devidutt Kabdwal)

One year, an older devotee arrived at the ashram in Padampuri a day before the festival of Mahashivratri. He was a pious man. Before reaching the ashram that evening, he committed a grave mistake and no one except Baba knew of it. When he came for darshan, Baba said, "You must be tired, go rest in the dharamshala. And by the way, please don't bless me with your darshan until this time tomorrow." The devotee was already feeling bad about his mistake and, on hearing Baba's sarcastic words, he felt even worse and headed to the dharamshala.

After he left, some of the other devotees present wondered why Baba had been so sarcastic towards him. Some of them went even further and thought that even if he had made some mistake, it would have been nicer if Baba had not spoken with him in that way. These devotees knew the man as someone with pure intentions and actions, so seeing him in that state made them sad. In their compassion, they forgot that no one loved the man more than Baba. After a while, they got busy with their work and forgot all about the incident.

The dharamshala had four rooms, two large ones and two smaller ones. The man went to one corner of one of the big rooms in the dharamshala where his bedding was kept. He sat and thought for a few minutes, and then suddenly was immersed in samadhi.

Back at the ashram, it was time for the evening meal. Everyone had their food, but no one remembered this man. There were around 150 devotees gathered that evening for the Shivratri event, but no one remembered him. Even when they went to the dharamshala to rest for the night, no one noticed him. There were about forty people sleeping in the big room in which he sat in samadhi, but strangely no one saw or noticed this man until the next evening, though several people went in and out of the room multiple times.

The next evening, about 24 hours after the incident, he opened his eyes and came out of samadhi. He felt very joyful and was very grateful to have experienced samadhi due to Baba's grace. He had no idea that a whole day had passed, but rather thought that it had been only a few minutes since he sat down. He remembered that Baba had said not to show his face at the ashram until the next evening. He closed his eyes again, thinking that it would be good if he could go back into samadhi and remain there until the next day by Baba's grace. No matter how much he tried, he could not get into that state again. He began to feel that he could not wait another minute to go meet Baba and receive darshan, so waiting until the next evening seemed impossible.

At that very moment, Baba told other devotees at the ashram that he had not seen this man since the previous evening, and asked someone to go check on him. When Baba said this, the devotees who had forgotten all about this man suddenly remembered him. They went to the dharamshala and found him sitting there in his meditation position, eyes wide open. They told him that Baba had inquired about him, but he did not believe them, saying that Baba had ordered him not to come to the ashram until the next evening, that is, on the evening of Mahashivratri. The other people replied: "Are you in your senses? Mahashivratri is today, and it is evening. Where were you since yesterday evening? We did not see you, and somehow we did not even think of you."

The man came out of room and started rubbing his eyes. He thought that there was either something wrong with him or that these other people were lying. He asked them again, "Are you speaking the truth, is today Mahashivratri?"

On hearing this, they replied: "What is wrong with you? Why would we lie to a good person like you and that, too, in Baba's ashram?" Finally he believed what they were saying and realized that he had been in samadhi for over 24 hours. He was deeply moved by Baba's love and how even his sarcastic comment was a blessing of grace in disguise.

The devotees who had come to bring him to the ashram did not understand why he was so emotional and wondered why he was crying. They asked him what had happened. When he replied, they could not believe how he had, without any previous practice or experience, sat in unbroken samadhi for over a whole day. So many people had come and gone in the room where he had been sitting, but no one had seen him. Then they realized it was owing to Baba's grace that he had this incredible experience.

The man had a bath, went to the ashram, and got busy with the work in the ashram. Baba did not ask him anything, but news of the story spread quickly among other devotees. Those who were his friends and had felt compassion for his condition the previous evening thought, "We thought we cared for him, but then we completely forgot all about him for a whole day! We felt bad about what Baba said to this man, but it turned out it was Baba who really cared about him, gave him this experience, and immediately after inquired about him." They realized that saints and God always have our best interest at heart. They also realized that by getting too attached to someone, we often end up forgetting what is beneficial for them and us.

TIME/SPACE TRAVEL?

(Contributed by Shri Govardhan Pandhe, Translation by Wing Commander H C Pant)

This event occurred in the year 1914 in the month of March. I was an officer with the Public Works Department and was stationed at Bhumiadhar. I had heard many stories about Sombari Baba, and was in awe of him. That particular day, I heard that the Executive Engineer was expected to arrive for an inspection in the area near Padampuri. In those days there were hardly any phones, so we often relied on news conveyed by travelers. I decided to go to the main area of the town to welcome the engineer. On the way, I passed by Baba's ashram and felt I should take the opportunity for darshan of this great saint. As I got off my horse and tied him up, I felt a sense of great joy and freedom. I went to Baba's hut and prostrated at his feet. I sat down next to him for some time.

After a while, I sought Baba's permission to leave. Baba said, "Come on, fellow, sit down. Where are you going so soon?" It was getting close to dusk, and I had to cross a dense jungle on my way to town. I started to feel tense, and told Baba that I ought to go since I had a long journey of nearly 12 kilometers to cover. I said I would come back when I had plenty of time on my hands. Baba scolded me and said, "Sit down, be quiet, and have some tea." He made me some tea and gave me some sweets to eat. It was beyond me to disobey the command of such a great being, so I did as he said. I must say that the tea was wonderful and I got great pleasure from drinking it. I cannot forget the affection and love that came through even as he scolded me.

Once I finished the tea, Baba himself asked me to leave, saying, "Now go, *saale!*" Baba would use the word "saale" quite often. Baba would usually scold those who were dear to him more than others, as he wanted them to learn quickly.

I bowed to Baba, bid him goodbye and set off. Across the road, I untied my horse and set off towards the main town gate. When I arrived, I suddenly realized that the time then was exactly the same time as when I had tied my horse up outside the ashram! Baba had literally made time stop! I felt bad about not having trusted Baba. If I had faith, I could have spent even more time in his blissful presence.

THE CONTRACTOR WHO PEEKED INTO THE ASHRAM AT NIGHT

(Contributed by Shri Govardhan Pandhe, Translation by Wing Commander H C Pant)

In those days, a contractor by the name of Shri Soni was working with me. He was engaged in contracts for various construction projects. I narrated to him some of my experiences with Sombari Baba and he too developed devotion towards Baba. Once he decided to go to Padampuri for darshan. On arriving there, he bowed to Baba with great respect. Baba asked him not to stay at the ashram after 9 p.m. Baba offered him tea and prasad, and then bade him to carry on with his journey.

For some reason, Shri Soni decided to go back to the ashram. However, since Baba had asked him not to stay there after 9 p.m., he decided instead to climb up a tree near Baba's hut. He was stunned when he heard melodious bhajans and saw divine beings dancing. Some time later, he went back home. The next day, he was going to Haldwani by bus. Along the way, he narrated his experience to people on the bus. Halfway through the telling the story, he suddenly collapsed and died.

It is said that one should never go against the instructions of a sage.

PROMOTION WITHOUT A DEGREE

(Contributed by Shri Govindram Kala, Ex-Deputy Collector)

When I was a sub-deputy inspector, I appeared for my B.A. examinations. I asked Baba if I would pass. Baba said, "How do you expect to pass without studying?" Then he continued, "Whatever was meant to happen after passing the exams will happen even without you passing them." As Baba had predicted, I failed in the exams, but a strange thing happened. It was mandatory to have some sort of degree in order to be promoted to the next level in my job. I was not eligible since I had failed in the examinations. However, it so happened that a spot opened up for the post and, for some reason, I was promoted even though I did not have a degree. From then on, I continued being promoted to higher posts without the issue of my lack of a degree ever coming up, and I eventually retired at the post of deputy collector.

REVERSING A FINE

(Contributed by Shri Govindram Kala, Ex-Deputy Collector)

A famous person in the area called Pandit Urvadutt Naithani was visiting a certain place, and all his arrangements had to be taken care of by a local police officer. For some reason, Pandit Urvaduttji was unhappy with the arrangements that the officer had made and complained to the Deputy Commissioner. As a result, the officer was fined ten rupees, which was a large amount in those days. On Baba's advice, the officer appealed against the fine. The Deputy Commissioner changed his mind and reversed his earlier decision to fine the officer.

SADHU RETURNS MONEY

(Contributed by Shri Govindram Kala, Ex-Deputy Collector)

A businessman from Kashipur once came to visit the ashram at Padampuri. A sadhu who was there at the time took 100 rupees from the businessman's coat pocket. Baba told me, "Govind, you are a policeman. Go make your inquiries."

I replied, "Yes, Baba, I will."

Three or four hours later, Baba said, "He has already spent five rupees. He will return in the evening with 75 rupees. He will already be feeling very bad about what he did, so don't say anything, just take the money." Exactly as Baba had predicted, the sadhu came back in the evening and returned 75 rupees to the businessman.

TROUBLE IN NEPAL

(Contributed by Shri Tikaram Bhatt, Bhowali)

In 1907, I came to Bhowali in the district of Nainital and started making bread to earn a living. A relative of a minister who served the royal family of Nepal used to visit regularly. One day he came to Bhowali for some reason and he tasted the bread made in my shop. I had gone to Bhimtal for a walk, but he left a message for me with a shopkeeper, saying that if I would like to go to Nepal for work, I should meet him at a place called Durgapur in Nainital district. I set out for Nainital the next day and was offered a job in Nepal, on a monthly salary of thirty rupees, with food and accommodation provided by the employer. I sought permission to bring along a helper and the man agreed. The helper's salary was decided at fifteen rupees per month, plus food and accommodation. Everything happened so quickly that I did not get a chance to visit Sombari Baba for darshan before leaving for Nepal.

On reaching Nepal, we set up four *tandoors* (traditional Indian clay ovens): one at the house of the minister, another two at the houses of two generals, and one near the king's palace. As part of my job, I would teach the local ladies how to make bread at each of these locations in turn throughout the day. After about ten months of working there, I returned to Bhowali.

In 1915, the minister asked me to come back to Nepal. He sent me money for the journey and also arranged for a visa. I was willing to go and decided to go to Kakrighat to meet Baba before setting off. It was about 8 in the night when I arrived. The dhuni was lit and there was no one at the ashram except Baba. Baba was performing puja, so I waited outside.

I happened to cough, and on hearing me, Baba asked, "Who is it?" I went in, prostrated at his feet, and offered two coconuts and flowers at his feet. Maharaj said, "Take some back as prasad." I started looking for a knife to take part of the coconuts as prasad. Without waiting for me to say anything, Baba said, "Are you looking for a knife? Don't worry, take everything. There's no one to eat anything here, except the crows!" Baba then seemed to get lost in thought for a moment, then asked, "Are you planning to go?"

Understanding that the question was about my decision to go to Nepal, I said, "Yes, Baba, I am planning to go." I do not know why, but I felt a chill go through my body at the time.

Baba thought for a moment and said, "It is written that you

will get into trouble. Crows and dogs will eat."

On hearing this, I asked: "So should I not go, Maharaj?"

Baba replied: "Go go, you must go. But there is trouble. Crows and dogs will eat." (The language used by saints is often cryptic and it is difficult to make logical sense from their words!)

I said, "Maharaj, crows and dogs might eat me here." He meant that trouble could occur anywhere.

On hearing this, Baba replied: "If it happens here, you are likely to go to Heaven along a straight road. If it happens there, you will have to go to Heaven this way . . ." and then he drew a long, circuitous route.

I asked again, "So should I not go, Maharaj?"

Baba said, "Of course you will go. But your future is in Bhowali. Trouble is written. Crows and dogs will eat." Baba applied vibhuti on my forehead and asked me to go home. I paid my respects and returned to Bhowali.

A few days later, my helper Lalmani and I set off for Nepal. On reaching Lucknow, we lost the visa. Somehow, we managed to reach a place called Virganj on the border, but without the visa, we were not allowed to enter Nepal. We sent a message about our predicament to the minister. We had to stay in Virganj for ten days and could hardly afford to eat as we had almost run out of money. After ten days, a new visa and some money arrived for us and we managed to reach Nepal. Throughout those ten days, I thought of Baba all the time.

On arriving in Nepal, we started our work. One day, Lalmani and I were going for a walk and noticed a strong bad smell. These were the days just after the festival of *Dussehra* (goddess Durga's victory over a demon), so we thought the smell might be from goats that are offered as sacrifice during the festival. By the time we reached home, Lalmani had developed a fever. The next day, I went to work alone, did my work, and returned home late in the afternoon. Lalmani was suffering from a high fever. Someone had given Lalmani three pills of some local medicine. He had already taken two, and kept the third pill aside to show me. As soon as I saw the pill, I was convinced that he would not survive. I stayed up all night watching him. In the morning when I examined him, there were blood clots in his eyes. He was infected by smallpox. At around 10 in the morning, he passed away.

I sent a message to the minister's court. They sent some money and also four Brahmins to help with his last rites. The body was taken to the Pashupatinath temple. While the body was being cremated, one finger fell out of the pyre. A crow came, picked up the finger and started pecking on it. A moment later, a dog jumped on the crow. The crow flew away, and the dog started eating the finger. I remembered Baba's words. Before leaving Bhowali, I had tried to convince Lalmani not to come to Nepal this time, but he did not listen. After the cremation rites, I returned to our house.

I was no longer interested in staying in Nepal and I came back to India. The minister was also in Almora at the time. I really wanted to go meet Sombari Baba. I reached Kakrighat. On seeing my eyes full of tears, Baba consoled me saying: "Don't worry, your future is good. Destiny cannot be avoided." He then gave me three herbs without telling me what they were. I used these herbs successfully to treat all sorts of diseases. I am living my life successfully the way he predicted. My only regret is that I forgot to ask him about my old age.

Quotes from Sombari Baba

THINGS DIRECTLY HEARD FROM BABA

(Contributed by Hiralal Sah)

1. "Once I was going to Amarnath for darshan. There was a lot of snow on the way, and my feet were sinking in it. Somehow I found a piece of wood lying half buried in the snow, pulled it out and picked it up. I put it down on the snow, sat on it, and slid on it. When it stopped, I found myself right next to the Ganga. From there, Amarnath cave is just half a mile away." (Hiralal Sah: It is possible Baba may have told me more on this incident, but I don't remember due to old age.)
2. He also said, "Whatever a being eats, he happens to find it somehow even in the forest." With this statement, Baba was teaching that the Divine takes care of all beings and fulfills all their needs. "I get engrossed in the company of saints and good people. I get money from the Lord, and spend it on serving such people. This has been a habit since my childhood."
3. "A *baniya* (trader) always has something extra on the side, like *palthan*." Palthan is dry flour used on the side while making chapatis. There are two teachings here: one, a wise person does not ask even for palthan from others, and carried the smallest thing he needs. The second teaching is that a wise and kind person may not necessarily need something himself (palthan is not a very useful thing to keep!) but he carries it anyway, in case he comes across someone else in need of it.

BABA'S THOUGHTS ON THE KUMBH MELA

(Contributed by Shri Hira Vallabh Pant)

One day many devotees had gathered at Baba's ashram and the topic of the Kumbh Mela came up for discussion. Everyone seemed to have their own opinions. Baba said, "Most of the people who turn up at the Kumbh Mela are not cleansed of their bad tendencies by having a dip in the Ganga. Among hundreds of thousands of sadhus who go there, there are hardly a few due whose presence purifies the Ganga herself."

"DO NOT WASTE A SINGLE MINUTE"

(Contributed by Shri Dhanilal Sah)

One of Shri Bhairavdutt Bhandari's sons passed away at a tender age. His heart was heavy with grief, and he set off for the ashram at Padampuri a few days before Holi. On arriving there, he spent a few days at the ashram and felt light in the heart. One day Baba said to him, "Bhairavdutt, *fakkads* (fakirs) have no home. We pass the time just like this. You are a family man. It is *Holi* (the spring festival, also called the festival of colors), and you should head home. Your family is waiting for you. They will be sad if you are not present." Then he added, "Do not waste a single minute on the way. You will reach your home in Ranikhet by this evening." Baba then gave Bhairavduttji some prasad, but much more than he usually did. Bhairavduttji bowed to Baba and set off from the ashram.

On the way he met some traveling traders at the hamlet of Champhi and, forgetting Baba's instructions, he wasted a few minutes listening to their idle gossip. He then continued walking and arrived at the main square in Bhowali. Just as he arrived at the square, he saw an army supply truck headed to Ranikhet pulling away. He even knew the driver of the truck. But before he could raise his hand or call out, the truck pulled off and drove away. He then decided to wait for another vehicle. But it was Holi and no other vehicle was to be found. Finally, at five in the evening, he started off on foot.

He stopped at a place called Niglat (near Kainchi). There was only a small shop there which was shut, and the shopkeeper let him in after much pleading. The shopkeeper had no supplies left, just some jaggery and black gram. Luckily, Shri Bhandari remembered the extra prasad that Baba had given him, and it saw him through the night.

The next morning, he waited for a vehicle to come by but there was none to be found, so he set off on foot again. By the time he arrived at the hamlet of Garamapani, it was late afternoon. Everyone there had already played Holi, and they were resting after having had lunch. Even there, he did not find any way of getting to Ranikhet and had to start off on foot again, eventually reaching Ranikhet at night. Not following Baba's instructions and wasting five minutes listening to gossip had cost him two days of difficult travel!

BABA READS A DEVOTEE'S THOUGHTS ABOUT HIS SHOE

(Contributed by Shri Dhanilal Sah)

Some devotees who worked in an office in Nainital had a custom of going to Padampuri after work on Saturday, staying there for the night and then returning to Nainital on Sunday evening. During one of these visits, a particular devotee woke up in the morning and, after taking his bath, sat down for his spiritual practice. While he was doing the practice, his thoughts wandered. The sole of one of his shoes had come off the previous evening and he started wondering where he might find a cobbler to fix it.

Baba suddenly remarked to one of the other devotees, "You know, the strange thing is that all sorts of people turn up here, such as cobblers! And then they spend their time thinking of all sorts of things even when it is time to do their spiritual practices!" Though Baba did not address anyone in particular when saying this, the devotee for whom it was meant got the point. After finishing his practice, he showed the other devotees his shoe and told them that the little pointer from Baba was meant for him.

TWO TOLAS

(Contributed by Shri Dhanilal Sah)

Pandit Laxmidutt Pande, an advocate who lived in Almora, was a devotee of Sombari Baba. His uncle, Hariram Pande, who was a famous lawyer, used to visit the ashram regularly, and due to his uncle's influence Laxmiduttji also loved Baba. Every Saturday after work, he would go to Padampuri or Kakrighat to meet Baba. His friend Mohanlal Verma would usually go with him. They would each take along two tolas of charas as an offering for Baba.

One Saturday, Mohanlalji went to Laxmiduttji and said that he could not go to the ashram that day. He handed Laxmiduttji two tolas of charas, asking him to give it to Baba. Laxmiduttji refused as it was illegal to carry more than two tolas and he was already taking two tolas of charas himself. There was no one else around at the time.

On arriving at the ashram, Pandeji paid his respects and offered two tolas of charas to Baba, who said, "Laxmidutt, you lawyers are so full of fear. If Mohanlal asked you to bring two tolas on his behalf, you could have done so. There was nothing to fear." Then he smiled and said, "But you did the right thing. When your heart does not want to do something, it is best not to do it."

Pandeji was stunned on hearing Baba's words. No one had overheard his conversation with Mohanlalji and he had set out for the ashram immediately after.

BABA CONSOLES HARPAL SINGH

(Contributed by Shri Dhanilal Sah)

A trader called Shri Harpal Singh from the village of Jeolikote had a young son who passed away suddenly after a short illness. Harpalji was very sad. After some days, he went to Baba's ashram at Padampuri. On arriving there, he saw that the ashram was quite full and devotees from all over the Nainital area were waiting to see Baba. Harpalji noticed a man sitting on the ground with his legs outstretched. Baba was far away and could not have physically seen the man through the crowd, but his voice boomed out, "Sit up properly with crossed legs. This is a place where fakirs sit, not a trader's shop." The man immediately straightened up and asked for forgiveness. Harpalji went closer to Baba and Baba indicated him to come up the stairs. Baba said, "Don't be sad. All the fruits that grow on a tree do not remain attached to it forever." Just hearing one sentence from Baba's mouth made Harpalji feel better.

He stayed over at the dharamshala that night. In the morning, after prasad, he prepared to leave. As was his custom, he went to the kitchen to meet the cook. There he gave the cook 50 paisa. He then went to Baba to pay his respects. Baba said, "What are you doing? Is this a hotel where you have to pay for food?" The kitchen was located far away from Baba's kutir, and there was no way he could have physically seen Harpalji give the money to the cook. Baba called the cook, Pandeji, and scolded him for accepting money from Harpalji.

"I NEVER FORGET ANYONE"

(Contributed by Pandit Devidutt Kabdwal)

A man who was about 38 years old once arrived at the ashram in Padampuri. Everyone else he knew had already had the good fortune of darshan, but being busy with some responsibilities he had never managed to go to the ashram. He had heard a lot about Baba from his friends and relatives, so one day he decided to go along with his friends the next time they went to the ashram. Accordingly, he set off early one morning with some friends to Padampuri.

The ashram was quite far from where they lived, so by the time they arrived it was already evening. Baba was sitting at the lower dhuni at the time, about to head for his evening bath. The other visitors who were accompanying this man had met Baba before, whereas it was his first time, so Baba did not say anything to anyone else but asked him, "Have you come to me before?"

The man replied, "No Baba, I have not had the good fortune to meet you before."

Baba said, "I never forget someone who comes to me even once, whether they come empty-handed or with a *battasha* (a small sugary sweet, quite cheap to buy) of one paisa."

On hearing Baba say this, the man thought, "I have never come here before, but from Baba's words it seems he thinks I have met him before. How can this be?"

There was no more talk that day. The next day, the man headed back home with his friends. This thought kept troubling him, so he asked some of his friends who were older and knew Baba well what he could have meant. They replied, "Baba probably meant you have met him before. But if you are saying you haven't, who knows what Baba is trying to say? He often speaks in cryptic terms." No one paid much attention to the matter, but this man continued to wonder, thinking Baba must have had a reason to say what he did.

When he reached home in the evening, he talked to his mother and told her what Baba had said. She replied, "Baba is right. When you were about four years old, I had taken you to the ashram in Haldwani for darshan. At that time, I purchased battasha for one paisa and got you to offer it to Baba."

On hearing this, the man was touched by Baba's love for his devotees and how he never forgot anyone. The next day he told all his friends the story behind Baba's comment. On hearing this story, people who had never had darshan felt a strong desire to go and meet Baba. Any person who even heard of Baba naturally felt a strong pull to go and receive darshan.

REFUSING MILK FROM GOPALDUTT

(Contributed by Shri Badri Dutt Lohani, Translated by Wing Commander H C Pant)

An officer named Gopaldutt was stationed in the village of Champhi near the Padampuri ashram. One day, he noticed a crowd of devotees at the ashram and thought he should also go for darshan. He went to one of the villages close by and announced, "I am going to visit Sombari Baba at Padampuri, please give me some milk to offer him." He asked for milk from several houses and, having collected it, headed to Padampuri.

When he arrived Baba said, "O Gopaldutt, why have you brought me milk from the poor and needy people of the village when they do not have enough for themselves? I am not in need of your milk. Look around. See how many devotees there are and how much milk there already is. Take your milk and go away. Give it to those who really need it. And after today, do not hurt innocent people by forcibly taking that which is theirs." Gopaldutt felt chastised and left.

POKING FUN

(Contributed by Shri Govindram Kala, Ex-Deputy Collector)

A man called Moti Singh ran a government shop in a place

called Peura. His wife gave birth to a child and, during the celebrations, he invited me for food. At the event he also offered me a sum of two rupees as a token (it is a tradition in India to celebrate joyful events by inviting people for meals and giving them some money as a token). I accepted the money, added two rupees of my own, and with the sum of four rupees I bought some raisins, almonds, and coconuts to take to the ashram. On arriving there, I offered them at Baba's feet. Baba said, "So! You buy food from money that is not your own. Not only do you eat it yourself, but also feed it to me!"

I said, "Baba, two rupees are from Moti Singh, but I added two rupees of my own, too. So some of the money used to buy the food was mine."

On hearing this, Baba laughed. He had a wonderful sense of humor and liked to poke fun at his devotees.

Predictions

PROPHECY ABOUT THE END OF BRITISH RULE IN INDIA

(Contributed by Hiralal Sah)

This incident took place around 1914, during World War I. One of my friends, Sri Basanaatlal Sah (also called Basanaat Baba Kotwal), who was about my age, worked as a teacher at the Philander Smith school in Nainital (there now is a Birla Vidya Mandir school in that location). The principal, Mr. Busher, was very happy with Shri Sah's work and appointed him the teacher of Urdu and Persian at the school.

At the time there was a student in the school whose father worked at the mint in Kanpur. Whenever a new series of coins was launched, after a visit to his father he would bring some freshly minted, uncirculated coins from the new series. This time, the student had some new shiny coins of one *anna* of nickel, which were not in circulation yet. The student showed them to Basanaat Babu and gave him some. After coming home from school, Basanaat Babu showed me the coins and I also kept some of them. When I went to Padampuri the next time, I took them along.

I had a chat with Baba as usual. Baba would ask people who arrived how things were with them and what was going on in their lives. We were sitting at the upper dhuni at the time. There was no one else, only Baba and me. Baba asked, "What else is new?" I put my hand in my pocket, took out the coins and put them on the ground. Baba asked, "What is this?"

I said, "Baba, these are coins."

Baba asked, "What metal is this?"

I said, "How do I know Baba? What do I know about metals! All I know is that this is how it sounds." I picked up the coins and tossed them on the floor.

Baba said, "They will make coins of two, four, and eight annas of the same cheap mixed metals instead of silver. Then they will make a one rupee coin from the same metals. When that coin is in circulation, this crown (the British Raj) will go."

Baba left his body in 1919. In 1946/47, a rupee coin made from those mixed metals came into circulation and the British Raj also ended around the same time. Baba's prophecy proved to be true, nearly thirty years after he left the body.

PROPHECY ABOUT PLAYING WITH A SIDDHA

(Story contributed by Hira Lal Sah, Hubba, Nainital)

We would go to the Padampuri ashram for darshan regularly.

Baba had often said, "There is a siddha in the form of a child in this area."

I said, "Baba, we travel all around this area, sometimes we even go into the forest to get wood, but we've never seen him."

Baba said, "*Arre* (an expression of frustration or exasperation), you will play with him later."

At the time, I could not understand what he meant. Two years after Baba left his body, a small boy yogi wearing a kaupin, with a face glowing like gold, was seen in a cave in front of the ashram. Devotees of Sombari Baba became his followers and he came to be known as Shri Bal Brahmachari Maharaj. Later I got to know him well, spent a lot of time with him, and also played cards with him. This was also Baba's prophecy: that I would play with the Siddha boy.

WHAT IS ANANDA?

(Contributed by Hariduttji and Habbaji)

This event took place in Padampuri, one or two years before Baba left his body. During one bhandara, Baba served everyone food with his own hands, as he often did. He paid individual attention to each devotee, asking them to eat more and more. Everyone was already very full, but Baba continued to serve them! When the devotees said they could not eat any more, Baba waited a while and then started insisting again that they should have a bit more. People said "Enough Baba, we have eaten a lot, we are full of ananda now."

Suddenly Baba stopped and became serious. Then he smiled and spoke: "You are talking about ananda, but do you even know what ananda is?" Then becoming a bit serious he said "Right now, Baba is feeding you and you're getting everything without making any effort, so you're happy. There could come a time when there will be so much devastation that you will only see lights flickering four *kos* (about 10 miles) away from each other. Humans will yearn to see another human being. Only after going through great trouble and traveling long distances will one person be able to meet another. At that time, they will know what ananda really means."

PREDICTING THE ARRIVAL OF DEVOTEES

(Contributed by Shri Ramlal Sah, Nainital)

We would go to Padampuri for Baba's darshan at least once every year, in the month of *Kartik* (November). Occasionally, when we were able to we went at other times as well. It happened several times that as soon as we decided to head to Padampuri, Baba would tell devotees present at the ashram in Padampuri that people from Nainital are on their way and arrangements for our stay would be in place before we arrived.

THE VALUE OF LOVE

(Contributed by Shri Hira Vallabh Pant)

One day, there was a discussion among devotees at the ashram on the topic that, these days, the love and respect for sadhus and for each other is reducing day by day. The devotees talked about how much they had seen this change in their own lifetimes and that, in present times, the pace of this change was becoming faster and faster: love was leaving the hearts of people and their hearts were becoming dry. Baba was also listening to these comments. He said, "You are talking about love now; there may come a time when the human population will drop to such an extent that a man will have to walk for 10 kos to meet another human being to talk to. That is the time when men will realize what love really means."

PREDICTING THE STORM

(Contributed by Shri Girwan Dutt Joshi, Nainital)

In the year 1911, I joined the Ramsay College in Almora. My father and my elder brother, Pandit Shri Krishna Joshi, were lawyers in Nainital. I would often visit Baba at Kakrighat when traveling to and from Nainital. Sometimes I would even travel to the ashram at Padampuri to meet Baba if he was there. During one of these journeys from Nainital to Almora, I stopped at Kakrighat for darshan. A friend was accompanying me.

Baba told me, "Prepare lunch at Kartigad, eat there, and then go ahead to Almora. During this time, the storm will also pass." (Kartigad is now called Suyalwadi). The sky was totally clear and there was only a light, pleasant breeze at the time. The person who was with me did not know anything about Baba, so he was a little skeptical. He had come along not so much for darshan but more because he wanted some prasad. Baba jokingly gave him four big laddoos and said, "Here, take these. You are a family man and need to eat more." The man was very happy at having received the laddoos, and started eating them as we continued towards Kartigad. As soon as we reached Kartigad, there was a big storm. We cooked and had lunch there as Baba had instructed. A couple of hours later, the storm passed as Baba had predicted, and we continued on our way.

BABA'S PREDICTION: YOUR UNCLE IS COMING HERE

(Contributed by Shri HariKrishna Trivedi, Editor, Hindustan Newspaper)

The presence of the great sage Sombari Baba in the land of Uttarakhand was a blessing for the people who lived in this area. He consoled and guided thousands of people who were tired, fearful, and worried from their experiences in life. He took away the pain of those who were suffering and guided those who were lost back to the path. Great wise sages who may no longer be in their body are still present in subtle form. Simply by remembering them and asking for help, one can receive their blessings, find inspiration, and have all doubts and worries resolved. Sombari Baba's blessings and grace are available to everyone even now.

I did not meet Baba personally, but my elder brother Shri Mathuradutt Trivedi had a wonderful experience with Baba, which he related to me often.

My brother was heading from Almora to Nainital to meet our maternal uncle, Shri Motiram Joshi. Our uncle held the post of sub-deputy of the education board at Nainital. There were no motor vehicles at that time; everyone would walk wherever they wished to go. As my brother was walking, the sun set. After it got dark, my brother felt a little fearful of walking alone in the forest and he thought it would be a good idea to make a brief stop at Baba's ashram. He paid his respects to Baba and sat there for a little while. He then felt a little hesitant to encroach on Baba's time and decided to continue his journey. Baba sensed this and said, "Son, where will you go? Don't go now, wait here."

My brother replied, "Baba, I have to go meet my maternal uncle."

Baba said, "But your uncle is on his way here."

On hearing this, my brother thought "How can this be?" Just a little while later, our uncle turned up at the ashram. My brother asked him, "How come you are here, Uncle?"

Our uncle replied: "I have been transferred from Nainital; this happened a few days ago." (Note that there were no phones or methods of sending messages quickly at that time). Then our uncle asked my brother how he happened to be there, and found out that he was heading to Nainital just to meet him. Had my brother not stopped at the ashram, or had he not waited there on Baba's insistence, he would have traveled all the way to Nainital for nothing and would have missed meeting our uncle. It was due to Baba's grace that he was saved the hassle of a long, tiring, and fruitless journey.

HELPING THE POLICE FIND A MURDERER

(Contributed by Shri Govindram Kala, Ex-Deputy Collector)

Once a man from Bhimtal murdered a potter in the village. The police officials were making inquiries in the area around the ashram. Baba said to them, "The person you are looking for is sitting on a big rock in the stream near Champhi. Go catch him." The officials did as instructed. They found the murderer, along with a bloodstained axe and the money that had been stolen from the potter.

PREDICTING THE BIRTH OF MY SON

(Contributed by Shri Govindram Kala, Ex-Deputy Collector)

When my wife became pregnant, Baba predicted it would be seven or eight months before the delivery (so the fetus would have been a month or two at the time) and that it would be a son. Sure enough, it was a boy!

BABA'S PREDICTION: YOU WILL STOP TAKING CHARAS

(Contributed by Shri Hira Vallabh Pant)

Shri Hiralal Sah Kumaiyya, who is popularly know as Habbaji, used to consume a good deal of charas and arkand (a refined and very expensive product made from charas, which includes things like musk. It had to be purchased from Nepal in those days and is not available at all these days).

Habbaji visited Sombari Baba often and had a great deal of love and respect for Baba. One day Baba mentioned to Habbaji that consuming too much charas causes cough during old age. He said, "You have already consumed a lot of it, and when the time comes you will stop."

One day, a few years after Baba had left the body, Habbaji was wondering how he could give up this habit. Arkand was no longer available by this time; often some local products would be passed off as arkand. Habbaji was used to taking a lot of arkand, which was less harmful than charas. But as the availability of arkand declined, he started compensating with charas.

Once, during the days of Holi, Habbaji consumed a lot of charas on the day of ekadashi and visited the famous temple of Gufa Mahadev at Krishnapur. He took a bath and offered prayers there. He prayed to Lord Shiva and asked to be freed from the habit of taking charas. Owing to the grace of Lord Shiva, he made a strong resolution to not take charas again. As a result of this decision and in order to help him stick to the resolution, he remained indoors in his house for a period of three months. After this period, he did not take charas again.

Baba's prediction that he would stop taking charas when the right time came had come true.

FORECAST OF DEATH

(Contributed by Shri Manoharlal Sah, cloth dealer, Mallital, Nainital)

Though this incident took place more than 50 years ago, it is embedded in my memory. I heard the words from Baba's mouth myself, so I can never forget them.

I was traveling from Nainital to Almora along with my mother. We had some porters with us to carry our luggage. We arrived at Kakrighat in good time. As we had plenty of time to complete the journey to Almora, I asked my mother to wait while I went to take darshan. I went to Baba's hut, paid my respects and sat down at his feet. Baba spoke: "Where are you going? The person you are going to visit passed away last night."

I was taken aback. Baba continued, "Don't say anything to your mother, there is no point. She will worry unnecessarily throughout the journey." Bear in mind that my mother was waiting far away, and I had not said anything about her presence to Baba. I bowed down to Baba and we carried on to Almora. On arriving there, Baba's words proved true: the person we were there to visit had passed away the previous night.

BABA'S PREDICTION: PRICE OF GHEE AT THE TIME OF DEATH

(Contributed by Shri Hira Vallabh Pant)

During World War I, the price of food was moving up and down dramatically and the price of ghee had reached between 8 and 10 *chatangs* (the measurement of weight in those days, there were maunds, ser, and chhatang) for a rupee. Baba said several times: "When the price of ghee reaches 6 chatangs for a rupee, it will be time to remove my *chasni* (large pot used to fry food) from the fire." At the time, people thought his words had something to do with the price of ghee becoming prohibitive; what they did not realize was that he was predicting that he would be leaving his body. And that is exactly what happened. Around the time Baba left his body in 1919, the price of ghee was 6 chatangs to a rupee, and the chasni was no longer used.

There is a saying that "*Purush ki maya aur vriksh ki chhaya usi ke saath chali jaati hai.*" ("Trap of worldly attachments of a person, and the shade of a tree, these go with them after their demise)." The teaching is that you came empty-handed and you had maya in this world, but on leaving nothing remains.

BABA'S PREDICTION: COMING BACK AS A BOY SADHU

(Contributed by Shri Hira Vallabh Pant)

When Baba realized that the time for him to leave his body was approaching, a few months before the day, he would occasionally ask devotees to collect some wood, even though there was no real scarcity or need for wood at that moment. Baba had been staying at the Padampuri ashram for five or six years by that time. In all this time, he had never asked devotees to collect wood, so they felt that something might be afoot and perhaps Baba was thinking of leaving his body. Once Baba even mentioned to people present: "In case someone decides to drop their body, there should be some wood for a pyre!"

Once Baba mentioned to people present, "I am considering going to Soron now, because the dharamshala has become old and is breaking down; it is a sin to stay in a run-down dharamshala. I will come back from Soron later." As was usual with Baba, no one could quite make out what he meant. Some devotees thought that Baba was talking about the dharamshala across the river from the Padampuri ashram, which needed some repair, and that he meant to say devotees would repair the dharamshala by the time he came back from a visit to Soron, a religious place (some think of it as the birthplace of Saint Tulsidas). But when he said it is not fair to live in a dilapidated house, he meant in an old body. The old devotees were very upset.

A few days later, Baba said, "I am a brahmachari and bodies of such people are cremated, not buried in a samadhi. Samadhis are supposed to be made for those saints who have taken *sanyas* after leading a worldly life." On hearing this, the devotees in the ashram became very worried. On seeing this, Baba said, "There is a mahatma here in the form of a child and you people will play with him."

A few days after this, Baba left his body and his devotees became very sad. Some days later, Hairakhan Baba met some of the other devotees and said, "My friend Sombari has left; now I will also go to the Himalayas." The devotees who had felt some sense of consolation at meeting Hairakhan Baba became even more desolate on hearing these words. After Sombari Baba left the body, the devotees were looking to Hairakhan Baba to console and support them.

One devotee managed to speak up and said, "Baba, we are already grieving at the loss of Sombari Baba and we were hoping you would bless us with your grace and wisdom. But if you talk of leaving us and going to the Himalayas, how are we supposed to carry on?"

The devotees realized the truth of two things that Sombari Baba had mentioned. Firstly, when he said, "I am considering going to Soron for a few days and will be back later," he was making it clear that he would be back. Secondly, Sombari Baba had said, "There is a mahatma here in the form of a child, and you people will play with him." Here was Hairakhan Baba confirming the same thing.

Two years after this event, a young boy with a divine countenance was seen in a cave across river. This boy came to be known as Badrinarayan Bal Brahmachari Maharaj. Sombari Baba's devotees believed that Bal Brahmachari Maharaj was a reincarnation of Sombari Baba, and they had plenty of proof to support this belief.

BABA GIVES AN INDICATION TO KRISHNA JOSHI

(Contributed by Shri Dhanilal Sah)

Shri Krishna Joshi, a devotee of Sombari Baba, was a pandit. He often recited holy scriptures in Baba's ashrams at Padampuri and Kakrighat. Once day, after completing his recitation at the Padampuri ashram, he asked Baba for permission to go home. Baba was in a good mood and asked him, "So, Krishna, when will you be back?"

He replied: "Baba, I will be back day after tomorrow."

On hearing this, Baba said, "Who knows what the day after tomorrow will bring?" That day, Baba left his body early in the morning.

Mahasamadhi

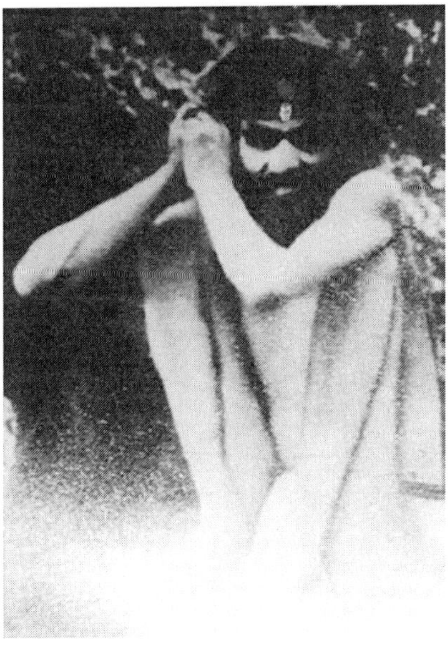

Sombari Baba in a relaxed mood at Padampuri
a few days before he left his body

DATES OF LEAVING THE BODY

(Contributed by Shri Krishnananda Shastri, Education Superintendent, Municipal Board, Nainital)

Baba left his body in the month of Poush (December/January) on the eleventh day of the waxing moon (called *Putrada Ekadashi*). The English date was January 2, 1919. The *barahwa* function (held on the twelfth day after the passing of a person) was held on *Makar Sankranti,* which fell on 14th January that year.

The last rites for Baba's body were performed by two of his great devotees, Shri Bageshwariji (also known as Amba Das) and Shri Hariduttji (Burju). To this day, a puja and annual *barsi* function is held at Padampuri on this day every year in Baba's memory.

A small temple was built at the place where Baba would sit. Sri Bal Brahmachari Maharaj, with the assistance of Devi Datt Kabdwal, had a beautiful marble statue made that looked so alive. The statue was installed there and it is worshipped every day. Though Baba is no longer in that body that was known as Sombari Baba, his ashrams and places where he stayed still vibrate with the beauty of his presence.

FINAL SAMADHI

(Collected by Shri Shankar Lal Sah as told to him by Haridattji)

For a few months before leaving the body, Baba had been giving hints to his devotees that the time for leaving the body was near. The evening before Sombari left his body, sadhus had visited the ashram. When food was served, they ate some of it and decided to save some for the next day. Baba was sitting far away at the time. He told a devotee, "Tell them to eat everything they can today, and as for the rest, offer it to the river. Don't keep any food for tomorrow."

According to Hindu tradition, if someone passes away, all the cooked food in the house is no longer fit for consumption and must be discarded. Baba arranged that there would be no food in the ashram when he died. Maharajji had given a clear hint to these sadhus. They did as he said and left nothing in the ashram to eat.

A small convoy of food and other cooking supplies passed by the road at the time of the cremation. The goods were being carried on mules, as was the norm in those days. At the time of burning his body, there was no bridge. People had to cross one river and then take the road that goes from Mukteshwar to Haldwani. All the vegetables, potatoes, everything used to be taken to Haldwani on Monday for the wholesale market. These mules were loaded with potatoes, and when they passed through that place where Maharajji's body was burning, they refused to move despite all the efforts of the people who were leading the mule train. They eventually gave up and informed the owner, who was close by. The owner came to check and immediately realized why the mules had stopped. He instructed his staff to take all the goods off the mules' backs and offer it to the ashram. He said, "Okay, this is Baba's instruction," and he unloaded all these potatoes right at the side of the river and it was stored in a room there. As soon as this was done, the mules started moving on.

On the 12th day ceremony, all the people of the vicinity were fed—relatives, friends, those who were known to the departed saints. Those huge sacks of potatoes were prepared and distributed in all the villages from Nainital, Mukteshwari, Almora, and Haldwani. Hundreds of people were fed with potatoes, puris, and halwah. Maharajji didn't want to put anybody into any kind of difficulty where they might feel there is no ghee, no water, no potatoes, so he had arranged everything in advance.

DEATH OF A DEER

(Contributed by Pandit Jagannath Joshi, ex-Municipal Commissioner, Nainital)

In the last two or three years of his life, Baba stayed at Padampuri throughout the year. One day during the last few months of his life, Baba was performing a *homa* (fire offering) and happened to burn his finger. He is reported to have said, "Agni Deva (the God of Fire) has caught hold of the body. It seems it will be time to change clothes soon."

A few days after this incident, a deer came to the ashram and started looking at Baba, ears upright, head held high, and with its tail wagging. On seeing the deer, Baba said, "From today, this deer should be given all the food and water it needs at the ashram." In accordance with Baba's instructions, the deer was given food and water every day. It partook of the offerings for one full week, and on the eighth day, it suddenly left the body. Baba instructed that last rites should be performed for the deer as it was an evolved soul.

PHOTOS OF BABA

(Contributed by Shri Hira Vallabh Pant)

Fortunately, there are a few pictures that exist of Sombari Maharaj. Many devotees had tried to take pictures of Baba, but did not succeed. The film would either turn out blank or the photos would not develop properly.

There were many people who would visit Baba for darshan in groups. Sometimes these groups would consist of people from a certain age group, and at other times, the groups would form based on their friendships. It was appropriate to travel in groups since at the time there were no roads and the devotees would have to travel about 15 miles on foot. Traveling alone in the forest was tiring and dangerous.

Shri Pratap Sah from the Mallital area of Nainital would go to visit Baba whenever he could and every time he would take along his camera, hoping to take a picture of Baba. But each time he could not find the courage to ask Baba for permission, nor he did not want to take a photo without Baba's permission. Baba could see what was in Pratap Sah's heart and he simply said, "The real image should be in one's heart!"

During one of these visits, Shri Sah decided, "Today I will take a photo of Baba, no matter what." He went to the dharamshala on the opposite side of the river from Baba's ashram and took three photos of Baba in different poses.

At the time when Shri Sah took the photos from the far bank of the river, Baba spoke, "O Bhoothnath, so at last, you did take a photo after all!" "Bhoot" in this context means a ghost and someone who works tirelessly and needs no rest, like a ghost, is called "Bhoothnath." Baba affectionately called Shri Sah "Bhoothnath" because he tirelessly kept trying to take Baba's photo. As Baba spoke, he stressed the word "at last." Within a few months of this incident, Baba left his body. It was then that the devotees realized why he had used the words "at last," and that it was owing to Baba's inspiration Shri Sah had mustered the courage to take the photos. Such is the grace of a sage. To this day, those are the only photos of Baba in existence.

BUYING WOOD WORTH 100 RUPEES

(Contributed by Lala Radheshyam in the cave at Soron)

In the autumn of 1918, a rich local man by the name of Jailal Sah had gone to Baba's ashram in Padampuri. There he made an offering of 100 rupees, which was a very large sum in those days. Baba called Shri Bageshwari and said, "Bageshwari, look, someone has offered this money. What will I do with money? I think it is going to be quite cold this winter, so why don't you go to the market and buy wood with this money." That was a lot of wood to buy! The ashram did not usually need that amount of wood. However, Bageshwariji followed Baba's instructions and purchased good quality oak wood with the money. There was so much wood that the entire storeroom of the ashram filled up.

That same winter, when Baba left his body in January, Shri Bageshwari realized that Baba had arranged for the wood for his funeral in advance, so as to not inconvenience his devotees with trying to find wood in the cold days of winter.

INCIDENTS FROM BABA'S LIFE

(Collected by Shri Shankar Lal Sah by listening to old devotees)

Here are some noteworthy incidents from Baba's life.

1. Once, Baba turned water into ghee and used it to fry puris.
2. When someone donated food with an unclean heart, Baba would refuse to accept it and instead threw it into the river.
3. If anyone who came to visit was not pure of mind, Baba would ask them to go take a dip in the river.
4. He knew people's problems before they spoke. He would tell them the cause of the problem, then he would give a solution and warn them not to repeat the behavior that had caused it.
5. Baba knew in advance when he was going to leave the body and made all the arrangements for his funeral personally.

6. Baba would use the word "saale" quite often. Literally translated, it means wife's brother, but it is also used as a mild swearword. Baba would usually scold those who were dear to him more than others, as he wanted them to learn quickly.
7. By applying a tika of vibhuti on a devotee's forehead, Baba would dissolve any forthcoming dangers and problems for his devotees. Baba applying a tika guaranteed that the devotee would reach home safely. Baba would often say, "If some one travels to me for darshan, it is my responsibility to make sure they get here safely and return home safely."
8. Once, a small pot of khichdi had been cooked at the ashram as prasad, enough for about three or four people. Suddenly, ten more devotees arrived. The cook was worried, but Baba told him not to worry. He instructed the cook not to look in side the pot and to continue serving. He also instructed the cook to keep the pot covered and to keep a stone on the lid between servings. The cook did as instructed and everyone ate their fill. When everyone was done eating, the cook was keen to see if there was any food left for him, so he opened the lid and peered inside the pot, only to find it totally empty. Baba scolded him saying: "If you don't have faith in the words of a sadhu, you will have to go hungry!"

MURTI OF SOMBARI BABA BROUGHT TO PADAMPURI

(Contributed by Gopal Dutt Joshi)

Some years after Sombari Baba had left his body and Bal Brahmachari Maharaj had been discovered, devotees in the area proposed that a murti of Sombari Baba should be made and installed in the Padampuri ashram. Bal Brahmachari Maharaj agreed to the proposal and personally went to Jaipur, where he arranged for a beautiful marble murti to be made. When it was ready, the murti was brought from Jaipur to Haldwani in the plains. It was winter, sometime in January. When the murti arrived in Haldwani, news spread and hundreds of people from the nearby villages started turning up to pay their respects. A big bhandara was held to celebrate the arrival of Baba's murti.

Some days later the murti was taken to Bhowali by bus. Beyond Bhowali there was no motorable road at the time, so the murti had to be carried by hand. On the day the party set out, there was heavy rain, hail, and snow. The murti had been packed in a lot of soft cotton and cloth and all the packing became wet from the rain, making it even heavier than it already was.

The first set of devotees carried the murti some distance, then others took up the task. The package was very heavy and the road had become very slippery due to the rain and snow. The task was so difficult that the devotees, despite their enthusiasm and sincerity, had to pause for breath. The hardest part of the climb to Champhi, Matiyal, and Padampuri still lay ahead.

Gopal Duttji and Devidutt Kabdwal moved ahead to take a look at the road ahead. Seeing this, Bal Brahmachari Maharaj said, "It looks like everyone is tired. Perhaps I should also help out a bit now." He started helping out. The devotees were moved to tears by seeing such a great saint helping with a simple physical task that they should have been able to do themselves. Gopal Duttji said that as soon as Maharajji helped, the journey to Padampuri flew by. No one felt tired, they did not need to stop to rest, and before long, the party arrived in Padampuri with the murti.

To this day, no one can explain logically what happened exactly. Such is the mysterious grace of the saints!

PADAMPURI AFTER BABA'S SAMADHI

(Contributed by local person from Padampuri)

Baba left his body in 1919. One of his great devotees, Shri Devidutt Kabdwal from Nainital, had this small marble murti of Baba installed at Padampuri, which radiates peace and inspires devotees who come to visit. To this day, many devotees come to the ashram at Padampuri to bathe in the confluence of the rivers and visit the temple for Baba's blessings. Before leaving, they go to Baba's dhuni and take some ash as blessings. The place itself has an atmosphere of great peace. Padampuri will forever be connected to Sombari Baba, and it is a part of India's great spiritual heritage. Though Baba is no longer in the body, his ashrams and places where he stayed still vibrate with the depth of his presence.

The ashram itself is not in very good repair. The effects of rain, sun, and wind are slowly wearing it away. The walls that protect the ashram from the water of the river are being eroded. There is no house for the priest who looks after the temple to live in. The dharamshala that was built for sadhus and visitors is no longer available, and the area around the ashram is neglected. Visitors who come to the ashram feel badly on seeing this state of neglect, and also notice the lack of basic facilities.

In the past few years, efforts have been made to restore the ashram. A trust called Shri Sombari Baba Smarak Trust has been established, and the Trust plans to restore the ashram in three stages, of which the first stage is already under way. The Trust has acquired some land in the area to expand the ashram and set up a dharamshala, and is also collecting money from donors in order to proceed with the work. With their efforts and Baba's blessings, the Padampuri ashram will be restored to serve the sadhus, devotees, and seekers who come here in search of spiritual peace and knowledge.

THE BRAHMINS AT BODHGAYA

(Contributed by Pandit Devidutt Kabdwal)

About ten days before Baba left his body, a devotee came to Padampuri with his family. He wished to go for a pilgrimage to Bodhgaya, the place where Gautama Buddha attained enlightenment. He thought it would be a good idea to meet Baba and seek his blessings before setting out on his journey.

After arriving at Padampuri, he had darshan, stayed overnight, and as he prepared to return home the next day he told Baba about his desire to visit Bodhgaya. Baba said, "It is a good thing to go on pilgrimage. After you arrive at Bodhgaya, feed four Brahmins on my behalf on the day of ekadashi. And since you are taking your wife and children along, if the food is prepared by her, that will be even better."

The devotee was touched on hearing this and felt very fortunate. He loved Baba very much and was always hoping that Baba would ask him to do something. Apart from very special occasions, Baba never asked anyone to do anything. One year, the kadhai in which khichdi was usually prepared developed a hole. Baba did not say anything to anyone and repaired it. The same kadhai was used for several months longer. Thought hundreds of people ate at the ashram every day, no one realized anything for four or five months, so it could be said that it was Baba's wish that the kadhai be used for some more time.

At another time, Baba's *angavastra* (cloth used to wrap the upper body) became so old and ragged that it developed two or three large holes. Baba continued to use it and did not say anything to anyone. Even though several new clothes were offered, he did not use them. One day a poor Brahmin devotee brought a rough cloth with great love, which Baba accepted. Only then did Baba get rid of the old torn angavastra. Knowing all this, the devotee whom Baba had asked to feed Brahmins in Bodhgaya felt very happy. He went back home and set out for Bodhgaya the next day.

Somehow he happened to arrive at Bodhgaya exactly on the day of ekadashi, with no such planning. He remembered Baba's wish to feed four Brahmins. As soon as he arrived in Gaya, four healthy-looking Brahmins approached him and said, "We are Brahmins on a pilgrimage. We don't want any donations of money; we only ask you to feed us."

The devotee was thinking of Baba's wish anyway and was happy that these people had turned up, which meant he did not even have to go look for Brahmins. He decided to go to the market, intending to buy some puris and sweets from a good clean shop to feed them. He had just walked a few steps when they said, "One more thing. We will only eat if someone from the family cooks the food. We cannot eat food from a shop in the market."

This reminded the devotee of Baba's instructions to cook himself, which he had forgotten. He thought: "Of what seva can I possibly be to Baba; it is he who does things through us. I had forgotten his second instruction, and he has reminded me through these people." After this, his wife made some food with great love and they fed the Brahmins.

On reaching home after his pilgrimage, the devotee heard that Baba had left his body and felt very sad. He then remembered the incident at Gaya and his sadness lifted. He thought, "A great soul like Baba will never leave those who love him; where will he go?" Later, he found out that Baba had left his body on ekadashi, the same day that he had arrived at Bodhgaya with his family. He told other devotees how he had arrived exactly on ekadashi, how the four Brahmins had turned up, and how they had reminded him about cooking the food.

On hearing the story, everyone present realized that Baba was very much still with them.

ANNIVERSARY OF BABA'S PASSING

(Contributed by Hira Lal Sah, Hubbaji)

This incident took place exactly one year after Baba left the body, on his first death anniversary.

Shri Bageshwari, a great devotee of Baba, had observed a strict set of practices called barsi for a full year in Baba's memory (this involves things like taking a bath every day, feeding a cow, making a water offering, and so on). After completing one year of practices, the first death anniversary is also called barsi (or barasi). Exactly one year after Baba left the body, on the day of barsi, the sky was clear all day. Around evening, a single cloud could be seen in sky and it started to rain heavily. A lot of water flooded the river quickly and it rose to the level of the ashram steps. No one had ever seen so much water and such a flood there before. Even large trees were floating downstream. A calf started floating in the water. Cows are sacred in India. They give more than they take, and ever since ancient Vedic times all slaughter and violence against animals for food has been forbidden in the Hindu diet. How could a cow be killed on this day of all days?

Bhavdeva, who had been standing by the river, took off his clothes and, wearing just his loincloth, jumped into the swollen river. He managed to grab the tail of the calf and float with it in the raging current. Some 100 or so feet ahead, he managed to bring the calf ashore, thereby saving its life.

To this day, a puja and barsi function is held at Padampuri every year in Baba's memory. Krishnananda Shastriji performed the annual rites for Baba until his own death.

Part IV
After Sombari Baba

Hairakhan Baba

Hairakhan Maharajji holding a Tibetan wheel

ABOUT HARIAKAHN MAHARAJJI

(Contributed by Shri Dhanilal Sah)

One day, a recitation of the Gita has been arranged at the ashram. Sombari Baba had asked for three seats to be prepared. One seat was for the wise man who was going to recite the Gita. Another seat was for Sombari Baba. No one knew who the third seat was meant for. That day Baba was acting impatient from the morning. He would constantly look out over the entrance of the ashram as if he was expecting someone.

Just as the recitation was about to begin, the great sage Hairakhan Baba arrived, wearing his *kanchopa* hat (a cap covering the ears). Sombari Baba rushed to greet and welcome him. Hairakhan Baba smiled, and they both sat and listened to the recitation of the Gita happily. After this, Hairakhan Baba walked a few feet away and then simply vanished. The large crowd of devotees who had gathered for the event were eyewitnesses to this incident.

HAIRAKHAN BABA'S WORDS

(Contributed by K.K. Sah)

A few days after Sombari Baba had left the body, Hairakhan Baba came to a place called Sipahidhara in Nainital. He was sitting in the kutiya of a saint called Garud Dasji. Hairakhan Baba's behavior was incomprehensible. Whatever prasad, fruits, and flowers were kept in front of him, he did not have anything to do with them. He did not care if someone left something or took something or whether someone ate some prasad or none. He would sometimes be quiet for a long time and sometimes speak for a long time. Sometimes he used foul language in speaking to his close devotees. He would speak partly in Pahari, partly in Gurkha Nepali, and partly in Hindi.

The night before Sombari Baba's mahasamadhi, my father

Hairakhan Baba and devotees

and Hubba and others were in Padampuri. Sombari said to my father, "What are you doing here? You have had my darshan. Go back to Nainital; your brother has died." It was a shock to my father, who indeed found his brother had died. In our religion, when there is death in the family, you are not supposed to go to temple or attend someone else's funeral.

Afterward the mahasamadhi, Hairakhan Baba was told everything that had transpired at the time. He said to my uncle Hubba, "Arre, why did you burn Sombari? He is in Surajkund, he would have come back!"

My father, Bhawani Das Sah, said, "Maharaj, I was not there at the time. Baba told me the day before he left his body that my cousin had died, so I had come back to Nainital. But if I was there at the time, I would also have thought that cremating Baba's body was the right thing to do."

K.K. relates a story about Hairakhan Baba: In 1911, a devotee of Hairakhan Baba, Sanskrit Scholar Pandit Aditya Ram Bhattacharya from Allahabad, requested Baba come to Allahabad. After arriving from Nainital, Baba took a bath at the confluence of the rivers in Prayag. Then a friend of the scholar, Major Basu from Allahabad, requested a photo be taken of Hairakahn. The photographer took one picture and immediately snapped another one. Hairakhan was dressed and wearing his usual cap that covered his ears. The pictures where taken at the same place, at the same time, while Hairakhan was seating on his asan. Then, when the photos were developed, one appeared showing him dressed and wearing his cap while the other one showed the upper part of his body naked. Before this miracle, other miracles were witnessed by so many devotees. Sombari Maharajji used to pay high regards to Hairakhan Baba. They met each other a few times.

Maharajji always used to say that he was a "*naisthick* brahmachari." Naisthick means strictly brahmachari. This is our faith. Two or three days before his mahasamadhi, he called Bageshwari Baba and said, "Bageshwari, look, I am going to leave my body. Don't worry. People will have different opinions about what to do with my body. Some will say bury him. Some will say give him *jala* samadhi (immerse his body into a lake). But I'm a naisthick brahmachari, so my body should be cremated. Don't listen to anybody else. These are my instructions: my body should be offered through fire."

These are the pictures taken of Hairakhan one immediately after the other.

Hairakhan murti made by Neils Olif Criscender in the presence of
Bal Brahmachari Maharajji at Kasar Devi in 1944 or '45

Bal Brahmachari Maharaj

Artist's rendering of Bal Brahmachari Maharaj

HOW WILL WE LIVE WITHOUT YOU?

(Contributed by Hubbaji)

Hubba said to Sombari Baba, "Maharajji, it is very impossible for us. How will we be able live without you? You are our parents; you are everything. We will become orphans if you leave your body."

Baba smiled. He said, "You people are fools. Siddhas never die. There is someone, a sadhu, who is in this area for the last so many years; he will appear in the form of a young boy."

Hubba used to take many liberties. He said, "Well, Baba, how will we be able to know, or to tell, or to believe that you are coming in the form of that baba (as a *balyogi*, child yogi)?"

Sombari used some abusive language and then said, "You will play with him." Hubba became quiet.

Two or three years after Sombari Maharaj left his body, a young sadhu with a shiny golden face appeared at Padampuri from a cave on that side of the river. At first, he was so shy that he would run away to his cave and hide if anyone showed up. But these old people remembered the words of Sombari Baba, so they tried to test this Bal Brahmachari Maharajji, and Bal Brahmachari used to say things as if he were indeed the incarnation of Sombari Baba. People started going to see him.

Whenever there was crowd, Bal Brahmachari would ask for his pack of cards and four people would start playing a card game of Trumps. One day a couple of old men happened to go to Bal Brahmachari Maharajji. He asked someone to bring a pack of cards. He said to Hubba, "I want to play with you." Hubbaji remembered the words of Sombari Baba, "You will play with him." He fell at Bal Brahmachari's feet. He could feel that Bal Brahmachari was the incarnation of Sombari Baba.

Bal Brahmachari Maharajji would say, "You don't have to do any puja to me." He had only one picture of Sombari. He said, "If you have to do puja, do it to him." This was one of many hints that he was the incarnation of Sombari Baba.

Gradually, gradually, he came near the takhat at Padampuri ashram. Bhageshwari was there. Everybody knew that Maharajji had said that a young boy would appear. Bageshwari suddenly got the thought in his mind: what if this boy might be that person? He requested, "Maharajji, take your seat on the takhat where Sombari Baba used to lie."

The boy said, "No. I cannot sit on that takhat." He never did sit on that takhat. But gradually people could confirm that he was indeed Sombari Baba.

Hubbaji

MILK FOR OFFERING

(Contributed by Hira Lal Sah, Hubbaji)

This incident took place about two or three years after Sombari Baba left his body and was the first time I had darshan of Bal Brahmachariji.

There used to be a special daily worship at the temple of Lord Shiva from the time when Baba stayed there: an offering of milk was made at the shrine every day. One evening, around 4 p.m., Shri Bageshwari started to sob and said, "It has been such a short time since Baba left his body and there isn't even milk to offer to Shivji today." Shortly after, a naked *avadhut* arrived. In a small lota he had brought along milk, which he kept at the dhuni. He was wet from the rain and was shivering from the cold. I looked inside the lota and saw the milk. I had never seen such beautiful-looking milk before. It was fresh and the color of light saffron. The milk was offered to Shivji.

I brought a dhoti and angocha and offered them to the avadhut. He refused and did not accept them. After a few minutes, he went to the cave across the river. I followed him. Shri Bal Brahmachari Maharaj was sitting in the cave. Maharaj said, "Get clothes for him."

I said, "Maharaj, I had just offered him some clothes but he refused."

Maharaj said, "Get the clothes, he'll wear them." From the corner of the cave, Maharaj brought a *janeu* (sacred thread) and put it around the avadhut's neck. It was a surprise for me to see the avadhut accepting a janeu from a young boy (a janeu is usually put on by an elder).

I went back to get clothes for the avadhut, and came back a few minutes later with the clothes and some other devotees. When I arrived, the avadhut was gone. Maharaj said, "He's left, go find him and give him the clothes." We started running fast to try and find the avadhut. We even split up and took different roads to try and find him, but we did not see the avadhut anywhere.

FIRST MEETING WITH BRAHMACHARI MAHARAJ

(Contributed by Gopal Dutt Joshi)

In 1926, I met Brahmachari Maharaj for the first time. I was in a village called Marhaura in the district of Chhapra from around November 1926 until around November 1927. I worked in a British-owned mill called Sunderland, and I had heard about Maharajji from some people at the mill. I used to chant the *Rudriya stotram (hymn in praise of Lord Shiva) every day. One day, a* mahatma came to my room and asked for five rupees. I had some money in my coat which was hung in the room, so I went to the coat and gave him five rupees. The sadhu said something about meeting again later and then left.

Soon after, I came to Nainital for the Durga puja holidays. There I met my relative, Jaidutt Joshi, who told me that Maharajji was in an area called Ghanipur. He suggested that I should take along his older son, Bhairavdutt Joshi, and go for darshan. Accordingly, I went there the next day and waited for Maharajji. In those days, a swami called Hiranand Swami was staying with Maharajji. He told me that Maharajji comes out of his dwelling at around 11 in the morning to make an offering of water to the sun, and that I could have darshan at that time.

At around 11, Maharajji came out as expected. His head and ears were covered, as was most of his face. I did not know who it was. Maharajji asked Bhairavdutt about me: who I was, what I did, and so on. When Bhairavdutt told him I worked in Marhaura, Maharajji said, "Oh, I have also stayed in Marhaura. It's near Sonpur, and they also have an annual fair." Maharajji then asked Hiranand Swami to make tea for us. That evening, I headed back to Marhaura.

BHAJANS WITH BAL BRAHMACHARI MAHARAJ

(Contributed by Gopal Dutt Joshi)

The following summer, I came to Nainital for the summer holidays. Jaidutt Joshi lived next door. On the evening of the second day of my stay, I heard him calling out to me. He said, "I met Maharajji last evening, and he told me that you have come to Nainital. He has sent some prasad for you." The prasad had some sweets, and interestingly, there were several fruits that were completely out of season at that time! Jaiduttji also told me that Maharajji was going to be there for some days, and that Maharajji liked bhajans. I liked singing bhajans and had a group of friends with whom I sang regularly. Jaiduttji suggested that I should go with my friends and sing bhajans for Maharajji. I liked the idea, so we went, and this became a regular event during my holiday. We'd stay with Maharajji until around 1 a.m. singing bhajans. Sometimes Maharajji would join us and play the *tabla* (drums). He was a fantastic player and never lost his rhythm.

BABA ASKED SHRI KABDWAL FOR CLOTHES IN A DREAM

(Contributed by Pandit Devidutt Kabdwal)

In 1919, when Sombari Baba left his body, his old devotee Shri Kabdwal felt very sad. When Shri Badrinarayan Bal Brahmachari appeared in a cave across the bridge from the ashram at Padampuri, news of this reached Nainital very quickly. Shri Kabdwal recalled the words that Hairakhan Baba spoke when Sombari Baba left his body: "Do mahatmas ever die? Sombari will come again. But this time he will come as a boy, so how will you recognize him?"

Shri Kabdwal felt a great urge to go and meet the child yogi, so he went to Padampuri within a few days. The moment he met the child yogi, he sensed that it was Sombari Baba. The child yogi nonchalantly brought up a topic that had been discussed between Sombari Baba and Shri Kabdwal, and Shri Kabdwal realized that he was indeed Sombari Baba!

After this event, Shri Kabdwal would visit Bal Brahmachariji regularly and partake in satsang. His devotion towards the child yogi grew. He continued his job with the government, working diligently, but every Saturday evening after work he would set off from Nainital to visit Bal Brahmachariji. Sometimes he would return on Sunday evening, but often, he would stay over and only return to Nainital on Monday morning. On public holidays and also during his vacations, he would go and spend time with Bal Brahmachariji.

One day, Shri Kabdwal had a dream. In the dream, Bal Brahmachari Baba said, "Devi Babu, it is winter and I feel cold. Could you please have an *ulfi* (a long robe worn by some sadhus) made for me?" In the dream Shri Kabdwal had the ulfi made and took it to Baba in Padampuri. The ulfi turned out to be too long, so Kabdwalji said he'd take it home and shorten it a little. However Baba said, "No, don't worry, I'll fold it at the waist and tie it with a rope like this, see?" Shri Kabdwal soon forgot all about the dream.

Some months later, he was visiting Bal Brahmachari Baba in Padampuri. Baba said, "Devi Babu, winter is coming, and the days are getting cold. Could you please get an ulfi made for me?" Shri Kabdwal did not remember the dream at that time. Things proceeded exactly as they had in the dream: the ulfi turned out to be too long and, when Shri Kabdwal offered to have it shortened, Baba said exactly the same thing about tying it with a rope. That's when Kabdwalji suddenly remembered the dream! He was overwhelmed and tears welled up in his eyes. He was about to speak, but Baba gently looked at him and said, *Bhava ko mun mei rakho.* "No need to say anything out loud; the deepest feelings are meant to be treasured in the heart."

Thus the old Sombari Baba devotees started having faith in Bal Brahmachari Baba, and others also came to believe in him.

Shri Kabdwal was a very practical person, and did not have much time for emotional spirituality. Often when a group of people would be together discussing high philosophy, he would interject saying they were getting carried away. But when it came to certain sages, he lost all sense of this "practical" side. One day he got emotional in this way in the presence of Bal Brahmachari Baba and Baba teased him, saying, "Devi Babu, it seems you are working too hard in the office these days. Your eyes are watering. They need rest!" Shri Kabdwal was left speechless on seeing the depth of Bal Brahmachari Baba's love, even through playfulness.

In 1921, Shri Kabdwal visited the shrine of Badrinath along with Bal Brahmachariji and some other devotees. His faith in the child yogi increased day by day. In spite of this, sometimes he would get into disagreements with Bal Brahmachariji. The behavior of the child yogi was mysterious and it was difficult to understand his actions based on the expectations and views of the practical world. However, when the time was ripe, Bal Brahmachariji would usually unveil the reasons for his actions.

BAL BRAHMACHARI BABA IN VARANASI

(Contributed by Pandit Devidutt Kabdwal)

Bal Brahmachari Maharaj was in the habit of going away for long periods of time and no one knew his whereabouts during these periods. Once he had been gone for a long time and Shri Kabdwal felt a strong urge to see Baba. He decided that he would find Baba no matter what and with this intention in mind he set off from Nainital. After many months of traveling he was in Banaras, where he stayed in a dharamshala for a week hoping to find Baba. Towards the end of the week, he became dejected, packed up, and headed to the railway station. All of a sudden, he heard a familiar voice: "Devi Babu, when did you come?" There was Bal Brahmachari Baba, standing right in front of him! "How long have you been here in Varanasi?"

Shri Kabdwal replied: "I have been here for a week, looking for you, Maharaj."

Baba replied: "Oh, really? I have also been here for a week." Strangely enough, Baba had been staying in the same dharamshala all that time, quite close to Shri Kabdwal's room! This incident made Shri Kabdwal realize that a sage can only be found when he wishes to be found, when he decides to bless someone with his presence. A decision to find them made from an egoistic point of view is unlikely to succeed, but when we seek them with love, they heed the call.

SHRI KABDWAL AND THE BABAS

(Contributed by Pandit Devidutt Kabdwal)

Shri Kabdwal was very particular about being punctual. However, in the presence of sages like Sombari Baba, Bal Brahmachariji, and Neem Karoli Baba, he would completely lose track of time. One day in 1948, he went to visit Neem Karoli Baba. When it was time to leave, he got up. Baba asked him to stay for a while longer, but he refused, saying he had to go. Later, he had a strong urge to go and take darshan of Sombari Baba. Though he wasn't feeling well, he walked all the way to the village of Gethia where Baba was at the time. When he arrived, Baba simply laughed and said, "What happened, son? You never go anywhere without an appointment and unless it is time, right?"

The ways of the sages are mysterious!

After about fifteen years of service in the government office, Shri Kabdwal decided to take voluntary retirement from active service. However, owing to his short service, the pension due to him was quite low, only about ten to twelve rupees a month. He studied the rules of the pension scheme and found out that the government could grant him a special pension of up to twenty-five rupees a month. He applied for the special pension and, after some correspondence with the government, he retired in 1928 having been granted the special pension. After retiring from active duty, Shri Kabdwal continued to spend time with Bal Brahmachariji and took advantage of his free time to be with satsang.

A BRIEF DESCRIPTION ABOUT SHRI 1008 BADRI NARAYAN BAL BRAHMACHARI MAHARAJJI

(Contributed by H.B. Pant Govindpur, Kausani, Almora)

Shri 1008 Badri Narayan Bal Brahmachari Maharajji was first seen by a Kumaon, Sri Madhu Sudan Joshi Shastri, in Madhobagh Park at Bombay in 1922. How this man met the Bal Yogiji is a mysterious event. He was going out for a walk along with some of his friends on a road passing by the Madhobagh Park when he suddenly heard some unknown voice calling him by his name thrice—Madhusudan! Madhusudan!! Madhusudan!!! This unknown voice came from the direction of the park.

The man, therefore, looked toward the park and saw a young robust yogi Maharaj of about 15-16 years of age. He was very much impressed at the first sight of the Bal yogiji from a distance, merely by the unusual health and well-built body of the Bal yogi's lustrous body. Unmindful of the voice, he proceeded on along with his friends. The voice was only heard by him and by none of his friends accompanying him.

When the whole party, slowly walking and chatting, had covered a distance of about half a mile from the park, it struck him that he should have gone for the darshan of the Bal yogi, whom he could only see from a distance and from which direction the voice was heard by him. As he was already very much impressed by the young, robust, and lustrous body of the Bal yogi, he wanted to meet him face to face. He made some excuses and took leave of his friends and turned back to the park.

On reaching it, he saluted the Bal yogiji with folded hands and a bowed head. The Bal yogi then inquired of him about the welfare of the Padampuri ashram of Shri 1008 Sombari Babaji, a great yogi. Why an unacquainted person whom the yogi Maharaj meets for the first time and inquires about an ashram which had not been previously visited by him is a mystery. However, this man replied in an ordinary way that Shri 1008 Sombari Babaji had left his physical body and a man known as Bageshwari was looking after the Padampuri ashram. He stayed for about fifteen minutes and saw that some well-to-do devotees were assembled there, and a lot of fruits, sweets, and dry fruits offered to the Bal yogi were in big heaps.

After he replied to the Bal yogi's query cursorily, and stopping a little while, he took leave of the Bal yogiji to go back without any inquisitiveness. When going back to his house and passing a distance of about half a mile, it struck him that he ought to have asked the Bal yogiji as to how he was acquainted with him and how he was acquainted with the Padampuri ashram. With this idea in his mind, he went back to the park again. On reaching the park, he found that neither the Bal Yogi was there nor were the devotees and heaps of fruits, sweets, and dry fruits had disappeared. He had to come back disappointed.

After this mysterious event, when this man returned to the

hills and was going home, he heard people say that a young Bal yogi had of late arrived at the Padampuri ashram. On hearing this, the whole scene of Bombay came to his mind and he thought that the Bal yogi must be the same one he had met in a park in Bombay. He decided to find out whether the Bal yogi was the same person. On meeting the Bal yogi, he found out that he was the same yogi he had seen in Bombay, and he therefore had some talks with him about the Bombay affair.

The Bal yogi with a smile gave him no definite reply, but only said that he did not know him (Madhusudan) till then.

In the course of time, the Bal yogi was considered an incarnation of Shri 1008 Sombari Baba of the Padampuri ashram by his followers or devotees on the strength of prophesies already made by the two well-known great saints of this period, as follows:

After the demise of Shri 1008 Sombari Baba of Padampuri, one of the greatest saints or mahasiddhas, known as Shri 1008 Hairakhan Baba, told some of his and Shri Sombari Baba's devotees that real saints do not die and Sombari Baba would again come. But how would people know him if he came in Bal-roop, a very young age? Shri 1008 Hairakhan Baba told this to his devotees on their expression of sorrow at the demise of Shri Sombari Baba.

The other prophesy was made by Shri 1008 Sombari Babaji himself in a roundabout way: that the dharamshala (by which meant his body) had worn out and he wanted to go to Soron (a religious place) and would come back soon. This was said by him a few months before his demise and his devotees could not make out the real significance at the time. Shri Sombari Baba told one thing more: that the place, Padampuri, is a *siddha bhumi* (a place where there are siddhas) and saints roam about in *Bal-swarup* (young age). He added that some *Mai-ka-lal* (or siddha) would come there (Padampuri ashram).

For many years the Bal yogiji lived a very simple life. He lived quite naked with a kaupin or loincloth and a piece of cloth on his head. He rubbed ashes on the whole of his body and took cold water bath thrice a day, very early in the morning at about 3 or 4 o'clock, the second in the midday, and the third in the evening. He took only fruits, vegetables, and milk as his diet. His body was well built and very robust, with exceptional health as well as a commanding and attractive personality. He performed Gayatri japa, *havan* (a fire ritual), and *pranayam* (breathing practices) as his daily routine. He performed his pranayam practice in an almost airtight underground box for 2-3 hours daily.

The Bal yogi's relations with the general public and his devotees were intimate and loving, so much so that everybody felt that he loved him the most. At the same time, in spite of his intimate and loving attitude, he had a natural awe-inspiring and commanding personality and nobody dared gainsay him face to face in any matter whatsoever. He possessed a marvelous psychic power and could do anything he liked easily and in no time. It was easy for him to read minds of different people, yet he never showed that he could read minds. There were occasions when certain people tried to judge him without themselves possessing any faculty to do so. Towards such people, his dealings were quite peculiar and haphazard and they returned empty-handed with the impression that the Bal yogi knew nothing.

He later on began dressing, wearing boots and a turban. He also started the amazing practice of playing cards to put off the undesirable element trying to judge him or yogis in general.

Sometimes the Bal yogiji used to say to his sincere devotees almost impossible things, which they could not make up, so they naturally questioned him to remove their doubts. He used to say that they should have blind faith in him and say "yes" to whatever he said and then they would know the secret of the things in due course.

While playing cards (Trumps) with his sincere devotees, he solved their problems in a very subtle manner in the language of playing cards, so that only the man concerned could understand him and no one else. For instance, in one case there was a great tussle going on between two parties for procuring the last (seventh) hand. He won the last hand and addressed his partner smiling, "Now I have saved! Now I have saved! and you are a fool to worry."

The younger brother of his partner was seriously ill and that is what the partner was worried about. He was convinced by the Bal yogiji in this subtle manner that his brother had been saved by him, while others could only understand that the last hand was taken by him and the defeat was saved. He did such things in the case of his devotees who had sincere and implicit faith in him, and in a very subtle and secret way. He did not care at all to utilize his tremendous powers in general for the sake of a mere show or winning favor of the general public, as many sadhus do. He cared little for the general opinion of the public at large, whether they praised or defiled him, yet he never lost his equilibrium of head and heart. He never hated anybody at heart nor did he think ill of anybody.

On the other hand, he scolded his sincere devotees bitterly if they wished ill of anybody or denounced anyone defying Bal yogi in any way. He told them to analyze themselves and try to improve their own defects or shortcomings instead of finding faults in others. This was one of his main teachings to his sincere devotees. He said that there are shortcomings in everybody, so one must try to remove or improve one's own defects first of all and then alone one can make some progress in the spiritual path, otherwise one is nowhere and gets entangled in the worldly sanskaras and gets into the cycle of births and deaths for a very long spell of time until he gets, by the grace of God, a really good guru to guide him along the spiritual path.

One European gentleman (Swedish, an art director named Nils Olaf Chrisander), tried to see the Bal yogiji many a time but could not succeed in his efforts. One day the Bal yogiji himself sent him word that he need not be worried and he (the Bal yogiji) would give him an opportunity of seeing him whenever he thought fit. This European gentleman lived at Kasardevi (a temple of the Goddess) some three to four miles away from the town of Almora proper. He practiced yoga there for about four years between 1942 to 1946.

At last one day Shri Bal yogiji game him an opportunity to see him (Bal yogi). He talked with Nils on the subject of yoga and gave him some hints which he needed. There were talks on other subjects as well. In course of the talks, Shri Bal yogiji showed him a photograph of Shri 1008 Hairakhan Baba and asked him if he could make a statue of the saint to resemble the photograph exactly. On this the gentleman replied that he would try his best to do so. He added that Shri Hairakhan Baba had given him and his wife darshan in Moscow when they were there on some business. This fact was corroborated when both the husband and the wife met together. Shri Bal yogiji entrusted him with the job of preparing a statue, which the latter did with difficulty. It took him a considerably longer time than usual. The difficulty being that only the front pose of the photograph was available while different poses are required in preparing a statue.

Though the gentleman felt difficulty and took a longer time in preparing the statue, it is doubtless a very nice and lively one that he made at last. The fact is that this artist had had the fortune of having the darshan of the saint in Moscow and was helped in his meditation from time to time to get impressions in his mind of different poses of the saint while preparing the statue. This statue has now been installed in a temple at Govindpur ashram of Shri 1008 Bal yogiji near Kausani in the Almora district. Mr. Chrisainder once visited this ashram when Shri Bal Brahmachariji was there. He stayed there for a night. He took rice, curry, and vegetable as prasad, which was cooked by Shri Bal Brahmachariji himself, and he relished the same too much.

This gentleman and artist, while intending to leave India for his mother country in 1946, asked Shri Bal yogiji as to how and when he would be able to see him or have his darshan again. On this the Bal yogiji replied that he would appear before him if and when he sincerely remembered him.

BAL BRAHMACHARI MAHARAJ REMOVES A DEVOTEE'S DESPONDENCY

(Contributed by Shri Nityananda Mishra)

According to Shri Nityananda Mishra in an article in *Ramlila Smarika* (1996, issue 17), in the year 1919, after Sombari Baba left his body, Bal Brahmachari Baba from Nepal arrived at Baba's ashram in Padampuri. Before this he used to stay in a place called Janakpuri in the plains of Bihar. In 1920, Bal Brahmachari Baba was wearing a strange getup—a fancy coat and breeches instead of the simple clothes of a sadhu. He had an attractive personality and looked like a handsome prince. Instead of being engrossed in prayer or meditation, he would play cards with the people who had come to the ashram. I wondered: "What kind of sadhu is this?" I did not think a person like this deserved my respect, so after a quick look, I left.

Twenty-six years later, in the year 1946, I spent a terribly cold winter in Nainital. The second World War had made a great dent on the Indian economy, and I was quite dejected with the lack of money and opportunity. One Sunday in February 1946, I set off from home towards Mallital. There had been hail earlier in the day and the sky was still overcast. The wind was cold and biting, but I did not feel like remaining indoors, so I set out. Along the way, near the Mallital post office, I came across Shri Devidutt Joshi, who was the principal of the regional college. Shri Joshi was a learned man: a wonderful teacher, a music composer, a much loved actor, as well as an accomplished sportsman. He was always in good humor and was well-liked by everyone in the community. On seeing me, he smiled and asked: "Mishraji, where are you going in this kind of weather?" When I said that I was going out for a walk to lift my spirits, he asked me to go along with him towards Bhowali. I replied that I did not have the spirit to walk five or six miles in such cold weather. But Joshiji insisted, saying that he would very much like the company and that we'd be back by dusk. I could not refuse him. He purchased some sweets at a shop and we both started walking towards Bhowali.

Along the way, Joshiji mentioned that he had heard Brahmachari Maharaj was going to be at the area called "The Pines," where the police Circle Inspector Shri Bhawanidas Sah (K.K.'s father) had an orchard. We arrived at the ashram of Brahmachari Maharaj at around two in the afternoon. There was no one to be seen there. The sky was very dark, it was raining hard, and a high wind was blowing. We happened upon Shri Bhawanidas Sah's wife in Bhumiyadhar village; she was cleaning some rice grains in a plate. She mentioned that the gardener had gone to a shop close by to get some milk. We asked her where we could find Brahmachari Maharaj, and she told us that he was meditating close by. We headed towards his meditation spot.

It was a strange sort of place: a hole about three to four feet deep and eight or ten feet wide. There were some steps to walk down to the bottom. In this terrific cold, in the middle of the rain, I saw

Maharaj sitting in the lotus position deep in meditation, lost to the world. To avoid disturbing him, we went back to the hut quickly. Joshiji asked Mrs. Sah how long Maharaj had been sitting in meditation. She replied he had been meditating since around ten, so about four hours. She also said it was almost time for him to return, and asked us to wait inside by the dhuni. We sat there for three quarters of an hour waiting for Maharaj to come back. When he arrived, I saw that he only had a small dhoti around the waist, a simple shawl around the shoulders, and a piece of cloth on the head. That day, I saw a completely different side of the person I had seen in regal attire 26 years ago.

We both bowed and, after paying our respects, we sat down before him. I was afraid that he might ask me about our previous encounter so many years ago. Maharaj only looked at me once and then started speaking with Joshiji. I sat quietly, listening to them talk. My mind was spinning with thoughts and worries. Appearing to pick up the topic from Mrs. Sah's activity of cleaning the rice, Maharajji said, "Grains have become very expensive these days, which is causing problems to many people. Some greedy merchants have hoarded a lot of grain, causing misery to tens of thousands. I wonder what kind of people these are!"

At that time, a great famine was sweeping through the eastern province of Bengal. Maharaj continued: "When the heart is pure and the mind is open, only then can good sense prevail. Purity of the heart can be achieved by meditation and by helping others. By exercising discernment, the mind becomes more open, and then people can tell the difference between right and wrong. In the presence of selfishness, the mind does not work well. We have to be strong. A calm mind helps us to face and solve all problems. The results of past karmas have to be borne, but we should not lose our discernment and fall prey to selfishness."

With these few short sentences in the middle of a seemingly normal conversation, Maharaj answered all my questions and guided me without even appearing to do so. We had some tea and then Maharaj asked us to set off for Nainital as it was beginning to get dark. This was my last meeting with Brahmachari Maharaj.

Something else notable happened after this meeting. My despondent mood lifted, I felt enthusiastic towards life, found new strength, and was able to think of solutions for my problems, which then resolved themselves one by one. I followed Maharajji's advice of being honest and clear in thought, speech, and also in my dealings with everyone. I did well in life. Even 30 years after the event, I still remember the joy that rose in my heart after spending a short amount of time with him, and how it changed my life.

Bal Brahmachari Baba had many devotees all over the country. One of the devotees recounted an event when Brahmachari Maharaj met Anandamayi Ma in Lucknow. Both of these great saints lost themselves in spiritual discussion. The devotees present there were saying to themselves and each other, "The waters of transcendental knowledge are flowing generously tonight. Fill up your containers as much as you can!"

BRAHMACHARI MAHARAJ PLAYS THE ROLE OF A SON

(Contributed by Shri Nityananda Mishra)

Pandit Chandravallabh Durgapal taught at the Humphrey High School in Nainital (now C.R.S.T. College). He was a very dedicated teacher and put in a great effort in teaching his students. He was also a very strict disciplinarian. He had a son who had, owing to a disagreement with his father, left home at a young age and never returned. Shri Durgapalji went to visit Brahmachari with his old wife. On seeing Brahmachari Maharaj, she exclaimed: "This is my son!"

Maharajji and many of the other people around tried to ex-plain to her that this was not the case, but she was insistent. She became very sad and started weeping when they tried to reason with her. Finally Maharajji smiled and said, "Since you have considered me your son, I am obliged to treat you as my mother and be like a son to you."

When that lady became old, Maharajji was at Banaras with K.C. Tewari and two or three other devotees. Brahmachari said, "The lady's time has come. She is going to die. I don't want to stay here. I will go to Nepal." He asked K.C. and Joshi to purchase a shawl. When she died, they were to put that shawl on her body.

Maharajji said, "I will go and select the shawl myself from a shop." He picked a very costly shawl. At that time, no one had much money with them, so they asked the shopkeeper to hold the shawl and they would come the next day to pay for it and take it. The shopkeeper insisted, "No, you take. I trust you. You take it today and you pay me tomorrow." Finally they agreed and took the shawl with them. The next day Bal Brahmachari Maharaj left for Nepal. He asked K.C. and Joshi to pay for the shawl the next day.

Tewari went to that shop, paid for the shawl, and asked the shopkeeper, "We are so confused. Hundreds and thousands of people come to Banaras, coming and going, coming and going, so how do you give this kind of credit?" The shopkeeper, an old guy, laughed loudly. He said, "How long have you been with that person who came with you? We have seen him doing puja or yoga at Manikarnika Ghat (the main cremation ghat of Banaras) for many years, and you say who is this?" It blew their minds.

After three or four days in Banaras, the lady died. They put the shawl on her to be burned with her. This became a big subject for K.C. and Joshi. They later told Brahmachari Maharajji what the shopkeeper had said. Maharajji said, "No, no, he might have misunderstood. It must have been some other person who he had seen doing puja or worship at Manikarnika Ghat. I was not there."

K.C. was saved by Brahmachari Maharaj. Tewari had a lung problem, so he was staying in Lucknow. Brahmachari asked him to go to the Gomti River every day in the morning—and it was very cold in the early morning—and take one lota of water, carrying it without spilling. It was a difficult sadhana for him. After spending two months like that in Lucknow, he was cured.

THE SADHU AT THE RAILWAY STATION

(Contributed by Gopal Dutt Joshi)

My brother-in-law, Bhairav Dutt Pande, worked in the Food Control department and was posted at Darbhanga near the border with Nepal. Once, I went there with Maharajji and a group of devotees. We spent some days visiting holy places in the area. Bhairavduttji suggested that we should go to a particular shrine, and we set off. Part of the journey was to be made by train, via a place called Janakpur. Bhairavduttji's wife gave us trunk full of supplies, such as spices, food, items for havan and puja, and so on. Maharajji would often give everyone *thandai* (a tasty and cooling drink) to drink, along with a very small quantity of *bhang* (charas) mixed in, so she also kept all the material needed to make the thandai in the trunk. For the number of days that we had stayed at Darbhanga, she had made note of all the things that Maharajji needed for his daily use and insured that all those supplies were provided for our journey. Bhairavduttji also came to see us off and accompanied us until the next station.

When we arrived at our destination, we went to all the holy spots there. We then went to a dharamshala and Maharajji instructed us to prepare food while he did his daily practices. As food was being served, Maharajji said, "First serve the food on a large *pattal* (a plate made of leaves) and if you see a sadhu outside, give it to him." I did as instructed. I had just stepped out of the house and climbed down a couple of steps when all of a sudden a sadhu showed up, grabbed the plate from me, and started eating immediately.

When I came back into the house, Maharajji asked "Did you give it to someone? Who was it?" I narrated what had happened. The next day, we prepared to head back. I noticed the sadhu from the previous afternoon following us at a distance. We arrived at the railway station and took our seats on the train. I told Maharajji about the sadhu, and that he was the same person who had accepted the plate of food the previous afternoon. The sadhu came to the platform and started looking towards Maharajji. A railway officer came by and told the sadhu that the platform was meant to be used only by travelers and tried to get him to leave. The sadhu would leave for a little while, then come back to the platform and try to be near the carriage in which Maharajji was sitting.

Exasperated, the railway officer asked him: "If you are not going anywhere, why do you come to the platform again and again? Go away."

The sadhu replied: "Do you not see? There is a divine being traveling on the train. I have come for darshan."

Maharajji gave me a little charas and asked me to give it to the sadhu, who was very happy to receive prasad from Maharajji. When the train set off, I kept watching the sadhu till he vanished from sight. I could make out he was looking continuously at the train and Maharajji all this time.

SHRI RAMNATH AUGAD BABA OFFERS FLOWERS TO MAHARAJJI

(Contributed by Gopal Dutt Joshi)

In 1928, Maharajji was in Ghanipur. One day, a person came by and told us that a saint was coming to visit. It turned out that the visitor was a very famous saint by the name of Shri Ramnath Augad Baba from Kashipur. Maharajji asked us to prepare an asana for the saint.

A few minutes later, the Baba arrived. He was a magnificent sight to behold, carrying a walking stick, with a red vermillion mark on his forehead. When he came close to Maharajji's room, his face took on a different countenance. I noticed that he was plucking flower petals from the garland around his neck and offering them to Maharajji. It was done in such a subtle way that most people did not notice what was going on, but I managed to see what he was doing. A little later, tea was served and some bhajans were performed. After staying for around half an hour, the Baba left. It made me think: Maharajji must be a very great soul for such a great saint to offer flowers from his own neck to Maharajji. And here were were, spending time in his presence, without even realizing how blessed and lucky we were.

RAM NAVAMI IN AYODHYA

(Contributed by Gopal Dutt Joshi)

One year we were visiting Ayodhya for the festival of Ram Navami (the celebration of Lord Rama's birth). It was very crowded because of the celebrations. Maharajji asked us to make thandai. When it was ready, he asked us to fill a glass and give it to him, saying he had to go give it to someone. We did as instructed. Maharajji took the glass, went off, and did not return till the next morning. When we asked him where he had been, he tried to fob us off by saying he got stuck somewhere, but did not tell us exactly what had happened. In our group, we also had Shri K. C. Tiwari and his uncle. The uncle had a long beard. The funny thing was that the day when Maharajji was away, several people came to visit us, and they thought that the uncle was Maharajji; they offered respects and left.

THE MAN IN VRINDAVAN

(Contributed by Gopal Dutt Joshi)

Maharajji wrote me a letter on the event of *Raksha Bandhan*, saying that he was going to Vrindavan in a few days and invited me to meet him there. He had also written where he'd be staying. I arrived, but Maharajji was not there. I waited for quite some time, but when Maharajji did not turn up I decided to take a dip in the holy river Yamuna. After my bath, I roamed around the entire day looking for Maharajji: on the ghat, in temples and in dharamshalas, but I could not find him.

Then it started to rain, so I went to a large temple called Shri Govindji and took shelter there. Quite a few people had gathered to shelter from the rain, so it was somewhat crowded. In the crowd, I noticed someone's back: it looked like Maharajji from a distance. However, I could not see his face. I started making my way to this person slowly. Strangely enough, the closer I got to the person, the more the person moved away from me.

The rain stopped and people started leaving. The man headed off, too, and I ran after him, but I lost him in the narrow bylanes. I went in the direction where I thought I had seen him go. Suddenly, I came across a man who started talking to me. I found out he was from the family with whom Maharajji was staying. He said Maharajji had told him that I had arrived, and that he should go find me and bring me home. On reaching the house, I told Maharajji the entire story of my day, and the person at the temple who had led me to the lane. Maharajji laughed and said, "Yes, yes, if you're looking for someone, everyone seems to look like the person you are looking for!"

MAHARAJJI SEES GOPALDUTT IN KANPUR ... FROM BANARAS

(Contributed by Gopal Dutt Joshi)

Maharajji was in Banaras while I was in Kanpur doing my practice of the Rudriya. In those days, it would take me a month to complete the practice, and during this time I would not cut my nails or shave my beard. Once Maharajji saw me in that state. He sent for a barber and made me shave! At this particular time, I got a letter from Devidutt Joshi saying, "Maharajji said, 'Gopal is doing his practice of the Rudriya in Kanpur sincerely.'" Maharajji knew what all his devotees were up to, no matter where he was!

THE JOURNEY FROM ALLAHABAD TO BANARAS

(Contributed by Gopal Dutt Joshi)

I got a telegram from Maharajji calling me to Allahabad to attend the Kumbh Mela. The telegram said that he would be staying at a place for the *juna akhara,* the largest sect of sadhus in India. When I arrived at Allahabad, it was raining heavily and water had collected up to knee height. With great difficulty, I managed to reach the place that Maharajji had mentioned and made my way to the juna akhara tent. There, I saw Maharajji with many great saints, such as Shiv Puri, Amananand Giri, Ram Dayal Giri, Kananand Giri, and the heads of several maths. I found out that everyone had been wanting to go for a dip in the holy *sangam* (confluence of rivers), but Maharajji had made them all wait, saying, "Gopal is on his way; once he arrives, we'll all go together."

On the way back from the sangam, the road was very slippery. When we arrived at the tent, Maharajji offered me the chillum. This was the first time I had tried it. By this time, the water had nearly reached the tent. We had to move the rugs in the tent to save them from getting wet. We decided to travel to Banaras the same day. There were about twenty or more of us: a mix of students, sadhus, and other people.

Maharajji sent the students to buy tickets for whatever train was arriving next, and depending on how many tickets they were able to get, he sent off some people from our group on that train. Between 1 p.m. and around 6 p.m., Maharajji sent off most people from the group in this fashion. Finally, only Maharajji and I were left. When our train arrived, Maharajji got on first, then he helped me to climb in through the window as the train was very crowded. We arrived at Banaras station around 4 or 5 the next morning. On coming out from the platform, we found that all the people we had sent off earlier were all waiting together in one place. All of them had just arrived, even though they had left many hours before us!

NEEM KAROLI BABA AND MAJOR T.D. JOSHI

(Collected and told by Bhagwati Prasad Pande, teacher)

Bal Brahmachari Maharaj was quite strict. Once a devotee, Major T.D. Joshi, came at midnight to have the darshan of Neem Karoli Baba in the bazaar house. He was a bit drunk when he bowed down at Baba's feet. Babaji smiled and said, *"Mast aa gaya"* (*mast* is that high stage of ecstasy when the person is lost in the vibrations of bliss). The god-intoxicated one has come.

Joshi was emotional and said, "Babaji, I knew that you would be at Sah's house, so I drank only half the bottle." Maharajji was laughing. Then he sang a bhajan (devotional song) and while singing became emotional.

Then the Major said to Babaji, "It's strange. When I come to you, I can hold your feet, I can sit close to your takhat, but when I go to Bal Brahmachariji, I cannot dare to sit even at a distance from him. Why is it like that?"

Babaji replied in Hindi, *"Brahmachari ko nahin pahchante ho."* "You do not understand the Brahmachari. When Sombari left his body, everyone was sad. All these people were crying. Brahmachari fooled every one of you. You couldn't recognize him."

BAL BRAHMACHARI AND NEEM KAROLI BABA

(Told by K.C. Tewari)

When Bal Brahmachari Baba finished his pranayam or meditation, nobody could look at his face. His face was red and his eyes bulged out for a while, then he became normal. Once in Lucknow, Neem Karoli Baba and Bal Brahmachari Baba met together. They went inside a room by themselves and locked it from inside. They were there for no more than five or ten minutes. When Brahmachari came out, his face was blood red, then he became normal again. When Neem Karoli Baba came out, people saw him like a big ball of light.

Before their devotees and the public, they acted like normal people, but who knows what they were like in that room away from every else's eyes. During that meeting, some devotees were present there. They couldn't speak! They had drowned into the ocean of ecstasy.

Epilogue

The accounts in this book can be read like stories, but to hear their essence you have to bring them into your spiritual heart and allow them to resonate. The simplicity, love, faith, and joy that exists in telling these stories is as present today as when they occurred. I hope the reader has treasured them as much in the reading as I have in passing them along. The teachings contained in them remain timely, as people continue to seek their own inner essence. May the great love these beings have for humanity become the truth of our own being.

I have done whatever I could to portray the depth of spirit these saints and siddhas radiate, but the task is inevitably beyond my limited ability. As Tulsi Das says in the *Ramayana*, "Even the speech of deities like Brahma, Vishnu, and Shiva, poets and men of wisdom, falters in depicting the glory of pious souls."

In this present age, it is difficult for a common person to undertake strenuous spiritual practices. It is also very difficult to have the good fortune of being in the physical presence of saints and siddhas for very long, although even when they have left their bodies, their ashrams still carry their vibrations. Siddhas are great yogis in whose presence a person's spiritual upliftment takes place without any effort. Even if the siddha does not speak, look at, touch, or interact with a person in any visible way, being in the presence of such a being completely transforms the seeker. However, simply by reading about or listening to stories of these great siddhas, like you have in this book, you can also benefit from their company.

On the path of bhakti yoga, the yoga of devotion, it is essential to know about the life of the saints, their journeys, struggles, and the grace they experienced and shared with us. This creates celestial bliss in the heart of seekers without needing to undertake any other practices.

If God comes before us in a physical manifestation, it is almost impossible for a common person to converse with Him/Her in a normal way; the experience is overwhelming. However, a seeker is able to speak normally with a siddha like they would with any other human being, expressing their fears, worries, dreams, and questions, and having all these issues resolved. It is even possible for us to have all sorts of fun with a siddha without having to concern ourselves about behaving in what is considered an "appropriate" way, very much like my relationship with Neem Karoli Baba Maharajji!

God is indeed all powerful and able to do anything, but He/She generally doesn't "do" anything in an active way, allowing life to take its meandering route. A siddha, on the other hand, will go beyond what can be reasonably expected of anyone—even someone close to us—and do things for us that are far beyond our comprehension. The unconditional grace they shower on us is not just in the spiritual aspects of our life, but in every single aspect, including our everyday mundane life, because a siddha makes no distinction between this aspect of life or that, just as they make no distinction between one seeker and another, their own body and another's. They are connected with the Divine at such a deep and high level of vibration that all distinctions cease to exist for them; as Maharajji often taught: *sab ek,* meaning All is One.

We have now come to the end of this book. But the story of life goes on. Do not for a moment think that this is the end of the miraculous journey. Siddhas and their unconditional grace have been our companions since time immemorial. It is not just about the past, but it continues even now.

In every time throughout history, siddhas have always been in our midst to guide mankind. We may not recognize them, may not be able to meet them in person, or may not even acknowledge them. It takes great fortune to meet a siddha, to recognize them, and to delight in their presence. Just like the fortunate people who shared their experiences in this book with us, remember, there are people even today who are having these kinds of experiences with siddhas from "the past" and also those in "the present." I use these terms in quotes because time is not a barrier for the grace and love of the siddhas.

Remember, these experiences and stories are not about someone else, somewhere else, in a different time and place; they are just as relevant today as they have always been. The grace of siddhas is accessible today, here and now, to everyone who seeks it.

Glossary

Amla – fruit

Ananda – bliss

Angocha/angavastra – Small piece of cloth used to clean the hands, generally for rough use

Anjali – Offering of water with joined open hands

Anna – Coin out of circulation, 1Rs was 16 annas at the time

Annapurna siddhi – Abundance of food through the blessings of Goddess Annapurna

Arkand – a refined, expensive product made from charas

Arre – Exclamation similar to oh!, what have you done?

Arti – ritual of offering light (from wicks soaked in ghee) to one or more deities or saints

Asana – Seat or posture or clean carpet for a saint to sit on

Ashram – Literally translated, "place of rest." A place where sages stay, usually has some arrangements for visitors to eat, rest, and practicc.

Ashwin – month in Indian calendar, around October

Atma – True self or soul

Atta – Wheat flour for making chapatis and puris

Avadhut – a type of mystic or saint who is beyond ego-conscious ness, totally lost in his own self

Baati – hard thick piece of unleavened bread generally used by saints or sadhus

Badmash – rascal, generally used in an affectionate exchange

Balyogi – child yogi who has adopted the path of yoga since childhood

Bal swarup – saint or god physically appearing in the form of a child yogi
Baniya – trader
Barahwa – ceremony held on the 12th day after someone's death (mooning period)
Barasingha – a deer with antlers
Barsi/barasi – death anniversary
Battasha – small and cheap sugary sweet
Bhandara – A celebration conducted in a holy place, like an ashram, that includes serving food to all present.
Bhakti – the path of devotion
Bhang – crude form of charas
Bhav – devotional feeling
Bhajan – devotional songs
Bhakti – devotion
Bilva – leaves from a tree offered especially in Shiva puja
Brahmachari – a male who practices living according to Hindu Vedic scriptures and is celibate
Brahmin – the priestly caste

Chapatis – round flat breads
Chasni – large pot for frying food
Chatangs – measurement of weight
Chatti – ceremony held on the sixth day after birth
Chillum – pipe for smoking ganja (marijuana) or charas (hash) mixed with tobacco
Chimta – fire tongs used by sadhus
Chir – pine wood for use as a torch and firewood
Chola – long gown
Compunder – assistant to medical doctor

Dadankhan – Pinda Dadankhan (N.W. Frontier Punjab), the place where Sombari Maharaj came from in the 19th century

Dal – lentils

Darshan – blessed vision or sight. It is considered a blessing to meet and see great beings.

Dhams – significant holy places

Dharma – the principle of cosmic order and righteousness, also holy duty

Dharamshala – hostel for pilgrims to stay in, usually free of charge.

Dhoti – long cloth wrapped around the waist

Dhuni – sacred fire set up by a sadhu. A dhuni is very holy and is considered to be a living being.

Diwali – festival of lights

Dussehra – festival that marks the victory of the goddess Durga over the demon Mahishasura; also celebrated on the day when Ram killed the demon Ravana

Ekadashi – the 11th lunar day of the bright or dark fortnight of every lunar month

Fakir/fakkad – a kind of wandering monk who has no possessions, also used for sadhus

Ghee – clarified butter

Gopi – Embodiment of devotional love for lord Krishna, generally they are from Vrindavan milkmaid families

Gram – brown lentil or channa in Hindi

Gudaria – torn dirty quilt

Gunas – the qualities of sattva (balance and harmony), rajas (passion and activity), and tamas, (chaos and disorder)

Hadpiya – wooden jar used to store ghee
Halwa/halva – sweet confection prepared with refined flour and ghee
Havan – a fire ritual
Holi – spring festival of colors, usually in March, when everyone is taken on the same level, no caste. It is an exchange of love by smearing the color powder on each other's face
Homa – same as havan

Jaggery – concentrated brown sugar, also called gur
Jala samadhi – after death, the body is immersed in a river or a big lake, especially for sadhus and saints of certain sects
Jamalgota – strong laxative
Janeu – sacred thread worn by devotees who repeat the Gayatri Mantra
Janmashtami – Krishna's birthday
Japa – reciting a mantra or name of God on a mala
Jeev samadhi – Leaving the body willingly in full consciousness
Jeth – May/June in Indian calendar
Jhola – shoulder or hand bag
Jnani – one who follows the path of knowledge
Juna akhara – one of the largest sect of sadhus in India, many of them Naga babas
Jyoti – oil lamp, usually lit morning and evening, also means flame

Kachoris – deep-fried puff pastry with spicy moong dal stuffing
Kadhais – large iron cooking pots, called large woks in the West
Kamadhenu – the cow of plenty, always giving
Kamandalu – water pot generally made of copper
Kanchopa – hat that covers the ears
Karma – spiritual principle of cause and effect that influences the

future of an individual
Kartik – month of November on Indian calendar
Kaupin – loincloth
Kheer – rice pudding
Khichdi – a one pot meal of rice and lentils, sometimes with vegetables added
Khukri – a large and dangerous knife common in Nepal
Kos – ancient measure of distance, 1 kos is about 2.25 miles
Kshatirya – warrior caste
Kumbha mela – a mass pilgrimage that takes place every 12 years mainly for taking holy dip in the sacred rivers
Kund – pond
Kutir/ Kutiya – small hut

Laddoos – A sweet treat, round in shape. A laddu can be of many dif ferent varieties and colors depending on the ingredients.
Leela – divine play
Lingam – a stone symbol of Lord Shiva
Lok-sahitya – folk literature
Lota – open container with narrow mouth for water

Mahalakshmi – the goddess of wealth
Mahant – head of a sect
Mahasamadhi – when a siddha leaves his body
Mahatma – great soul, this term is used to address sadhus and great beings.
Mahashakti – the great divine feminine
Mahashivratri – festival worshipping Shiva
Mai-ka-lal – siddha, a person who holds something extraordinary in him

Mala – rosary beads
Malpuas – sweet fried bread
Mandi – wholesale market
Makar Sankranti – marks the transition of the sun into the zodiacal sign of Makara (Capricorn) on its celestial path. It has astro logical significance.
Marghshirsha – October-November in Indian calendar
Maryada – strict code of conduct
Mast – god-intoxicated
Math – hermitage, a certain type of ashram
Maya – power of illusion
Mewa – dry fruits
Moong – yellow lentil
Misri – rock sugar
Mithai – sweets
Mukti – liberation
Murti – statue of a great being, especially of a deity or saint
Muskut – warts

Naga – naked sadhu
Nagraj – king cobra
Naisthick – strictly
Naula – a depression with a little spring, used for collecting drinking water
Navratri – 9-day festival in Spring and Fall in honor of the Divine Mother, also known as Durga Puja. During the Spring Navratri, the birth of Lord Ram is celebrated.
Neebus – large lemons
Niyam – Acts and laws of nature and human behavior, also constitu tional laws

Pagall – crazy one. It is also used in an affectionate way directed to a simple or shy person

Pahari – hill dialect or hill man

Paisa – equivalent to 1/100th of a rupee

Pakoras – Fried cake-like snack made with gram flour sometimes mixed with vegetables

Palthan – dry flour used while making chapatis to prevent the dough from sticking to the pastry board

Pancha maha yagna – offering to the 5 elements, mainly during a fire ceremony

Panch pallava – leaves from 5 sacred trees, including the banyan, peepul, fig, crown flower, and flame of the forest.

Panjeri – sweet and bitter tonic to keep the body warm and to protect it from colds and other ailments

Paramatma – the supreme soul

Pashmina – fine quality male's shawl

Pattal – plate made of leaves

Peepul – sacred fig tree

Pind – a word generally used for village in North West Punjab

Poush – month of November-December in Indian calendar

Prarabdha – the part of past karma that creates the present body; destiny

Pranaam – To pay respects with folded hands, joining the palms together, and bowing. Joining the palms indicates keeping the five senses in check, and bowing indicates honoring the divinity in a person.

Pranayam – breathing practices

Prasad – blessed, consecreated food

Puja – worship

Puranas – ancient Sanskrit scriptures

Purna siddha – a fully awakened yogi or saint who has attained perfection
Puris – fried flat bread, usually made from wheat flour

Raksha Bandhan – festival that celebrates the love and duty mainly between brothers and sisters
Ramnaam – repeating the name of Ram
Ram Navami – the celebration of Lord Rama's birth
Ratti – very small measure of weight, a quarter ratti is the same weight as a mustard seed; masha is a slightly larger quantity. Equivalent English words would be "iota" or "jot."
Raukhad – rocky place where nothing grows
Rishi – sage
Rupa – appearance
Rudriya stotram – hymns in praise of Lord Shiva

Saale – wife's brother, also commonly used to call a close friend or someone close to get their attention
Sab ek – All is One
Sadhu/ Sadhaka – one who is on the path of sadhana
Sadhana – spiritual practices
Sahib – a polite form of address for a man, like "sir"
Samadhi – when a saint leaves his body, also used for the graveyard of saints and sages Sangam – the confluence of two or more rivers, also used for meeting of holy people
Sanskaras – the history and traits that influence a person
Sant mahatma – a plural word for saints and sages. sant – saint and mahatma – great saint
Sanyas – renunciation
Sanyasi – renunciate

Satsang – a holy company or meeting of devotees

Ser or seer – measure of weight; A ser is a little over two ounces, and a little less than a kilo.

Seva – service

Shikha – small lock of hair on the top of the head

Shishir – winter months

Shloka – couplet in Vedic verse

Siddhi – spiritual power

Siddha – A great being who has no karma of his or her own and comes to the world just for the upliftment of other souls.

Siddha bhumi – place where there are siddhas

Snan – bath

Sombar – Monday

Sooji – a dish made from semolina

Subji – vegetable

Tabla – Indian drums

Takhat – or tucket, a wooden platform

Tandoor – traditional Indian clay over

Tapasya, tapas – spiritual practice or austerity to attain liberation

Tapasvi – one who does tapasya

Tarpan – Gratification, libation of water to the names of the diseased ancestors with mantras

Tehsildar – tax inspector in charge of a part of a district

Thandai – tasty cooling drink

Tika/tilak – sacred mark on the forehead made of colored powders or ash

Tikkar – a kind of bread made by grilling flour in a fire just like baati, generally prepared and used by sadhus

Tirth yatra – pilgrimage to spiritual places

Tola – measurement around 11.6 grams, mainly for gold
Tonga – horse cart
Tulsi – holy basil

Ulfi – long robe or chola worn by some sadhus
Urad – type of black lentil

Vaidya – Ayurvedic doctor
Vedanta – one of the philosophical schools of Hinduism, based on the Upanishads, the Sutras, and the Bhagavad Gita
Vibhuti – sacred ash
Vidya – Knowledge in a broad sense, or a knowledge of a specific field
Virakta – free from worldly attachments, totally detached
Vyaghcharm – tiger skin

Yatra – journey, when the journey is to holy places it is a pilgrimage

Acknowledgments

Dear Readers,

I started this project and collected the material for it with sincerity and great enthusiasm. The inspiration originated on a visit to Padampuri with my elder cousin S.L. Sah, my sister-in-law Bhabhi, and my sister Bina. S.L., on seeing the deteriorating condition of Sombari Baba's ashram, suggested that a book would be a good way to preserve his memory. My legacy of family connections to these saints and siddhas provides a shared viewpoint across generations. I feel privileged to have grown up literally in the lap of these siddhas.

Devotees of Shri Neem Karoli Maharajji from the U.S. started coming to Nainital. I would talk with them about saints, my family, the hallowed places of Kumaon. All these talks created a keen desire of knowing more and more. Together we visited some of these ashrams. One day I told them about my desire to have a book published on Sombari Baba, for which I had a collection of authentic stories. The western satsang showed great interest and gradually began to put pressure upon me to finish this book.

After some time, all the material was ready, but it needed to be translated and made coherent. It's like all the ingredients for a dinner were now ready, and all that remained was to bring them together and cook the meal. I would like to admit honestly that after the initial burst, I had become a bit lazy!

Sometimes I would remember my discussions with Maharajji (Neem Karoli Baba), the stories he had shared with me, and also the historical and factual information he had shared with me about these saints and the places associated with their lives. At such times,

I would think: "I have collected all this material in the last 20 to 30 years; I really should do something with it now!"

Occasionally in my conversations with Ram Dass he would remind me to work on the book. In India, it is considered impolite to talk about death, but Ram Dass has no such compunctions. "K.K.", he would say "Think about what will happen to all this beautiful knowledge if you pass away. It will be lost to the world!" That would motivate me for a while to work on the book.

Here, I would like to mention Raghu Markus, who kept pushing me on with the work. At first I tried to convince him that I was working on the book, hoping that would satisfy him. But he would not let it rest. It got to a point where I had to say: "Raghu, each time you call me I start getting palpitations in the heart!" I also came up with a new trick: as soon as I knew it was Raghu calling, the first thing I'd say was "Raghu, you will be very glad to know that I am working very hard on the book." Raghu would then laugh, knowing what I was up to, but he did not let up the pressure!

Katya Langmuiir came along to scan all the material into digital format. She turned up one evening to do this work and I said to her "It's quite late now; why don't you do it tomorrow morning?" She insisted on doing it immediately and created a disc with all the scanned material and gave it to me.

Next came our satsang friend Mangesh Mahale. He stayed in the mountains for two months in 2013, and I must admit that at first I was very reluctant. During this time, Mangesh often drove all the way from Almora to Nainital to see me and work on the book, but I was often busy with other things, so we did not get much done. The next year he came again and stayed at Nainital, so I could not escape. Sometimes I would say to him: "Enough for today. Let's do this tomorrow." He would reply: "No way, we're doing it today, and now." A lot of the material was in the local Pahari dialect, so it had to be translated into Hindi first and then into English.

Then came Parvati Markus, who edited it all into a coherent narrative. Durga Julia Sanchez helped me in India with corrections and photos. And Brij Mohan Joshi is a photographer from Nainital who volunteered his time and effort to take pictures of old pictures and make copies of these saints.

I would like to thank all these people from the bottom of my heart, and hope that the love and joy from my heart reaches straight to theirs. It has been a delight and honor to work on this project, and to relive beautiful memories from the lives of great siddhas.

I would also like to acknowledge all those who contributed stories. I verified all of these stories as first-hand accounts and have implicit trust in the transmission of these accounts. Many of them came from my father and guardians, devotees who actually met and witnessed the leela of Sombari Baba. If I have forgotten to mention any name in this acknowledgments, I beg their pardon. There are no words to express my gratitude to all those who have been in one way or another associated in the publication of this book. My pranams to everyone.

Contributors

Those who are keen about the publication of this book with their loving blessings:

Dr. S.C. Agarwal (Ret'd. J.T. Commny)
M.L. Sah (Evelyn Hotel, Nainital)

Those who are no longer alive but their blessings were of great value and inspiring:

Hiralal Sah
Hira Vallabh Lohni, Municipal Ranger, Retired, Nainital
Pandi Devidutt Kabdwal
Pandi Jagannath Joshi, ex-Municipal Commissioner, Nainital
Pandi Khimananda Suyal, Kumaon
Shri Badri Sah (lawyer)
Shri Darshan
Shri Dhanilal Sah
Shri Girwan Dutt Joshi, Nainital
Shri Govardhan Pande
Shri Govindram Kala, Ex-Deputy Collector
Shri Harikrishna Trivedi, Editor, Hindustan newspaper
Shri Hiralal Sah (Hubbaji)
Shri Hira Vallabh Pant
Shri I.L. Sah
Shri Kaka Kalelkar
Shri Krishnananda Shastri, Education Superintendent, Municipal Board, Nainital
Shri Nityananda Mishra, article in *Ramlila Smarika* 1996 issue 17
Shri Manoharlal Sah, (cloth dealer, Nainital)
Shri Ramlal Sah, Nainital
Shri Shankar Lal Sah
Shri Surendranath Jauhar (Fakir), Sri Aurobindo Ashram, Nainital
Shri Tikaram Bhatt, Bhowali

Photo Credits

Cover photo by Rachael Fisher.

All photos of Shri Sombari Baba were taken by a close devotee named Pratap Sah, whom Babaji nicknamed Bhootnath.

The two side-by-side photos of Hairakhan Baba were taken in Allahabad by Major Basu. The other photos of Sri Hairakhan Baba and the group with Hairakhan Baba (taken at Sepoy Dhara, Nainital) were obtained from Ms. Gangi Sah, photographer in Nainital.

Photos of Bagheswari Baba at Padampuri, K.K. with Neem Karoli Baba at Kainchi, and K.K. with Ram Dass in Nainital were taken by M.L. Sah.

Photos of Haridatt Burju, Haridatt with K.K.'s family members, Hubbajji (in Kausani), the ashrams of Padampuri and Kakrighat, and S.L.'s family group at Padampuri were taken by K.K. Sah.

The photo of K.K. with Hanuman murti in Brindavan was taken by Bhawan Singh, pujari, in the presence of Shri Neem Karoli Baba Maharajji.

Photos taken in the U.S. with Ram Dass and family were taken by Rameshwar Das.

Resources

For more devotees' stories about the saints, Neem Karoli Baba in particular, go to https://www.ramdass.org/category/gurus_grace/